Traditional Industry in the Economy of Colonial India

The majority of manufacturing workers in South Asia are employed in industries that rely on manual labour and craft skills. Some of these industries have existed for centuries and survived great changes in consumption and technology over the last 150 years. In earlier studies, historians of the region focused on mechanized rather than craft industries, arguing that traditional manufacturing was destroyed or devitalized during the colonial period, and that 'modern' industry is substantially different. Exploring new material from research into five traditional industries, Tirthankar Roy's book contests these notions, demonstrating that, while traditional industry did evolve during the Industrial Revolution, these transformations had a positive rather than a destructive effect on manufacturing generally. In fact, the book suggests, several major industries in post-independence India were shaped by such transformations.

TIRTHANKAR ROY is Associate Professor at the Indira Gandhi Institute of Development Research, Bombay. His recent publications include *Artisans and Industrialization: Indian Weaving in the Twentieth Century* (1993).

Cambridge Studies in Indian History and Society 5

Cambridge Studies in Indian History and Society will publish
monographs on the history and anthropology of modern India. In
addition to its primary scholarly focus, the series will also include work
of an interdisciplinary nature which will contribute to contemporary
social and cultural debates about Indian history and society. In this
way, the series will further the general development of historical and
anthropological knowledge and attract a wider readership than that
concerned with India alone.

Traditional Industry in the Economy of Colonial India

Tirthankar Roy

CAMBRIDGE
UNIVERSITY PRESS

PUBLISHED BY THE PRESS SYNDICATE OF THE UNIVERSITY OF CAMBRIDGE
The Pitt Building, Trumpington Street, Cambridge, CB2 1RP, United Kingdom

CAMBRIDGE UNIVERSITY PRESS
The Edinburgh Building, Cambridge, CB2 2RU, UK
http://www.cup.cam.ac.uk
40 West 20th Street, New York, NY 10011-42, USA   http://www.cup.org
10 Stamford Road, Oakleigh, Melbourne 3166, Australia

© Tirthankar Roy 1999

First published 1999

Printed in the United Kingdom at the University Press, Cambridge

Typeset in 10.12pt Plantin   [CE]

A catalogue record for this book is available from the British Library

Library of Congress Cataloguing in Publication data

Roy, Tirthankar.
Traditional industry in the economy of colonial India.
      p.   cm. – (Cambridge studies in Indian history and society: 5
ISBN 0 521 65012 7
1. Industries – India. 2. Industrial policy – India.
I. Series.
HC435.1.R69 1999
338.0954 – dc21   98–44110   CIP

ISBN 0 521 65012 7 hardback

Contents

Illustrations

Maps

Tables

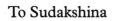

To Sudakshina

Acknowledgments

Since this book was taken up, I have been a frequent visitor at the library of the Gokhale Institute of Politics and Economics, Pune, to use its rich collection on small-scale and traditional industry. I would like to thank the library staff and the institute faculty, especially Smriti Mukherji, for their help during these visits. In addition to the Gokhale Institute, I have worked in a number of other libraries, of which the National Library at Calcutta, the Royal Commonwealth Society collection at Cambridge, and the India Office at London have been especially useful.

Among those who read the draft and helped improve its quality, I should mention first of all the referees of the Cambridge University Press. Dharma Kumar read and edited an earlier version of chapter 6, which was published in the *Indian Economic and Social History Review.* She has also encouraged me in this line of work from long before the idea of this book took shape. Association with Douglas Haynes has benefited this work, especially on the interpretation of and sources for textile history. A fellowship at Cambridge in 1996 gave me access to some of the sources available in the UK, and the right environment to complete the first draft of the book. I am grateful to the Charles Wallace India Trust for the fellowship, and to Gordon Johnson, Raj Chanda-varkar and C. A. Bayly for making my stay a productive and pleasant one. Key arguments of the book were presented in four seminars. Two of these were at the Centre of South Asian Studies, Cambridge, and one each at the Madras Institute of Development Studies and the Indira Gandhi Institute of Development Research, Bombay. Each seminar was an occasion to rethink the main ideas and write them up with more clarity than before. A summary of some of the ideas appeared in an article called 'Music as Artisan Tradition' in the *Contributions to Indian Sociology.* Sections in the book dealing with the same themes benefited from comments and editorial suggestions received from the journal.

My employer institution, the Indira Gandhi Institute of Development Research, generously supported my local travel and other needs connected with the work, for which I am grateful to the Director, Kirit

Parikh, and the Acting Director, Jyoti Parikh. Members of Dastkar supplied some of their field data, which are used in chapter 7. For the photographs, I am obliged to the Librarian of the University of Mumbai (Fort campus), Messrs Mitter Bedi and Hamilton Studio (Bombay), Rusheed Wadia, and A. K. Banerji, and for the maps to Prasad Gogate. Sudakshina Roy saw me through the final stages of typescript preparation.

1   Introduction

The questions

Two sets of problems motivated this study on traditional industry, or the artisans,[1] in colonial India. The first arises in South Asian historiography, and the second in comparative development. The experience of the artisan has long been used to illustrate opinions about the impact of British rule on the economy of India and, therefore, has been a controversial topic in Indian historiography. The evidence on the artisan, however, is ambiguous. There are too many variations by region, industry and period to permit easy or uniform generalizations. The question remains: can a sufficiently general and convincing account of the artisanate be found? The book is primarily an attempt to answer this question. The answer proposed here leads to a desire to see South Asia in a larger context. The book suggests that traditional industry modernized and played a creative role in Indian industrialization. That traditional industry can play such a role is a familiar theme in the economic and social history of early modern Europe and prewar East Asia. A question naturally follows: which elements in the South Asian story are special to the region, and which shared with industrialization in general?

The period of the study is, roughly, from the 1870s to the 1930s. Occasionally, more recent trends will be cited for comparison. The raw material consists of descriptions of industries in which artisan enterprise was significant in this period, and remained so beyond the period. There are five such studies, on handloom weaving, leather, brassware, carpets, and gold thread (*jari*). Two of these industries, handloom weaving and *jari*, were deeply influenced by exposure to imported substitutes.

---

[1] In this study, the term 'artisan' or 'traditional industry' refers to industries that combine three loosely defined features: tool-based technology, non-corporate organization, and precolonial origin. In some contexts, 'artisanal' may refer to industries which are today run with electric power, but have artisanal origins, and reflect the connection in aspects of industrial organization.

1

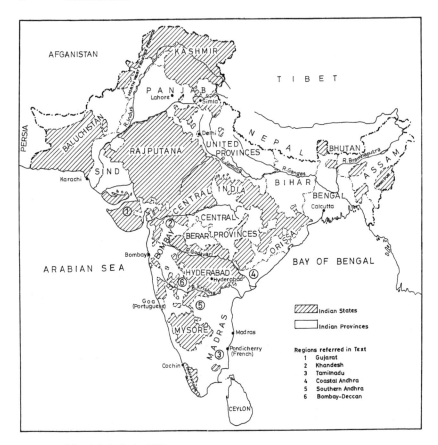

Map 1.1 India in 1939

Brassware illustrates two processes: the integration of the home market and the creation of an export market. Carpets and leather emerged as major exportable goods in the colonial period. The experience of several other industries will also be cited occasionally, but they do not appear here as independent studies.

At one level, the cases are no more than simple narratives of a kind of enterprise deeply rooted in the region's economic life and yet neglected by historians. At a more analytical level, they illustrate a view of change which, simultaneously, disputes the most widely known position available on artisans in British India, and enables India to be compared with other cases of industrialization. Accordingly, the agenda of the introductory chapter are to describe the thesis developed here in opposition to the received view, and to consider the thesis in a comparative context.

The next two sections deal respectively with the significance of artisans for South Asian economic history, and the significance of South Asia for models of industrialization.

The proposal

The general line of argument followed in the book can be explained simply. There is little dispute among historians with the statement that economic contact between India and industrializing Europe had both a destructive and a creative impact on Indian industry. In the most influential view, the destructive impact has tended to be overemphasized. This book, by contrast, considers the creative impact the more important. A view in which the destructive impact dominates would imply that the industrial history of the colonies and that of the colonizers are essentially dissimilar. For example, it tends to suggest that industrialization in Britain meant 'de-industrialization' for her colonies. A view in which the creative impact dominates, by contrast, proposes that the two histories are similar in certain core aspects. It will be argued here, for example, that there are similarities in the effects of long-distance trade on the artisans.

In either view, the dominant source of change was long-distance trade. The sixty years between the opening of the Suez Canal (1869) and the Great Depression (1929) witnessed an almost continuous growth of external and internal trade, and changes in the nature of trade in India. Foreign trade became an immensely more powerful economic variable than ever before. Exports expressed as a ratio of national income increased from small amounts in the precolonial period to 10–11 per cent in the interwar years.[2] The region was integrated in an expanding world trade and payments system. The basic pattern of comparative advantage, which has not changed much till today, became established. In this new international division of labour, India's exports came to consist of natural fibres, leather, agriculture, a number of goods

[2] The ratio is a rough measure of the importance of trade. In 1925, it was about 11 per cent, or merchandise export of Rs. 4 b on a national income at current prices of Rs. 34 b. The value of exports increased 50 times between 1834 and 1925, and possibly over a hundred-fold between 1760 and 1925. Notwithstanding possible adjustments for changes in prices, the currency system, and real income, it is unlikely that nominal national income could have risen by a comparable magnitude between these dates. Under realistic assumptions, the ratio was much smaller than 11 per cent in 1760 and in 1834. Trade figures are from K. N. Chaudhuri, 'Foreign Trade and Balance of Payments' in Dharma Kumar (ed.), *The Cambridge Economic History of India*, vol. II, *c.1757–c.1970* (Cambridge, 1983). 1925 income is from S. Sivasubramonian, 'Revised Estimates of the National Income of India, 1900–1901 to 1946–47', *Indian Economic and Social History Review*, 34, 2 (1997).

intensive in craftsmanship, and labour itself. The process was initiated by commercial and industrial revolutions in the West, but secured by political and administrative means.

Within India, a national market emerged in a number of basic goods and services that were imperfectly if at all traded before. Agricultural goods are one example. Labour, which became much more mobile than before, is another. Political stability and unity aided internal economic contact. Perhaps for the first time in India's history the political centre was overwhelmingly more powerful than the periphery. Economic integration was also aided by safer passage, a judiciary meant to define, honour and enforce contracts, a uniform monetary system, and uniform fiscal regulation. Faster and cheaper transport brought about agglomeration of trade, occasionally of consumers as well. Where the commodity in question was an exportable, its trade gravitated towards the ports where most railroads in India originated from, and converged in, until recently. Increased access to the world market often meant access to inexpensive imported inputs and, therefore, a shift of material trade towards the ports or the railways. More generally, easier communication discriminated the favourably located against the remoter territories in terms of access to information about buyers, sellers, processes, and technologies. All these changes had older antecedents, and they continued later, but the core infrastructure needed to hold a market economy together was more or less completed in these sixty years.

The effects of extended trade and infrastructure have engaged the greater part of economic history scholarship on the region. The usual questions considered include why goods and services earlier gifted away or bartered became commodities, what it meant to market structure and organization, whether it made the participants better or worse off, and what role the State played in the entire process. Agrarian history has examined how peasants responded to a world demand for Indian raw material and grain. Where marketed surplus became sufficiently large to motivate changes in levels of production or productivity, historians have looked for the growth-inducing effects of markets, or explained their absence where they did not appear. Both of these explanations involve studying the interactions between markets, and the social, cultural, ecological, and demographic contexts in which they appear.[3] Business history similarly has examined the sources of capital in the first mills,

---

[3] For a selection of recent and reprinted essays on these themes, see K. N. Raj, N. Bhattacharya, S. Guha, and S. Padhi (eds.), *Essays on the Commercialization of Indian Agriculture* (Delhi, 1985); D. Ludden (ed.), *Agricultural Production and Indian History* (Delhi, 1994); and S. Bose (ed.), *Credit, Markets and the Agrarian Economy of Colonial India* (Delhi, 1994).

and the markets where their output was sold. Usually, these were trades of relatively recent origin.[4]

By contrast, artisans represent one major form of occupation on which the effects of this process have remained more or less unexplored. Industry probably employed about 15 per cent of the workers in the middle of the nineteenth century, that is, about 10–15 million persons. Industry was not only numerically a large sector, but contained producers known worldwide for craftsmanship. Such scale and such quality must have been affected in complex ways. Yet, studies that show, with convincing and diverse examples, how they were affected, remain scarce.

Nevertheless, a coherent position on the artisans, the only available 'theory' where artisans are seen in relation to the overall economic environment, does exist. A Marxist tradition in development scholarship has consistently argued that the destructive impact of economic contact with Europe on the modern Third World outweighed any possible creative or productive impact. Two types of evidence are commonly used in support of this view: the distress of the Indian textile artisan facing competition from British cloth and yarn in the nineteenth century; and a decline in total industrial employment in India in the census period, 1881–1931. In a criticism of this view, some authors have pointed out that industrial income per head did increase in the colonial period, so that the decline in artisanal and overall industrial employment cannot be read as a sign of economic regress.[5] It is possible to go further, and suggest that the evidence on the artisan has tended to be rather simplified. On three main grounds, some of them already articulated in the relevant literature, this book disputes this evidence.

First, the experience of textiles is ambiguous. Cotton textiles, the largest industry in the region, did have to cope with competitive imports from mills in England. Hand tools were pitted against machinery, and, in the ensuing battle, hand tools lost much employment and income. And yet, qualifying this story, recent works in textile history have shown that, in handloom weaving, competitive decline was not a general occurrence, but specific to certain types of market and apparel. Non-competing hand-woven cloths, on the other hand, experienced long-distance trade not as a debilitating force but possibly as a creative one

---

[4] The cotton mill industry in western India, for example, owes its origin to profits from the export trade in cotton and opium from Bombay, and trade in British products brought to India. See Morris D. Morris, 'The Growth of Large-Scale Industry' in Dharma Kumar (ed.), *The Cambridge Economic History of India*, vol. II, *c.1757–c.1970* (Cambridge, 1983), 573–4.

[5] The Marxist position and its critique are more fully discussed in chapter 2, where all citations appear.

(chapter 3). Moreover, in industries other than cotton textiles, competitive imports are more or less an exceptional feature. A general model of transition, therefore, needs a wider sample of industries than textiles, and needs to deal with the effects of economic exposure other than external competition and competition from mechanized industry.

Secondly, the evidence on employment is ambiguous too. The censuses do suggest a decline or at best a stagnation in the total numbers engaged in industry. Male employment in industry remained close to 9–10 million between 1901 and 1931. But these totals probably hide contradictory tendencies. The more detailed censuses conducted after independence (1947) found that employment in industrial units mainly using family labour has steadily declined between 1961 and 1991, both in absolute terms, and relative to employment in units using wage labour. A part of the increase in wage employment occurred in mechanized industry, but the bulk of it occurred in units not officially classified as 'factories', units that tend to be highly labour-intensive and non-mechanized, or 'artisanal' by our definition. There is no reason to believe that this tendency started after 1947. More realistically, it was set in motion by structural changes in the colonial period. Since family labour is likely to be less specialized than wage labour, the trend implies rising average productivity despite the stagnation in overall employment. Consistent with this finding, national income statistics of both pre- and post-independence periods show a growth in industrial incomes and productivity even with low growth rates in industrial employment.[6] In other words, the stagnation story suggested by census employment totals is misleading. Any worthwhile story about industrial transition must consider technological and organizational changes within artisanal industry.

Finally, the received view is inconsistent with the long-term character of industrialization in India. In 1911, 95 per cent of industrial employment was located outside officially registered factories. In 1991, 71 per cent of industrial employment is still located outside registered factories. This informal employment consists of 6.8 million persons in the shrinking household industry and 13.4 million in unofficial factories. The latter include various forms of wage employment not directly influenced by the regulatory regime. The share of the latter in industrial employment has been growing very rapidly in recent years.[7] In some of the densely industrialized cities where this growth is concentrated,

---

[6] See chapter 2 for a more detailed treatment.

[7] Between 1961 and 1991, the share of factories in industrial employment increased from 15.3 per cent to 28.6 per cent, that of unofficial factories from 24.6 per cent to 47.7 per cent, and that of household industry fell from 60.2 per cent to 23.7 per cent: India, *Statistical Abstracts for India* (Delhi, various years); and India, *Annual Report 1994–5*, Ministry of Labour (Delhi, 1995).

industrial clusters specialize in activities that began well before independence. A closer look suggests that, in all of them, capital and labour have mainly agricultural or artisanal origin.[8] The most famous example is the conversion of handlooms into power-driven small weaving factories.[9] There are similar examples from leather, metals, glassware, and ceramics. Of course, in the long run, artisanal industry has seen many changes in product composition, organization, and to some extent in technology. But overall, it has not just survived, but shaped the character of industrialization both in colonial and post-colonial India.

This is the broad message of the five examples studied in this book. Artisanal activity survived in India for the same reasons that it has done elsewhere in the world: consumer preference, absence of mechanized alternative, or favourable factor endowment. But the survival was not static. For artisans needed to adapt to changing conditions of demand and supply from the nineteenth century onwards, induced mainly by the extension of long-distance trade. The effects of long-distance trade appear neither as purely deleterious, nor as simply expansionary. Bearing broad parallels with other historical instances, the effects were mainly qualitative. Competition increased. Patronage and old 'moral economies' collapsed. New types of trade, merchant, and financier arose. Division of labour and specialization increased. Systems such as putting-out and factories spread. More locally, there arose merchant-manufacturers, and 'industrialists' in some of the modern senses of the term,[10] though this last movement was restricted both in scale and in spirit.

Because artisanal technologies were under no immediate threat, the most visible dimension of these changes was institutional. New and distant markets led to efficiency-enhancing changes in industrial organization. The examples in this book suggest two specific sources of organizational change. First, new or distant markets made capital and

[8] Some examples are, Surat, Bhiwandi, Salem-Erode area in small-scale weaving of cloth on the powerloom; Agra, Dharavi, and the Madras suburbs in leather; and metalworking and woollens in western Uttar Pradesh, Punjab, and Haryana. For a survey of the literature and a study on the artisanal roots of industrial entrepreneurship in modern India, see Tirthankar Roy, 'Capitalism and Community: A Study of the Madurai Sourashtras', *Indian Economic and Social History Review*, 34, 4 (1997). On agrarian roots of enterprise in small-scale industry and trade, a useful survey of the literature is Mario Rutten, *Farms and Factories* (Delhi, 1995), chapter 1.

[9] Probably the single largest industry in India today, such factories, called 'powerlooms' in India, employed about 4 million persons in 1991. This figure accounts for 20 per cent of wage labour in industry, and 33–35 per cent of wage labour in the informal sector industry. Factories employed 8.7 million in 1991. Wage labour in industry numbered 21.9 million. See Tirthankar Roy, 'Development or Distortion? Powerlooms in India, 1950–97', *Economic and Political Weekly*, 33, 16 (1998).

[10] See on 'The Industrialist: A New Man', the review in the first chapter of François Crouzet, *The First Industrialists. The Problem of Origins* (Cambridge, 1985).

information scarcer resources, thus enabling or forcing those in possession of these resources to control production. And, secondly, 'asym-
metric information' between buyers and suppliers made possible
opportunistic behaviour on the part of the supplier. In the skilled crafts,
where the main consumers were formerly the local bosses, opportunism
was earlier kept in check by the political superiority of the consumer.
Long-distance trade and the anonymity of the buyer removed these
checks and initiated a 'regulatory vacuum' in which problems of quality
and delivery became acute.[11] New organizations were often local experiments with regulation.

The hypothesis that trade had a creative impact on the artisan is not a
new one. That long-distance trade could transform artisanal enterprise
in ways that might enable the latter to raise productivity is a theme
common to early industrialization in Europe, and late industrialization
in Japan. The story outlined here in part belongs in this larger narrative.

South Asia in context

Although the term 'Industrial Revolution' has sometimes been questioned, most economic historians would agree with the idea of a major
discontinuity between industrial conditions in Britain and Western
Europe before the late eighteenth century, and those after. The discontinuity can be seen in technology, organization, sources of demand, the
role of long-distance trade, and the intersectoral transfer of capital and
labour. It is also, however, a received wisdom that the early stage of this
transition, despite the great inventions that came towards its close, is
distinguished not by the general adoption of machinery, which
happened selectively and slowly, but by the incremental but historically
unprecedented rise in productivity within the older manufactures. For
Britain, Maxine Berg has shown that conventional examples of technological breaks, cotton, metals or the generalized use of steam power,
were the rather more dramatic cases in industrialization. The general
case was a rise in productivity and output in a number of industries
based mainly on hand tools, such as leather, wood-working, and construction.[12] We see here the extension of industrial capitalism primarily
in 'a change in organization and not in the apparatus of production', to

---

[11] The term is taken from the introduction in C. Sabel and J. Zeitlin (eds.), *World of
Possibilities* (Cambridge, 1997), 27.

[12] 'A more effective division of labour force, and the reorganization of commercial and
mercantile networks surrounding the production process could all generate gains in
productivity, even on their own.' Maxine Berg, *The Age of Manufactures, 1700–1820.
Industry, Innovation and Work in Britain*, second edition (London and New York,
1994), 40.

use Paul Mantoux's words.[13] The adaptations in modes of work and methods of production were cumulative, but sufficient in making possible a rise in average incomes. In several countries of the European continent, early expansion in demand for industrial goods generated a 'dualistic' development of craft-based and machine-based industries. The dualism has persisted into the modern period.[14] In a different way, the accent on institutional choices and the resultant gains in flexibility reappears in the literature on European 'proto-industrialization', which has described capital accumulation based on domestic production in the countryside. A central idea of this literature is the comparative advantage of the 'family economy', a composite of putting-out, household production and rural industry.[15]

Bearing parallels with these reassessments of how industrialization 'began', a recent literature on firm strategy in historical perspective has 'reassessed the idea of a triumph of mass production ... to the point of obliteration'.[16] The story of Western industrialization which thus takes shape allows decentralized production a key role, and sees organizational change not in terms of clear choices between the old and the new, but in terms of 'hybrids'. In most historical and several contemporary examples, the strategy involves an economy of diversification, or a certain 'open-endedness' of the final output.[17] This economy tends to be large for small firms using tools or generic machinery and skilled labour, and small in large firms with specific machinery and narrowly skilled labour.[18] It is this economy which preserves a role for artisanal

[13] Paul Mantoux, *The Industrial Revolution in the Eighteenth Century* (London, 1928). The introduction defines the revolution mainly in terms of the extension of factories, which involved a separation of capital from labour. Mantoux criticizes Karl Marx, among others, for making an artificial distinction between 'manufacture' and 'factory' and identifying the latter with the use of machinery.

[14] See the contributions in M. Teich and R. Porter (eds.), *The Industrial Revolution in National Context. Europe and the USA* (Cambridge, 1996).

[15] For a recent survey of the historical patterns of rural industry, see Robert S. Duplessis, *Transitions to Capitalism in Early Modern Europe* (Cambridge, 1997). On institutional aspects, see the discussions in S. C. Ogilvie and M. Cerman (eds.), *European Proto-industrialization* (Cambridge, 1996).

[16] For a review of this line of work, see the introduction, 'Stories, Strategies, Structures: Rethinking Historical Alternatives to Mass Production' in Sabel and Zeitlin (eds.), *World of Possibilities*.

[17] Michael Piore, 'Technological Trajectories and the Classical Revival in Economics' in Michael Storper and Allen J. Scott (eds.), *Pathways to Industrialization and Regional Development* (London and New York, 1992). The use of this strategy has revived in the industrial countries after the 1970s for a number of reasons. See also the introduction to this collection of essays.

[18] The former usually appears in the form of dense collections of small firms transacting between themselves for input requirements. The vertically integrated firm illustrates the latter.

industry, organized in myriad hybrid ways, in economy-wide accumulation of capital.

In Europe, transregional demand was a crucial impetus to industrialization. So it was in late-nineteenth-century Japan, though the impact of long-distance trade, being the outcome of a delayed exposure, is much starker in Japan. As in South Asia, there was decay and dislocation in the older crafts, notably in segments of textiles, but there was also adaptation in other crafts and other segments of textiles which became successful exporters.[19] The sources of competitiveness of traditional industry had several bases. One was cheap but skilled labour. The other was the flexibility with which labour could be utilized for markets that valued differentiation. In this process of primary accumulation, which lasted in Japan well into the interwar period, neither mechanical invention nor mass production, nor even fundamental adjustments in the composition of industry, was the key feature. The key, almost invariably, was the creative use of labour in traditional industry under new systems of production and exchange. In broad outline, the same message reappears in the examples from India presented in this book.

However, to suggest a similarity in experiences does not amount to proposing a single evolutionary model, nor to ignoring differences. One obvious difference is in the outcome of the transition. The industrialization built on the basis of traditional industry clearly did not generate prosperity or development in South Asia comparable to that in Europe or Japan, 'development' being defined as a sustained rise in average income. Income and productivity did increase in absolute terms, but slowly in comparative terms in the long run. What was missing? Nothing in our examples supports a Marxist answer to this question. Trade, markets, or colonialism as such did not play a regressive role in South Asia. The answer, therefore, is to be found in the quality of the South Asian soil where industrialization was born, but did not attain maturity.

Indeed, European or East Asian evidence does not suggest that artisanal enterprise is the same thing as industrialization in the modern sense. They are certainly related. The former creates new organization, new towns, and new methods; it enables accumulation of capital, and facilitates factor markets – all of which assist industrial maturity. But the evidence also suggests that mature industrialization based upon mechanization, formally trained labour, and a rapid growth in labour productivity, needs much more than enterprising artisans. For example, demographic maturity is necessary to alter the factor mix, that is, the proportion of available capital and labour. Government intervention is

---

[19] A fuller discussion of the East Asian experience appears in chapter 2.

necessary in a number of areas, most importantly, in universal education, public finance, and financial development. Structural change in agriculture is necessary to create a home market for industry and to supply cheaper material. If some of these conditions remain weak, the result will be an industrialization unable to break free of its roots; one which not only begins with, but also continues to be reliant on, the artisans and manual labour. This, as chapter 2 in this book will argue, is more or less what happened in South Asia in the last century or so.

Plan of the book

The book consists of six main chapters, and a brief conclusion. Chapter 2 presents a more detailed outline of the economic history of the Indian artisan. The outline generalizes from the material of the industry examples, and compares India with other industrializing regions. Chapters 3 to 7 present the five examples. Each chapter is roughly divided into two themes: market extension, and industrial organization. On the former theme, the experiences of various industries overlap. But, on the latter aspect, that is, old and new systems of production or sale, they seem to differ a great deal. One of the main tasks for this book, therefore, is to boil down the industry descriptions to a more abstract account of organizational change. The greater part of chapter 2 is devoted to that task.

2 Markets and organization

This chapter will describe the main features of the transition that took shape in colonial India. It will also try to see the transition as part of a larger tendency. The transition involved, on the one hand, conditions in which the products of traditional industry were sold, and, on the other, conditions in which these were produced. 'Markets' and 'organization', therefore, are the core themes of this chapter. A convenient point to begin is an influential argument about 'markets', specifically about the impact of economic exposure during the colonial period on the Indian economy, in which argument the artisan has played a central role. This is taken up for review in the next section. The review will conclude with the proposal of an alternative reading of the evidence. The rest of the chapter is divided into eight sections. The first six describe the main elements of this alternative story. The remaining two compare India's experience with that of others to discover where they conformed and where they deviated.

The received view and its critique

The most coherent position available on the impact of economic exposure on artisans finds expression in a Marxist tradition in development literature. It involves an interpretation of nineteenth-century economic history that can be summed up in three propositions:
1. Economic contact between the European nations and their colonies in the modern developing world created a new international division of labour.
2. The process destroyed or severely damaged pre-existing industry in the colonies, but created new types of enterprise in their place.
3. The creative role of contact did not compensate for the destructive, indeed even aided regress, so that an economic retardation resulted from trade, investment, and colonial administration.

'De-industrialization', a term familiar to historians of South Asia, literally refers to proposition (2), but in fact represents a model of

12

economic transition that incorporates all three propositions. The direct evidence of regress comes from the destruction of industry, Indian industry being, in the words of Paul Baran, 'the outstanding case in point'.[1]

Karl Marx's essays on India contain the original statements of propositions (1) and (2).[2] Twentieth-century writers on development inspired by these essays added proposition (3), and thereby turned an argument about impact into a theory of the origins of underdevelopment.[3] Underdevelopment no longer mirrored the pre-development state of rich nations, but a condition created in the course of dealing with them, a condition described in terms such as 'deformed', 'stunted' or 'distorted'.

Both Marx and the Marxist tradition in development cited, along with other effects, the 'ruination' of Indian textile artisans as an example of the adverse effects of contact. More specifically, it was stated or implied that the process rendered many artisans unemployed who had 'no alternative save to crowd into agriculture',[4] which presumably was already overcrowded. Paul Baran states the general argument thus:

On few historical subjects is there so much agreement among students of widely differing perceptions as on what happened to India after Western capitalism appended her to her chariot ... [T]he British administration of India systematically destroyed all the fibres and foundations of Indian society. Its land and taxation policy ruined India's village economy ... Its commercial policy destroyed the Indian artisan ... Its economic policy broke down whatever beginnings there were of an indigenous industrial development.[5]

The reference to 'commercial policy' suggests the cause of the decline: competition from British manufactured goods sustained by policy. André Gunder Frank, who has offered probably the best known version of the Marxist theory of underdevelopment, cites 'the systematic destruction of the Indian textile industry' as a key piece of evidence.[6]

---

[1] Paul Baran, *The Political Economy of Growth* (Harmondsworth, 1978), 277.
[2] Marx's intention was to illustrate the 'vegetative' economy that precolonial India represented for him, by referring to the forces that destroyed it for the better: 'English interference ... sweeping away both Hindoo spinner and weaver, dissolved these semi-barbarian ... communities, by blowing up their economical basis, and thus produced the greatest ... revolution ever heard of in Asia.' 'The British Rule in India', *New York Daily Tribune*, June 25 (1853), reprinted in Marx and Engels, *Collected Works*, vol. XII (Moscow, 1979), 132.
[3] Most explicitly done by André Gunder Frank, *On Capitalist Underdevelopment* (Bombay, 1975). In this author's words, 'Marx may be partially pardoned' (p. 22) for being too optimistic, and not having foreseen the creation of underdevelopment (that is, proposition (3)).
[4] R. P. Dutt, *India To-day* (Bombay, 1947), 103.
[5] Baran, *Political Economy of Growth*, 277–83.
[6] Frank, *On Capitalist Underdevelopment*, 22.

Another eminent contributor, Immanuel Wallerstein, explains growing inequality between developed and developing nations in our times with 'such earlier phenomena as the deindustrialization of many areas of the world (starting with the widely known example of the Indian textile industry in the late eighteenth and early nineteenth century)'.[7] A. K. Bagchi's text on development contains another statement of the argument and the evidence.[8] In the 1970s, the widespread anti-trade and protectionist sentiment behind development policy was shaped by this reading of history, as the following statement from a textbook by Michael Barratt-Brown suggests: 'that ... handloom weavers in India suffered long-lasting damage from textile machinery introduced in England ... provides an understandable motive for protection'.[9] The 'destruction' thesis made the task of explaining South Asian underdevelopment so simple that it continued to pervade, even became a fixation, in modern thinking on development. For one among many examples, Alice Amsden's impressive work on Korean industrialization thus generalizes about India: 'artisanal production ... expired in the face of coercion and competitive imports from more advanced countries ... The British Crown legislated the decrepitude of the handloom weaver in India ... and then free trade furnished the final blow.'[10]

Marx cited only the weavers and spinners. But in Marxist writings a generalization is made routinely. Gunder Frank states that 'virtually the entire Indian handicrafts industry was severely crippled if not destroyed', which in turn 'severely and unfavourably affected all of rural society and its structure'.[11] Baran, in the citation above, talks about 'the Indian artisan'. Barratt-Brown switches freely between textiles and 'handicrafts'. Bagchi generalizes from textiles to 'handicrafts industries' on the basis of the rather feeble supplementary evidence of gun-making in Monghyr and saltpetre refining.[12]

What is the empirical foundation on which the various versions of this view have been based? Marx relied on rather impressionistic contemporary reports. The sources for most of the later writers, surprisingly, boil down to Marx himself. Two post-war socialist treatises, by R. P. Dutt and by John Strachey, and a well-known nationalist critique of

---

[7] Immanuel Wallerstein, *The Capitalist World-Economy* (Cambridge, 1979), 56–7.

[8] A. K. Bagchi, *The Political Economy of Underdevelopment* (Cambridge, 1982), 24, 34–5.

[9] Michael Barratt-Brown, *The Economics of Imperialism* (Harmondsworth, 1974), 36.

[10] Alice Amsden, *Asia's Next Giant* (New York and Oxford, 1989), 194.

[11] Frank, *On Capitalist Underdevelopment*, 22.

[12] Bagchi, *Political Economy of Underdevelopment*, 82. Saltpetre was a minor item of export from Bengal around 1800. Its share in export value was 2–4 per cent. In 1901, it engaged about 25,000 persons in an industrial workforce of approximately 15 million. Illegal gun-making in Munger (Monghyr), paradoxically, is known to be one of the few industries still flourishing in the otherwise bleak industrial landscape of Bihar state.

British policy by Romesh Dutt, are also cited.[13] Romesh Dutt's aims were more political than scholarly, and he wrote before the main body of published sources on the artisans became available. R. P. Dutt and Strachey do little more than reproduce passages from Marx. Wallerstein and Barratt-Brown for the most part do not worry about substantiation. Bagchi is more factually based, a dataset to be cited shortly.

When attention turns from development literature to Indian data and scholarship, a richer set of material can be found against which 'destruction' of Indian handicrafts can be tested. The rest of this section takes up the material for detailed treatment. To anticipate, while not disputing the fact of a decline in industrial employment, the data leave room for rethinking on why it happened and what it means.

Any discussion on the factual basis of growth or decline in industries must begin with the employment statistics of the population censuses. There are six pre-independence censuses, which give occupational distribution of the workforce for the period 1881–1931. However, these six are poorly comparable. There are three main problems. First, the 1881, 1891–1901, and 1911–31 censuses use different occupational classification systems. Secondly, the data on women workers are known to be suspect in almost all the censuses: there was a systematic confusion between workers and dependants, and one over intensity of work; and both involved women relatively more. And, thirdly, the 1931 census used a definition of worker much stricter than its predecessors.[14] There is a further problem with the 1881 census, namely, the existence of an ambiguous category called 'manufacturers-cum-sellers'. They were classified under industry or trade in the 1911–31 censuses according to primary occupation. These problems jointly imply that inferences on trends in occupational structure should (i) treat the male workforce data as the more reliable; (ii) treat 1931 figures as a possible underestimate compared to 1911 and 1921; (iii) avoid comparing detailed occupational data beyond the period 1911–31; and (iv) consider industry and

---

[13] R. P. Dutt, *India To-day*; John Strachey, *The End of Empire* (London, 1959), 52–3; R. C. Dutt, *The Economic History of India*, vol. I, *Under Early British Rule, 1757–1837* (London, 1901); and R. C. Dutt, *The Economic History of India in the Victorian Age* (London, 1906), various chapters. For a survey of contemporary nationalist views, see Bipan Chandra, *The Rise and Growth of Economic Nationalism in India* (New Delhi, 1966), chapters II and III.

[14] See B. G. Ghate, *Changes in the Occupational Distribution of the Population*, Office of the Economic Adviser, Government of India (Delhi, 1940), 4–5; J. Krishnamurty, 'Changing Concepts of Work in the Indian Censuses: 1901–61', *Indian Economic and Social History Review*, 14, 3 (1977); J. Krishnamurty, 'Occupational Structure', in Dharma Kumar (ed.), *The Cambridge Economic History of India*, vol. II, *c.1757–c.1970* (Cambridge, 1983).

trade figures jointly. Subject to these caveats, the census data suggest a few conclusions unlikely to be controversial.[15]

1. In the period of the censuses, the proportion of male workers engaged in industry declined, from about 10.6 per cent in 1881 to about 8.4 per cent in 1931.
2. The proportion of women workers in industry declined somewhat more rapidly.
3. If industry and trade are considered together, the proportion of male workers engaged in these sectors fell from 15.5 per cent in 1881 to 14.1 per cent in 1931. Thus, while trade and commerce did employ an increasing proportion of workers, the increase was not sufficient to offset the fall in industry.
4. In absolute numbers, the male industrial workforce fell between 1881 and 1901, was constant between 1901 and 1921, and rose between 1921 and 1931.
5. The number of women industrial workers was in continuous decline.
6. Between 1901 and 1931, both relative share of industry and absolute numbers engaged in industry changed rather little.

To conclude, therefore, there can be hardly any dispute over the existence of a decline in male industrial employment, in absolute and relative terms, between 1881 and 1901. The fall continues thereafter, but not in absolute numbers, and slows down in relative terms. The situation with female workers is unclear, given the low reliability attached to this data. However, there has been no claim so far that the actual trend was the opposite of what is observed. These aggregate statistics from the censuses have been interpreted to mean industrial regress in well-known works on comparative development.[16]

Between 1911 and 1931, detailed occupation classes become more comparable. These data, as mentioned before, are subject to the qualification that the 1931 definition of workers is too restrictive. In this period, occupation statistics suggest where the decline in male employment may have concentrated. Going by major industry groups, wood, metals and leather show little change (Table 2.1). But textiles, ceramics, food industries, dress and toilet articles, and the building industry suffered falls. Going by specific crafts, employment fell in cotton, silk and wool weaving, among potters and braziers, and among oil extractors

---

[15] The description that follows will draw mainly on Krishnamurty, 'Occupational Structure'; and Daniel Thorner and Alice Thorner, '"De-industrialization" in India, 1881–1931' in *Land and Labour in India* (Bombay, 1962).

[16] For example, Colin Clark, *Conditions of Economic Progress* (London, 1951), 423.

Table 2.1 *Male workers in industry*

Industry group	1911 (millions)	1931 (millions)
Textiles	2.685	2.531
Cotton	1.921	1.761
Silk	0.078	0.057
Wool	0.103	0.064
Metals	0.658	0.660
Brassware	0.101	0.084
Leather	0.247	0.257
Wood	1.312	1.306
Ceramics	0.768	0.728
Pottery	0.652	0.601
Food	0.806	0.706
Rice-pounding	0.128	0.103
Dress and toilet	2.676	2.566
Building	0.752	0.528

Note: Figures are for 'actual workers' for 1911, and 'earners and working dependants' for 1931.
Source: Census of India, 1911 and 1931, *India*, vol. I Part II (Delhi, 1912 and 1933).

and rice-pounders, to mention the main industries. In textiles, the loss of the hand industry was partially compensated by the growth of mills. The 1911–31 censuses also contain some information on the proportion of workers from major artisan castes engaged in their traditional occupation. 1911 and 1931 are only approximately comparable. Subject to that qualification, the percentages are in uniform decline for five major groups: weavers (Julaha, Tanti, Koshti), tanners (Chamar, Chakkiliyan), potters (Kumhar), oil-extractors (Teli, Ghanchi), and blacksmiths (Lohar). The extent of decline is smaller for those groups who had already diversified by 1911. Thus, the percentage of workers pursuing traditional occupations for tanners and oilmen was 13–24 per cent in 1911, and did not change much in 1931. But, for all others, the decline is sharp and of similar magnitude. Interestingly, among weavers, potters, and oilmen, the proportion of workers who practised their traditional craft on the side increased marginally.

There are relevant occupational data from sources other than the censuses. In the period between 1809–13 and 1901, Bagchi has estimated a fall in non-agricultural employment in eastern India.[17] Twomey has estimated a fall in notional employment in cotton textiles in the second and third quarters of the century.[18] Another estimate for a slightly different period suggests a decline in share of industry in total employment, but a rise in absolute numbers.[19] There is also qualitative evidence on the fate of the artisan. These again suggest exit on a large scale. Artisans supplied labour to the mills that were started in the nineteenth century, so that studies on industrial labour deal with groups who gave up their traditional occupation.[20] Artisans were prominent among groups who migrated to the plantations in Britain's tropical colonies.[21] Sources on the famines of 1876–8 and 1896–8 discussed the extreme vulnerability of the rural artisan to conditions of food scarcity.[22]

Coming to interpretation of these data, two questions need to be asked in relation to the Marxist thesis. Were these declines and dislocations caused by imports? Were they symptomatic of a regress? The answer to the first question, whether competitive imports can be blamed, must be negative. The fall in employment was more general. Textiles alone among major industries faced competitive import. But there were also falls in the numbers of potters and braziers, rice-

---

[17] A. K. Bagchi, 'De-industrialization in India in the Nineteenth Century: Some Theoretical Implications', *Journal of Development Studies*, 12, 2 (1976) shows this for Gangetic Bihar, and claims general validity for India. Marika Vicziany criticized Bagchi's estimates in 'The Deindustrialization of India in the Nineteenth Century: A Methodological Critique of Amiya Kumar Bagchi', *Indian Economic and Social History Review*, 16, 2 (1979).

[18] M. J. Twomey, 'Employment in Nineteenth Century Indian Textiles', *Explorations in Economic History*, 20, 3 (1983).

[19] Dharma Kumar and J. Krishnamurty, 'The Evolution of Labour Markets in India, 1857–1947', mimeo, Employment and Rural Development Division, World Bank (Washington DC, 1981).

[20] For a general statement

> [T]he textile mills have many weavers from families that, for generations previously, worked at handlooms; the village worker in hides and leather, the carpenter and the blacksmith are all being subjected to pressures from the factory. In many cases the easiest, and perhaps the only, way out of the difficulty is for the village craftsman to transfer his allegiance to the rival which is supplanting him.

Report of the Royal Commission on Labour in India (London, 1931), 15. On artisanal sources of textile mill labour, see Morris D. Morris, *The Emergence of an Industrial Labor Force in India: A Study of the Bombay Cotton Mills, 1854–1947* (Berkeley and Los Angeles, 1965), 81; Rajnarayan Chandavarkar, *The Origins of Industrial Capitalism in India: Business Strategies and the Working Class in Bombay, 1900–1940* (Cambridge, 1994), 146; Ranajit Das Gupta, 'Factory Labour in Eastern India: Sources of Supply, 1855–1946. Some Preliminary Findings', *Indian Economic and Social History Review*, 13, 3 (1976), 320, 322.

[21] Konrad Specker, 'Madras Handlooms in the Nineteenth Century', *Indian Economic and Social History Review*, 26, 2 (1989), 158.

[22] *Report of the Indian Famine Commission* (Simla, 1898), 298.

pounders and builders, and in a whole range of quasi-services classified under 'dress and toilet'. None faced competition from British goods. Their decline must be seen as an effect of an as yet poorly understood macroeconomic transition. The transition may have been aided by British 'commercial policy', but only indirectly.

On the second question, whether decline in employment should imply economic regress, a well-argued critique exists. In 1962, the Thorners clarified that 'there can be no dispute with a flat statement that India's traditional handicrafts have declined'.[23] But, then, 'industrialization' by definition includes the prospect of machinery replacing the handicrafts. The process does not mean a fall in industrial income. Real income per worker in industry increased during the period 1900 to 1947.[24] In fact, it increased steadily and significantly at an approximate compound rate of growth of 1.7 per cent per year. The approximate rate of growth of real income per capita was 0.7 per cent in the same period. Based on this evidence, a non-Marxist interpretation of the decline in the handicrafts becomes possible. Deepak Lal states the position thus:

If . . . we consider the hallmark of the industrial revolution to be the substitution of fixed for working capital in industrial production as we move from the mercantile, handicraft, putting-out type modes to the fully fledged industrial, mechanized, and factory-based modes of industrialization, India had begun to experience the first stirrings of this revolution by 1851. Far from being a century of de-industrialization, the British century marked the beginning of modern industrialization in India.[25]

There are, indeed, several examples of substitution of handicraft by mechanized industry. Cotton spinning is a classic example of decline in non-specialized and low-productivity manual workers, replaced by workers in mechanized processes. Cloth is partly an example of mechanization. Rice-pounding is another. In some other cases, tastes changed from one type of good made with relatively labour-intensive techniques to others made with less labour, such as from earthenware to metals.

Despite such examples, the non-Marxist position in the version stated above is rather simplistic. Any story of the displacement of traditional industry by machinery amounts to a serious misreading of the long-term pattern of Indian industrialization. Enterprises answering to the description 'fully fledged industrial, mechanized, and factory-based' have

---

[23] Thorner and Thorner, '"De-industrialization"', 70.

[24] Krishnamurty, 'Occupational Structure', 534–41.

[25] Deepak Lal, *The Hindu Equilibrium*, vol. I, *Cultural Stability and Economic Stagnation: India 1500 BC–1980* (Oxford, 1988), 186.

always accounted for a small proportion of industrial employment in India. The share of officially registered factories in industrial employment did increase, but from 5 per cent in 1901 to only 10 per cent in 1931. The percentages engaged in mechanized industry were smaller still. In the interwar period, the combined share in industrial employment of the new mechanized industries (cotton and jute mills, sugar, cement, paper, woollen mills, brewery, and steel) was in the range 4–5 per cent. Their share in factory employment actually fell over the period of 1919–39.[26] What remained of factories, and all of non-factory industry, was largely based on manual work, and to a significant extent, derived from traditional industry such as tanning, carpentry, metalwork, food-processing, or weaving. Given its marginal weight in employment, it is not credible that the increase in industrial productivity could arise mainly from the rising share of the mechanized sector. After independence, the situation has changed, but not in any fundamental way. The share of factory and mechanized industry in employment and value-added was higher in 1991 than in 1931, but not very much higher. In fact, the share of factory work in employment, 31 per cent in 1971, has been falling since 1971. In short, machinery substituting manual and tool-based work happened on too limited a scale in India, colonial or post-colonial, to be treated as a universal or predominant historical process.

The naïve non-Marxist position cited above, therefore, needs to be improved. An alternative is the hypothesis that the crafts did not decline at all. The decline in employment is symptomatic of a reorganization that improved their capability. To establish this, it needs to be shown that productivity can and did increase *within the crafts*. If there was such a trend, it must have been led by changes in industrial organization rather than in technology, for, by definition, crafts continued with relatively unchanged technology.[27] Thus, a tendency towards greater specialization can improve output per worker by means of increased work intensity or efficiency of those who remain in the industry. A substitution of family labour inside household units by wage labour inside small-scale factories can have this implication. This happened

[26] Tirthankar Roy, 'The Pattern of Industrial Growth in Interwar India', *Journal of Indian School of Political Economy*, 6, 3 (1994).

[27] The term 'organizational change' will be used in this book to refer to three spheres of change: division of labour and specialization, location and access to economies of agglomeration, and in common with the disciplines of organization theory and industrial organization, the nature of the firm. The last subject, in this context, consists of two sets of relationships: exchange of goods and services (for example, spot-sale, putting-out), and employment of labour (for example, household, factory). The significance of organization in this study is that it is affected by long-distance trade, and, in turn, it can affect efficiency.

extensively in handloom textiles.[28] It has been happening on a national scale in post-colonial India (chapter 1). It is a strong inference that it happened in the crafts as a whole in colonial India. That productivity did increase in the crafts can be inferred from national income data. Real income in 'small-scale industry' increased by 72 per cent between 1901 and 1947, whereas employment declined. The approximate rate of growth of average income in this sector was 1.1 per cent per annum. The average rate for 'large-scale industry' or the registered factories was *smaller* at 0.9 per cent. The exact percentages are subject to a large margin of error. But the basic conclusion, that productivity increased significantly in the crafts, is not likely to be upset thereby.

The same tendency can be seen in the experience of several major industries for which we have reasonably good quantitative data. Consider, for example, handloom cotton and silk weaving, tanning of hides and skins, and weaving of carpets and rugs. In terms of yarn equivalent, handloom cloth production increased from 259 million lbs in 1904–8 (annual average) to 419 million lbs in 1934–8 (annual average). Exports of carpets and rugs increased from 1.6 million lbs to 9.9 million lbs between the same pair of dates. Exports of hides and skins increased from possibly less than 10,000 tonnes in 1870 to 91,000 tonnes in 1910–14 (annual average).[29] Major raw materials of the silk handloom industry, raw silk and silk yarn, began to be imported from the turn of the century. Together, import of the two items increased from 0.5 million lbs in 1904–8 to 2.2 million lbs in 1934–8 (both annual averages). Some of it may have been in replacement of domestic production of these materials, but only some. There was no sign that the domestic silk industry declined to the extent that imports increased. To the best of our knowledge, the number of handlooms engaged in cotton and other fibres fluctuated around 2 million in the first half of the twentieth century, though regional experiences followed divergent trends. The fourth row in Table 2.1 above suggests a decline, or at best stagnation, in 'actual workers' engaged in the textiles using wool, a major component of which category was carpet weavers. Direct estimates of the number of carpet looms are not easily available. A plausible inference is that the major carpet-weaving region, United Provinces, engaged possibly a little less than 1,000 looms in the first decade of the century, and about 5,000 in the 1930s. On the other hand, there are

---

[28] Tirthankar Roy, *Artisans and Industrialization. Indian Weaving in the Twentieth Century* (Delhi, 1993). See also the related discussion and citations in chapter 1 of the present book.

[29] From this level, the trade shrank somewhat until the Depression, and dwindled rapidly thereafter, as domestic demand for hides replaced external demand.

numerous reports of decline in marginal carpet towns from all over northern and central India in the same period, so that the aggregate loomage may have increased more slowly. Neither the United Provinces looms nor this inference about the aggregate number suggests an increase comparable to that of carpet export. Employment in leather in the late nineteenth century is impossible to compare with that in the 1911–31 censuses. Crude data suggest a decline; a decline is also suggested by the fact that members of the traditional tanning castes were known to have been leaving their traditional occupations almost continuously during this time.[30] In all these examples, therefore, there is evidence in favour of a significant rise in labour productivity.[31]

Both the Marxist position and the naïve non-Marxist position treat the cotton textiles as prime evidence in their favour. But, in fact, recent textile scholarship in India has consistently argued that the real picture in textiles is much more complex than has been painted by these writers. The textile data suggest three facts on which there is not much disputation today: (i) the gradual extinction of hand-made yarn; (ii) a possible decline in handloom weaving in the middle of the nineteenth century; and (iii) the expansion of weaving in the first half of the twentieth century.[32] The first two findings are consistent with the Marxist thesis. But, what about the third? It is indeed possible that Indian crafts and British machinery produced identical cloth. But the crafts could partially offset their handicap in labour productivity and survive by accepting lower wages, adjusting skill downward, and altogether by

---

[30] The sources for these output and capacity data are, Table 2.1 above; India, *Annual Statement of the Sea-Borne Trade of British India with the British Empire and Foreign Countries*, vol. I, Director of Commercial Intelligence and Statistics (Calcutta, various years); Roy, *Artisans and Industrialization*, chapter 1; and chapters 6 and 7 in the present book.

[31] This work does not deal with the quasi-services. Examples of both mechanization and exit of vulnerable workers come from the services. One rare work on this sector is Dharma Kumar, 'The Forgotten Sector: Services in Madras Presidency in the First Half of the Nineteenth Century', *Indian Economic and Social History Review*, 24, 4 (1987). In the sources consulted in this study, there are isolated descriptions on how occupations which involved processing of material, and were thus between services and industry, were changing. One general change was for numerous unskilled services formerly integrated with the domestic and agrarian economy to detach from the agrarian context and partially to mechanize. Grain- and oil-processing are prominent examples. Carpentry and smithy relocated from the village to the towns, and were reapplied from agricultural implements to new products, such as furniture and cutlery. Several such shifts are described in A. C. Chatterjee, *Notes on the Industries of the United Provinces* (Allahabad, 1908).

[32] Cited, in the context of a theoretical critique of de-industrialization, by Morris D. Morris, 'Towards a Reinterpretation of Nineteenth Century Indian Economic History', *Indian Economic and Social History Review*, 5, 1 (1968).

becoming an industry of the poor for the poor.[33] The condition can be called a regress, visible not in employment but in incomes. Wage trends in weaving are difficult to generalize on. Careful surveys and reconstructions have found no sign of a steady fall in real wages of *any* class of workers. Those most comparable in skills to the skilled weaver experienced a slow rise between 1857 and 1906, and a quicker rise between 1906 and 1947.[34] An index of a 20sx20s grey cotton cloth weaver's real earnings exists for about fifteen years in the interwar period, and consistent with the overall movements during that time, the index moved cyclically.[35] Trends apart, it is very hard to construct an average wage series because there was no such thing as an average weaver. Wage disparities between weavers have always been very wide, but the Marxists tend to ignore them. There were many types of weavers, and while some experienced long depression, several others did not compete with British cloth at all. Some cloths had specific markets, which the power-loom could not penetrate. Many others demanded 'flexible specialization'.[36] Recent writings on the industry have confirmed that such segmentations were an important feature of the industry, and that in several segmented and competing goods productivity improved. They have studied specific preferences of the Indian consumer, and discussed possible sources of productivity gains. Since the basic technology in artisanal production changes at best by small adaptations, productivity gains must be partly attributed to better organization.[37]

To conclude, the Marxists have read the basic 'stylized fact' about the scale of artisan activity in the nineteenth century too narrowly. A different reading, which acknowledges the survival of and reorganization

---

[33] Bagchi implies this option in his conclusion on how the Indian spinner and weaver survived British goods. See Bagchi, 'De-industrialization in India in the Nineteenth Century', 145.

[34] Deepak Lal, *The Hindu Equilibrium*, vol I, *Aspects of Indian Labour* (Oxford, 1989), chapter 2.

[35] Roy, *Artisans and Industrialization*, chapter 2.

[36] The ability to serve different tastes and market segments with general-purpose machinery or tools, and the ability to make adjustments in the tools to enable such adaptations. See Charles Sabel and Jonathan Zeitlin, 'Historical Alternatives to Mass Production: Politics, Markets and Technology in Nineteenth-Century Industrialisation', *Past and Present*, 58 (1985), and the recent collection edited by these authors, *World of Possibilities* (Cambridge, 1997).

[37] The proposition first appeared in Raj Chandavarkar, 'Industrialization in India before 1947: Conventional Approaches and Alternative Perspectives', *Modern Asian Studies*, 19, 3 (1985). Criticizing the idea of Indian industrialization as a process determined by large-scale industry, the essay cites handloom weaving to suggest that 'non-factory forms of production organization were capable of ... dynamism, expansion and ... innovation' (p. 641). The chronology and content of growth, decline and reorganization in weaving have been explored in detail mainly in a post-1985 scholarship on textile history. Fuller reference to this literature appears in chapter 3 below, notes 1–4.

in these industries, is necessary. What appears as a general decline is possibly a widespread exit of low-productivity workers. This was one result of the artisans trying to adapt to macroeconomic changes from the nineteenth century. What were the macroeconomic changes? Why did industrial organization change? What forms did the adaptation take? These are the questions that need answers.

To answer them, it is necessary to look beyond textiles. Textiles were undoubtedly the most important industry. But they are also rather unsuitable to generalize from. Cotton textiles were so widely dispersed in India, so polymorphous in product, techniques, organization, and social relations, that they hardly represent a simple model of transition. To cite textiles as typical of any other industry is out of the question. Further, cotton textiles tend to draw attention to the machinery-versus-tools battle. But, for industry as a whole, such a contest was not the most critical factor. Cotton textiles, in this sense, were an exception and not the rule. *Jari* was affected by competitive imports, but the competition was one on quality, rather than one between different technologies. Examples of obsolescence occur in products, like handmade paper or iron hardware, which were too minor to carry the weight of a general model of transition. To develop a different model of transition, one that can capture the creative effects of trade much better, a wider sample is needed. There do exist a few scarce narratives on industrial change using a wider sample of industries, especially noteworthy being D. R. Gadgil's book on industrialization.[38] It uses a limited range of sources; but the brief comments convey the sense of a many-sided change in rural and urban industries of nineteenth-century India, and hints at a programme of research. To start such a project, a broad view of what was happening to the craftsman's market needs to be developed. The concept used here is 'commercialization'.

---

[38] D. R. Gadgil, *Industrial Evolution in India in the Recent Times* (Delhi, 1971). Gadgil referred to the following processes. There were migrations of carpenters and smiths who faced declining rural demand due to technological change and, at the same time, diversified urban demand. The number of potters and oilmen shrunk as new raw materials substituted for old in the same uses. The order of customary dues crumbled in the rural economy to which several kinds of craftsmen and castes were more or less subject. And the late-nineteenth century famines caused massive dispersal of artisan populations. Another example of using non-textile data is J. Krishnamurty, 'Deindustrialization in Gangetic Bihar: Another Look at the Evidence', *Indian Economic and Social History Review*, 22, 4 (1985). The article concludes that mixed fortunes obtained for such industries of eastern India as silk and woollen textiles, leather, carpentry, blacksmithy, and pottery.

Commercialization

'Commercialization' in this study means one or more of three processes: (i) a shift away from production for one's own use, or for use as gifts and tributes, to production for the market, especially the non-local market; (ii) a shift from local to long-distance trades and (iii) the creation of infrastructure and institutions which aid such shifts. To these quantitative or institutional dimensions, a fourth and a more qualitative one can be added: a change in consumer and producer behaviour induced by the possibility of long-distance trade. Commercialization was a significant tendency in these senses in the examples studied here. The fact that real income in industry was expanding in the twentieth century suggests a fifth dimension for commercialization: an expansion in demand. However, for most individual industries, such an effect cannot be tested. It is also hard to claim that size of demand was a powerful impetus in the aggregate, for real per capita income rose too slowly. We shall return to this point later.

The most important example of outright market creation is leather, especially tanned hides and skins. This product became a major tradeable in the late nineteenth century, and the capital and expertise accumulated in this trade was the foundation for a diversified leather industry to build up later, now one of South Asia's leading exports.

Manufactured tradeables also included several skilled crafts. Markets for them were not non-existent, but mainly local, before the colonial period. Woollen carpets and engraved metals were earlier made in north Indian cities chiefly for local consumption. There are references to trade, but as exceptions than the rule.[39] Shawls were probably traded to a greater extent, but they too were rooted in local consumption. In crafts like ivory-carving, carpets, engraved metals, and wood-carving, the European residents became important buyers within India. The cloths made on the southeastern coast and known by the trade-name 'Madras', were an exportable from the precolonial times. But the trade grew or substantially revived in the interwar period, and the product began to be made and sold under systems that were of relatively recent origin. If India's accumulated competence in a range of craftsmanship was threa-

---

[39] Carpets were commissioned by officers of the East India Company. But the purchases probably came from the royal factories, and involved great difficulty. The trades are not known to involve specialist traders and trading networks. In the late nineteenth century, the difficulties had disappeared, and specialist traders had come into existence. On the Company's access to Agra and Lahore carpets in the middle of the seventeenth century, see John Irwin and P. R. Schwartz, *Studies in Indo-European Textile History* (Ahmedabad, 1966), 20–2.

tened by the decline of the courtly or temple elites of the precolonial era, commercialization partly sustained or revived it.[40]

Trade replaced local and home manufacture of several inputs. Cotton yarn, *jari* and dyes began to be imported. Raw silk and the silk substitute rayon were imported in the early twentieth century. In metals, imported sheets replaced locally gathered scrap. In glassware, blocks replaced scrap. A minor example is imported leather for some early attempts at making European-style shoes and saddlery by the artisans. In all cases, the imported input was cheaper than the local one, was easier to handle, gave rise to new trades, and to merchants specialized in these trades, who in turn influenced production of the final good. Eventually, imported inputs also induced attempts at import substitution. Jari, for example, is a story of import substitution by a mix of protectionist policy and innovation at the work-site.

In goods consumed at home, handloom cloth being the main example, long-distance trade was a far from new invention. But there are grounds to believe that long-distance trade in handloom cloth increased in extent in the colonial period. First, the introduction of mass-produced and mass-consumed cloth from England and the Indian mills increased the average scale of the cloth trade, and extended the networks of trade that were of recent origin. Secondly, the introduction of imported inputs extended the scale and network of input trade. Thirdly, production of artisanal cloth gravitated towards points of internal trade, towards the railways, and especially into towns where input trade was concentrated. Fourthly, as a result, the handloom industry urbanized, its most successful representatives were urban clusters that greatly expanded in loomage in the early twentieth century. Fifthly, systems of final sale tended to shift from spot to contractual. This shift will be discussed below.

Commercialization is illustrated in the quality of urbanization of industry. 'By far the largest manufacturing centres' in Mughal north India were Lahore, Delhi and Agra. These sites were centres of power and concentrations of demand. They signify that power and local

---

[40] Exports of manufactured goods were about 35–40 per cent of merchandise export in the middle of the1920s. Exports of the principal exportable crafts (leather, 'Madras' carpets, and metals) were possibly 3–5 per cent of merchandise export, and 10–15 per cent of manufactured export. For an earlier comparison, in 1760, manufactured exports (textiles) were 65–70 per cent of total exports of the English East India Company, and all of it came from the artisan. While the share of the crafts in exports declined, the nominal value of craft export in the middle of the 1920s was possibly ten times higher than the estimated total industrial export in 1760. The volume must be higher, too, if by a smaller multiple. The raw data are taken from K. N. Chaudhuri, 'Foreign Trade and Balance of Payments' in Dharma Kumar (ed.), *The Cambridge Economic History of India*, vol. II, *c.1757–c.1970* (Cambridge, 1983).

demand, and not exports, were the main influence on the location of skilled crafts.[41] The same point can be made with the towns that came into prominence in the eighteenth century: Farrukhabad, Lucknow, and Benares in the north, and Poona, Aurangabad, and Madurai in the south. In the colonial period, however, prominent craft towns were no longer centres of power, nor necessarily driven by local markets. Sholapur, Salem, Agra, Amritsar, Ludhiana, and Surat were sites that served non-local markets. Economics, and not politics, defined their comparative advantage over competing craft towns. The economic factors were sometimes directly observable: for example, savings in input costs drove handloom weaving into towns where mill yarn was made. Sometimes, they were the less visible commonly shared economies of agglomeration, such as infrastructure and information, on which small producers tend to be especially dependent.

Commercialization, finally, had a behavioural dimension. Tastes, especially for goods whose significance for the consumers exceeded their use-values, changed over long periods in response to social and economic changes that acted on these meanings. Cloth is the clearest case.[42] But in minor and less apparent ways, other decorative crafts were subject as well. Further, several types of customary rights on wastes and commons began to disintegrate when some of these goods became scarce and/or saleable. The two examples that reflect this clearly, but in different ways, were hide of naturally dead cattle and pastures that supported handloom weaving of woollen garments.

One type of behavioural change, so far neglected in historical scholarship, recurs with remarkable persistence and regularity in the evidence on the skilled crafts. In numerous decorative crafts, sources speak eloquently of a degradation of quality which commerce brought in its wake. A state of depreciation of craftsmanship was pervasive in the late nineteenth century. Specific reports from carpet, metal, *jari* and textiles will be discussed in the relevant chapters. A broad assessment, made in the *Journal of Indian Art (and Industry)* in connection with objects displayed in the Festival of Empire, 1911, should do here. 'It is, unfortunately, true', the article concludes, 'that most large collections

---

[41] H. K. Naqvi, 'Industrial Towns of Hindustan in the Eighteenth Century' in M. K. Chaudhuri (ed.), *Trends in Socio-Economic Change in India, 1871–1961* (Simla, 1969), 238–9.

[42] Examples of the changing message of Indian clothing appear in B. Cohn, 'Cloth, Clothes and Colonialism: India in the Nineteenth Century' in A. Weiner and J. Schneider (eds.), *Cloth and the Human Experience* (Washington and London, 1989), 325; and C. A. Bayly, 'The Origin of Swadeshi (Home Industry): Cloth and Indian Society, 1700–1930' in A. Appadurai (ed.), *The Social Life of Things: Commodities in Cultural Perspectives* (Cambridge, 1986).

illustrate almost every form of imperfection which is possible.'[43] Defects were classified under (i) bad design, or designs inconsistent with shape, awkward mixtures of oriental and European designs, of which printed textiles furnished many examples; (ii) overcrowding of ornamentation, seen in carpets, brassware from Moradabad and Bidar, and wood-carving, and partly attributed to the mechanical reproduction of old designs; (iii) mixed styles forced by new preferences, for example, 'colours of carpets have been changed in order to harmonize with those of the curtains of the purchaser'; and (iv) carelessness, inferior material, and hasty execution. Problems (ii) and (iv) made the objects not only unattractive, but unusable. Thus, overornamented metal plates became useless as plates, or beautifully decorated but porous pottery was useless as pottery.

Some of these complaints may have been a matter of perception. Better and worse goods were compared more closely in 1870 than 100 years ago because they were now sold in the same market. But that does not completely explain these complaints; it is hard to ignore the many specific observations about decay over a period of time. There were also several instances of a market crashing in response to uncertain and variable quality, as in the auction market for carpets in London. The kind of hazard listed in the *Journal* would have been unthinkable in, say, carpets made for mosques, courtly consumption, revenue payments or royal dowry, such as were made in the medieval manufactories. The decay partly resulted from the clash of distinct aesthetic sentiments when Europeans became the major buyers of Indian goods. Tastes were malleable, as the buyer continually attempted to compare, classify, and conceptualize a relatively unfamiliar product. The artisan, in turn, never quite understood or approved what was expected of him.

But, in the main, the decay derived from changes in behaviour enabled by commercialization. Consumers were now distant and anonymous. Thus, they were often uncertain about what is a really good work. The anonymity removed old restraints on experiments. There was propensity for fraud. To borrow a term from economic theory, 'moral hazard' was endemic; that is, unequal knowledge of buyers and sellers about quality, together with a predominance of transient buyers, could lead to systematic offers of poor quality. There was need to make cheap and worse copies of old masterpieces. When bad copies predominated, the buyers of good products could not be sure of what they might be buying, and tended to stop buying. Eventually the demand for the good article declined. There was a propensity to break conventions, but

<hr/>

[43] 'Defects in Indian Art Ware', *Journal of Indian Art (and Industry)*, 15–16 (1912–14), 48–50.

experiments rarely succeeded. Craftsmanship was imparted by learning-by-doing which could not deal in abstractions and notional innovations. Such attempts could not only be hazardous, succeeding only by chance or by rare individual talents, they could create an unhealthy competition in counterfeit knowledge. Sham secrets were common in all design-intensive crafts and in chemical processes like dyeing. Reflecting the same inherent problem, the artisan proved to be a poor engineer time and again. Whenever a product needed to combine an inherited with an acquired skill – weaving with dyeing, or carving with carpentry – the allied skill was as a rule carelessly performed. When demand for the composite good strengthened, the consumer tended to give up the artisanal good in favour of a better-engineered one, eventually de-stroying the decorative skill altogether.[44] Precisely when good designers were needed, informal systems of access to knowledge ensured that they were in short supply. North India had a master-apprenticeship system that involved a culture of proficiency. But the masters tended to compete, when they needed to, by the only way they could: hiding knowledge and refusing to encode knowledge. The problems were aggravated by the absence of guilds, and, where quasi-guilds existed, by their decay due to members who enjoyed the benefits but refused to meet the obligations. Probably the only example of a formal guild in north India is in the smelting of precious metals. To maintain purity, smelting used to be done in Lahore, Delhi, and Lucknow in common premises monitored by bodies like town councils. The maintenance of the furnace was done for a fee imposed on all members of the silver or *jari* merchant community. In the 1880s, it was found that the fee had no legal force. 'Renegades' took advantage of this, and, eventually, the payment ceased, weakening the very institution itself.[45] This 'free riding' problem was present even where sheer force of custom, rather than formal guilds, served to control quality.

Complaints of the nature described above become rare from the middle of the interwar period. Many craft towns did successfully deal with them, some by better quality control, and others by simplifying their product to suit mass markets. Examples of the latter come from Surat *jari*, Moradabad brass and Mirzapur carpets. But the depreciation of craftsmanship remained as a possibility whenever an old product tried

[44] An interesting example comes from wooden furniture in Bombay. The better-finished products of one Mr Wimbridge drove out 'the florid ornament associated with the Indian furniture of former days'. J. A. G. Wales, *A Monograph on Wood Carving in the Bombay Presidency* (Bombay, 1902), 9.

[45] E. Burden, *Monograph on the Wire and Tinsel Industry in the Punjab* (Lahore, 1909), 9–10.

out a new market. Many examples, in fact, can be found among the declining crafts in present-day India.

Having described commercialization, it is now possible to show cases of technological and organizational change as the effects of commercialization. The next five sections deal with these aspects.

From custom to contract

'Custom' in this context is a shorthand for the diverse initial transactional systems in the early or middle nineteenth century.[46] Before going further, it is necessary to give this term some substance with reference to the literature on precolonial commercial systems. First of all, a distinction needs to be made between 'transactions' and 'markets'. 'Transactions' is defined as any regular exchange of goods and services. The term includes 'markets' or exchange for prices, but it also includes tributes and customary dues or exchange for protection and sustenance. Any transactional system can be classified as a spot-transaction or a contractual one. The former does not involve prior agreement on prices and quantities. The latter involves agreement. The main reason agreement matters is that it brings the production relation nearer to wage employment. Also, the greater scale and regularity of long-distance trade tend to favour agreement, so that agreement is often a sign of long-distance trade. Both types can be performed on specific sites or can be siteless, that is, they may involve a marketplace or may not.

It is well known that seventeenth and eighteenth-century India possessed *all* these types. There was a whole hierarchy of sited spot-markets, from the rural regular *mandis*, irregular *mandis* and fairs, to the great sea-port bazaars in towns such as Surat.[47] A famous example of the siteless spot-market is the local peddlar. Contractual transaction included such forms as (i) rural customary exchange of artisanal goods for grain-share or rent-free land; (ii) direct transactions between courtiers or temples and urban artisans; and (iii) putting-out between merchants and artisans. Forms (i) and (iii) were typically siteless. Form (iii) alone was unambiguously market transaction. The most detailed

---

[46] The term comes from a classic theoretical treatment of the subject by John Hicks, *A Theory of Economic History* (Oxford, 1969). In Hicks, 'custom' has a more specific sense.

[47] Two important essays which describe and conceptualize precolonial commercial systems are B. R. Grover, 'An Integrated Pattern of Commercial Life in the Rural Society of North India During the Seventeenth and Eighteenth Centuries'; and K. N. Chaudhuri, 'Markets and Traders in India During the Seventeenth and Eighteenth Centuries'; both reprinted in Sanjay Subrahmanyam (ed.), *Money and the Market in India 1100–1700* (Delhi, 1994). See also the editor's introduction in the same volume, 40–2, for related discussion.

account of this form appears from sources on European trade in India, though it is known to exist in home trade as well. These forms were not exclusive: rather one often supplied another.

Between the precolonial period and the twentieth century, relative to mercantile contractual systems (form (iii) above), there was a decline in all other systems. Indisputable cases of decline are the peddlar, the customary dues, the fairs,[48] temple patronage and the royal factories or *karkhanas*.[49] On the other hand, already in the eighteenth century there were tendencies which favoured merchants and contractual work. For one example, the 'intermediate economy', constituted of the town bankers and merchants interested in artisanal goods, has been seen to have consolidated in eighteenth-century north India.[50] For another example, European trade had established mercantile networks that seem to have persisted even as the volume of trade declined. Thus, major sites such as Surat represent industrial-mercantile traditions that changed in form but not in importance. Some of the European firms dealing in exportable crafts in late-nineteenth-century north India were known to have shifted from exportables prominent in precolonial trade. A shift from indigo to carpet is an example.

In important aspects, the mercantile-contractual systems of the pre-colonial and colonial periods were different. First, the very scale of long-distance trade, where such networks flourished, expanded enormously in the colonial period. Secondly, precolonial trade was dependent on political power. Away from European trade, there are few examples of industrial centres which did not at all rely on consumption of the elites and protection offered by them. Within European trade, merchants would barely exist without collaboration with or effective deterrence to those who ruled the territories. This explicit role of politics in mercantile

[48] Probably the most important example, but not an isolated one, is the decline of the Maheji fair in Khandesh, and the shift of the textile trade it specialized in towards Yeola town. The shift is briefly discussed in J. Nissim, *A Monograph on Wire and Tinsel in Bombay Presidency* (Bombay, 1900), 9.

[49] Karkhanas will be dealt with later. By the nineteenth century, factories owned by rich customers were rare. However, they seem to have been replaced by a form of spot-sale with a clear trace of patronage in it. There is a rare description of this form of urban transactions in north India:

> Very few gentlemen condescend to make their own purchases; they generally employ their confidential domestic to go to the market for them; and with the ladies their women servants are deputed. In rich families it is an office of great trust, as they expend large sums and might be much imposed upon were their servants faithless. The servants always claim dustoor (custom) from the shopkeepers.

Mrs Mir Hassan Ali, *Observations on the Mussulmans of India*, W. Crooke (ed.) (London, 1917), 230–1.

[50] C. A. Bayly, *Rulers, Townsmen and Bazaars: North Indian Society in the Age of British Expansion, 1770–1870* (Cambridge, 1983), chapter 1 and 144–5.

operations disappeared in the nineteenth century. And, thirdly, precolonial infrastructure, from transport to monetary system to security of property, was crude enough to limit the scale and regularity of contracts relative to the nineteenth century.[51]

With the Industrial Revolution and colonial rule, the composition of buyers changed, the elites withdrew, buyers became distant and anonymous, and in need of cheap standardized goods. In turn, the space for a mercantile economy more free from political power could expand. In the crafts studied here, merchants specialized, proliferated, and subdivided. Europeans and Americans, some having multinational operations, entered the trades. Artisans themselves entered trade. Trade in mass-produced inputs became an important new field. And capital became more mobile than before. This last tendency has a parallel from agriculture. From about the 1860s, regional accounts continued for many decades to report migration and resettlement of mercantile-financial communities to finance cultivation, and to set up as shop-keepers in towns that lacked such services. New avenues of profitability and easier transit were not the only attractions. Previously, a village shopkeeper's banking services depended on a delicate balance between the creditor's literacy with accounts and the debtor's comparative advantage in brute power. With the latter somewhat curbed, banking became a more lucrative profession, and land exercised, directly or indirectly, a pull that dominated over most others. Such a movement can be seen in the crafts as well, but its character was different in two ways. First, there was agglomeration rather than dispersion. Secondly, there was greater coalescence of finance and production. Financing cultivation did not involve great knowledge, nor did grain require a costly search for markets. But the crafts did require special knowledge, and a search for markets. Thus, crafts demanded more than money capital, that is, traders willing to specialize. There was no place here for 'the' shopkeeper. To the extent specialization implied that the risks and returns from trade derived from the craft itself, and not from caste qualifications, it was easier for a producer to become a merchant or a financier. As a result, caste barriers to trade, which are usually preserved by privileged access to credit, were generally lower in the crafts. If the migrant Bania 'colonized' the village, the carpet or hide merchant came

---

[51] The point can be illustrated with a hypothetical example. Between trade on bullock carts and trade on railways, the *turnover* of contract increases manifold. Railways enables repeated transaction, which is qualitatively a different thing from isolated ones. A contract valid for one production cycle in a year matters little to a producer, for all the other cycles in the year remain dominated by spot-sale or non-market forms. But, a contract valid for *all* production cycles in a year can turn a producer into a quasi-worker.

to the town to be soaked up in a network of exchange in which the craft had absolute primacy.

Merchants were also dealing with different problems than before. The problem of decay in quality of the skilled crafts has been mentioned. Further, buying for distant markets required more working capital, the ability to coordinate between buyers and producers, the capacity to bear market risks, and access to information. In export trade, the usual system in the middle of the nineteenth century was for buyers to gather a certain quantity of goods from the bazaars, and send them to London for sale at whatever prices they would fetch in auctions. Auctions were the main system of final sale in the nineteenth century. Auctions existed in shawls, carpets, 'Madras', and possibly in leather as well. Bidding is a logical response when the final demand is unknown, or the output cannot be graded. But, on the negative side, an auction had a massive price instability built into it, which derived both from the imbalance in the quantity of demand and supply, and from the variable quality of the goods. Rich artisans, exporters and input merchants needed to reduce these risks and to enforce good work from the ordinary artisan. They needed, in other words, new transactional rules, here called 'contracts'. In general, spot-sale declined, and gave way to contractual buying. Exportable crafts witnessed a parallel change at the marketing end, the decline of auctions.[52] Forms of new contract at the site of production varied. One factor in the variation was whether the critical resource utilized in production was skilled or unskilled labour.

Forms of contract

The best example of a relatively unskilled craft in transition is tanning of raw hides and skins, which was a rural craft in the beginning of the period, performed mainly by outcast rural labourers. The unit of production was the individual or, more often, a group of families forming a tanner colony. Unskilled or degraded labour that had to locate close to the village for reasons of consumption or supply of raw material, tended to converge in the figure of the rural menial. This individual was primarily a labourer for the village, invariably an agricultural labourer, and occasionally a crude artisan on the side. The

---

[52] A few crashes later, auctions faded away from about the First World War, to give way to sale on confirmed order. Between the 1880s, when auctions were common, and the 1920s, communication had improved between the consuming and the producing countries, tastes had acquired a more stable character, specialized traders and their agents appeared at the site of production equipped with capital needed to hold sufficient inventory, and systems of contract were devised to monitor and regulate quality.

products were rarely sold, but were usually bartered for entitlements such as rights to reusable wastes or a very precarious right to subsistence. The users of such services were the peasant-employers. This hierarchy was fundamental, and made the practice of industry unfree for the artisans in a number of senses: unfree to specialize, to choose customers, or to set prices.[53]

During the period of study, this customary rural labour declined, and artisans migrated out of the peasant economy and into the urban tanyard set up by hide merchants. Exporters of hides found it difficult to transact with rural suppliers, though they did try at first.[54] The need to control supply and quality forced a relocation of slaughtering of cattle and of tanning itself to the trading cities. Further, tanning allowed economies of scale, so that in the cities it reassembled in factories, where the tanning castes performed wage labour. The tanners became free from the quasi-serfdom of the village, but remained unfree insofar as their lowly status limited access to entrepreneurial resources like credit. Besides, hierarchy continued within the factory, and enabled employers to pay small wages and permit poor working conditions.[55]

In the skilled crafts, we rarely see the old unit of production collapse so thoroughly as in leather. These trades too faced problems of supply and quality. New systems came into being, but were usually adapted from old ones. The reason behind such continuity is simple. Before the age of technical schools, training or the supply of skills and access to skills happened at the site of production. If the demand for skills remains strong, the production site cannot weaken all of a sudden. And yet it needed to change. To describe the nature of the change, it is necessary to digress briefly into the nature of the customary production site.

In our examples, institutions that served critical training functions, such as the creation, diffusion and conservation of skills, and that restricted access to skills, could be of two types. In urban north India, the most common unit of work seems to have been a hierarchical team

---

[53] This sphere of exchange does not seem to have been sufficiently studied. It was different from *jajmani* in that tanners were too lowly to be part of a 'sharing' arrangement. It had features in common with Weber's 'demiurgic' occupations, that is, non-market exchange among producers as opposed to inter-tribal exchange, and the presence of implicit compulsion. Max Weber, *General Economic History*, trans. F. H. Knight (New York, 1961), 124. The difference between Weber's context, manorial production in Europe, and rural India probably lay in the nature of the hierarchy.

[54] Commercialization of hides induced competition between the peasants and labourers for cattle hides. But neither could prevail in this competition, for, while the peasants controlled the supply of hides, the labourers alone could process them.

[55] '[T]he class of worker ... [is] from long social tradition ... peculiarly powerless to help itself': *Report of the Royal Commission on Labour*, 98.

of male Muslim artisans, sometimes related by kinship ties, but not necessarily so related. These collectives crystallized around master-apprentice lineages. A contrasting general type one encounters, usually in rural or semi-rural crafts, or among Hindu artisans, or in certain industries like ordinary cotton weaving, is a hierarchical team made up of parents and children. The former type may be called 'team-work', and the latter 'home-work'. These two broad types cannot be precisely defined with the material we have, but they can be described a little more closely.

Home-work was a production unit, situated within a unit of consumption and reproduction, a 'firm' if the head of the family took some part in sale, and had a division of labour governed by age and sex. By contrast, team-work was primarily a production unit alone, and it was too specialized in specific tasks to become a firm. It usually needed a merchant to coordinate tasks. The two types can be distinguished further on four other aspects: employment, instruction, gender, and hierarchy. These were interrelated, but the correlation was not always very strong. The core distinction perhaps is employment of children, between productive employment of young persons by the family in which they are born, as opposed to service outside of that domestic group. This particular contrast – between intra-family and outside service – is a well-known, widely used, and theoretically fruitful one in different contexts.[56] It has even been seen as culturally specific.[57] This duality corresponds to one in systems of instruction: of children by parents, and of servants by masters. A further correlation can be observed in respect of gender. Non-family apprenticeship, at least in India, rarely involved women. In the crafts in question, and especially in anything to do with metals, women were rarely employed. Finally, and it follows from the above, the hierarchy at work on the shop-floor, the primitive managerial paradigm, also presented a contrast: it was generational in one case, and formal or ideological in the other. A further contrast seems to be that, home-work identified itself with a workplace (homestead) more than did the employer of apprentices. Team-work identified itself more with skills and processes while the workplace tended to change. The apprenticeship unit was a *team*, not a *home*.

Classic examples of home-work come from ordinary, that is, relatively

---

[56] It is a common point of reference in developmental demography, and used to explain societal differences in average age of marriage. See J. Hajnal, 'Two Kinds of Preindustrial Household Formation System', *Population and Development Review*, 8, 4 (1982); and Jack Goody, 'Comparing Family Systems in Europe and Asia: Are There Different Sets of Rules?', *Population and Development Review*, 22, 1 (1996). These demographic implications, however, follow in the presence of several *other* conditions.

[57] See the debate cited in the preceding note.

unskilled and plain, cotton cloth weaving all over the country. The adult males operated the loom, and all others of working age processed the yarn. As the family expanded in means, there was a tendency to de-employ women and hire in labour. Yet, the work-unit for a long time retained its former integrity, originally derived from domestic division of labour. A factory which arose out of home-work tended to integrate processes, as in a household. Team-work can be seen usually as part of an institution called *karkhanadari* (described more fully below). *Karkhana* literally means workshop or factory. The average team con-sisted of male Muslim artisans arranged in a master–disciple relation-ship. Specific tasks were performed in sheds owned either by senior artisans or by merchants, or, until the middle of the nineteenth century, quite often by rich customers. Factories and workshops in this context arose as the size of the team grew, or several teams or tasks were brought together under one shed. One implication of this system was the de-integration of processes, and, therefore, a greater division of labour compared to home-work. Not surprisingly, many of the most refined craft skills were often preserves of Muslim artisans of northern India. These features were almost universal among Muslim artisans in a wide range of crafts performed in the towns of the upper Gangetic plains. Examples come from Moradabad brass, Benares *jari*, Agra and Amritsar carpets, Srinagar carpets and shawls, Lucknow *zardozi*, Benares brocade, Saharanpur wood-carving, Punjab's ivory-carving, and a number of other minor skilled crafts in the towns of United Provinces, Punjab and Kashmir.[58]

What was team-work really like? A mid-nineteenth-century descrip-tion of carpets and shawl weaving in Punjab illustrates:

The weavers are all males, commencing to learn the art at the age of ten years. In all transactions there are two parties, the master, or Ustad, and the scholar or Shagird, the former being the capitalist, the latter the mechanic.[59]

The passage goes on to describe the wide-ranging terms which bound

---

[58] The following is a selection of representative general descriptions of nineteenth and early-twentieth-century *karkhanadari* and apprenticeship: United Provinces, *Industrial Survey of the United Provinces* (Allahabad, 1922–4), volume on Farrukhabad district (on brassware and cotton carpet), Cawnpore (cotton carpet), and Lucknow (lace and embroidery); *Report of the Royal Commission on Labour*, 97–8 (Amritsar carpet); T. P. Ellis, *Monograph on Ivory Carving Industry in the Punjab* (Lahore, 1900), 7–8; R. H. Davies, *Report on the Trade and Resources of the Countries on the North-Western Boundary of British India* (Lahore, 1862), Appendix V, xxviii (Punjab shawls made by Kashmiri artisans); United Provinces, *Report of the United Provinces Provincial Banking Enquiry Committee* (Allahabad, 1930) (Benares brocade); and S. N. Majumdar Choudhury, 'Extracts from a Survey of the Small Urban Industries of Benares' in *United Provinces Provincial Banking Enquiry Committee*, Evidence vol. II, 371–2 (Benares brocade).

[59] Davies, *Report on the Trade and Resources*, Appendix V, xxviii.

these two parties together. For example, the remuneration ranged from wages, to quasi-wages (wages in another name), to fixed shares of revenue. The role of the *ustad* ranged from a capitalist and an employer, to a senior partner, to a trainer. The role of the *shagird* ranged from a scholar, employee, partner, to sometimes a 'bond-slave'. It will be suggested below that some of this ambiguity was an effect of time.[60]

Families and teams are, in different forms, universal in the pre-modern world. But the Indian apprenticeship had a peculiar feature. All systems of training need an authority, which decides when a student can start competing with the master. Parents are in a 'natural' hierarchy with respect to young persons. So are masters. But as apprentices grow up and learn, this authority needs to be replaced with one less natural and more formal. The ownership of capital in the skilled crafts, where craftsmanship itself was the capital and embodied in people, was not a secure basis to ensure authority. The means of command could be a guild, or headship of communities, or simply being a maestro. These various instruments of regulation in apprenticeship system implied a common source, the non-family transference of knowledge. Any well-developed apprenticeship, the most familiar historical instances of which come from medieval Europe, therefore, tends to be accompanied by some sort of a guild, or an employers' association.[61] The guild as such is a complex and many-sided institution. But one of its essential functions was the regulation of the mobility of the apprentice. If apprentices are free to compete, none would teach them; if they can never hope to be masters, none would demand instruction. Guilds neither prevented nor freed mobility, but bound it by rules.

In north Indian cities, this function was not altogether absent. The master peer group did have some say on mobility, but as individuals or as members of a loosely defined community.[62] Further, a visible and

---

[60] An earlier and briefer description of the same industry and conveying the same ambiguity in a simpler form is cited in John Irwin, *Shawls* (London, 1954), 8.

[61] These statements are based on the following studies on medieval and post-medieval Europe: Sylvia Thrupp, 'The Gilds', and H. Kellenbenz, 'The Organization of Industrial Production' in J. Habakkuk and M. Postan (eds.), *The Cambridge Economic History of Europe* (Cambridge, 1977), vols. III and V respectively. A more recent study on guilds has also been drawn upon: S. A. Epstein, *Wage Labor and Guilds in Medieval Europe* (Chapel Hill, NC and London, 1991), chapter 3. The latter study can be used to develop many formal similarities and differences between nineteenth-century Indian apprenticeship and the usual apprenticeship contracts in medieval Europe. The Indian system, by contrast, was far less extensive, less of a legal contract, though it tended to become one in some cases, had different patterns of mobility, and had sporadic similarity in the nature of remuneration (the presence of an entry fee or quasi-wages, for example). At bottom, however, both were a contract for teaching the craft.

[62] In sources from the colonial period, *panchayat* of substantial artisans in Benares has been mentioned: Majumdar Choudhury, 'Extracts from a Survey', 371. There is also a

enduring ideology of competence may have played a role in controlling mobility. This ideology can be called the notion of 'ustadhood', *ustad* being the Urdu term for masters, which still remains a familiar and powerfully evocative word in Islamic South Asia. However, no vestiges of a corporate body of skilled artisans can be seen in the nineteenth century. In fact, nothing in early colonial or medieval Indian history suggests the existence of corporate entities independent of public authority, of the kind many European guilds or even their remnants represented. If apprenticeship as such is defined as a composite of two attributes – non-family transference of knowledge, and masters formally controlling licence of competence to teach – the north Indian system possessed the first, but not the second.

The terms that described north Indian urban artisanal organization in the nineteenth and early twentieth centuries – *karkhana*, *karkhanadar*, *ustad* and *shagird* – were inherited from the precolonial period. Their origin suggests a reason why north India never developed a guild. The most famous usage of *karkhana* refers to royal departments under the Mughal courts. In practice, the term did not necessarily mean factories, but included factories along with stores and some administrative departments. Besides the imperial ones, the main north Indian towns developed a whole hierarchy of *karkhanas* owned by courtiers and individuals close to them, though much more is known about the imperial karkhanas.[63] Two features of this institution are important for the present study. First, by means of *karkhanas*, urban north India became culturally at home with the idea of collective work, which is the context in which apprenticeship develops. Secondly, while these *karkhanas* did not necessarily rule out private production for the bazaar, they did represent a subversion of the market. The extent of subversion varied over time, place and product. It was, however, significant enough to find mention in all major studies on the *karkhanas*. The subversion happened in three ways. There was implicit or explicit control of the courts on purchase of inputs. The output was rarely marketed but kept for royal use, gifts, even provincial revenue payments and exports organized by the court. And the *karkhanas* tended to recruit the best workers in the industries. The distinction between the rank and file and the elite among the

mention of *birádari*, literally brotherhood, among artisans of urban north India in one source on silk weavers: Abdullah Ibn Yusuf Ali, *A Monograph on Silk Fabrics Produced in the North-Western Provinces and Oudh* (Allahabad, 1900), 102. But, as Yusuf Ali himself qualified, nowhere did *birádari* mean formal rules and regulations. 'Organized guilds' in that sense 'are unknown': *ibid.*

[63] An excellent recent work on the subject is Tripta Verma, *Karkhanas under the Mughals* (Delhi, 1994).

artisans was mediated by proximity to power.[64] The word *karkhanadar* in this system referred to a supervisor, and *ustad* to the skilled master. In the early-nineteenth-century Kashmir shawl industry, John Irwin states, the term *karkhanadar* referred to *owners* of *karkhanas*, whereas *ustad* was still the master.[65] In the late nineteenth century, the term *karkhana* applied to almost all non-family workshops, large and small. The large ones were often owned by merchants; the small ones by the *ustads*. One would expect that, in that situation, the distinction between the *karkhanadar* and *ustad* would fade. This seems plausible from the evidence on the later *karkhanas*.

Thus, in precolonial urban north India, the skilled artisanate, even whole industries, functioned mainly in a relationship of *dependence* on public authority. This is where the Indian apprenticeship was the antithesis of the European. The *ustad* and *karkhanadar* originated in a relationship of dependence. They were not employers. The courts did not depend on them. They were not a source of tax revenue for the courts as their European counterparts were. They were employees or quasi-employees of the court.[66] Clearly, guild or endogenous systems of employer protection were not needed in such conditions. The master's power reflected that of the patron. We know little about how the *karkhana* survived in the eighteenth century. The history of some industries, such as shawls in Kashmir, suggests that the *karkhana* became a private firm catering to merchants in overland trade with Europe.[67] In those industries where long-distance trade developed early, *karkhanas* must have altered their nature earlier. But such early transition was almost certainly not the rule. By and large the concentrations of skilled artisans in the eighteenth century tended to be in cities with powerful regimes. The fundamentally non-market character of most

[64] This is hinted in a number of sources: see Verma, *Karkhanas under the Mughals*, 16, 24. The most famous description was given to François Bernier, who distinguished between two types of urban artisan. At one extreme was the bazaar artisan who was nominally independent, that is, not an employee of the rich and powerful, and yet a perpetually poor man, lowly skilled, and subject to all kinds of arbitrary bullying and exploitation by merchants or agents of the rich. At the other end was the elite among the artisans, the super-skilled artist, who was necessarily an employee of the *karkhana*. Thus: '[T]he artists ... who arrive at ... eminence in their art are those *only* who are in the service of the King or of some powerful Omrah, and who work exclusively for their patron.' François Bernier, *Travels in the Mogul Empire* (London, 1914), 256 (emphasis added). See also 228–9 on patronage.

[65] Irwin, *Shawls*, 8. The source is William Moorcroft's papers of 1821.

[66] In this sense, Indian skilled craft tradition can be seen to belong primarily in what Hicks has called the revenue economy, rather than a commercial economy, even though markets formally existed in both: Hicks, *Theory of Economic History*, 22–4.

[67] Irwin, *Shawls*, 8.

karkhanas might have diminished, but could not have withered until the nineteenth century.

To return to the nineteenth century, how were families and teams affected by long-distance trade? In general, there occurred a super-imposition of new exchange contracts on the old production unit. With home-work this took the shape of generic putting out, as in cotton handloom weaving. With apprenticeship, it took the shape of a putting-out involving *karkhanas*. In both cases, putting-out reflected the development of the mercantile economy earlier discussed. But what happened to the producers?

We again meet the *karkhana*, *karkhanadar*, and *ustad* in urban north India, but now in quite different senses of these terms. The word *karkhana* now meant *any* collective work, from large carpet factories to the sites where individual teams of wire-drawers, brocade-weavers or engravers settled down to work. *Karkhanadar* was again an intermediary, but not an elite employee any more. The word *karkhanadar* now combined three basic elements. First, the *karkhanadar* secured orders from dealers who owned shops in the cities and exported goods. Typically, in urban north India, such a dealer would be a Hindu, whereas the *karkhanadar* was a Muslim. Secondly, the *karkhanadar* owned a work-space where *ustad-shagird* teams came and executed contracts. And, thirdly, the person was almost invariably of artisanal origin. Merchants and *karkhanadars* tended to be socially distinct, whereas master-artisans (*ustads*) and merchant-artisans (*karkhanadars*) were very closely situated, at times almost indistinct. More rarely, the *karkhanadar* could be a small-scale raw material merchant. The word *karkahanadari* in this context meant a three-party contract, between merchants and *karkhanadars* on the one hand, and between *karkhanadars* and *ustads* on the other. The term *ustad* again meant the head of a work-team. But, on rare occasions, the *ustad* seemed the same thing as *karkhanadar*. The *ustad* was still an intermediary, but with a difference. The notion of being a teacher or master was subdued and mixed with that of being a labour-contractor, a kind of capitalist.[68]

Thus, the production unit was resilient, but not passive. In all industries, commercialization created opportunities for the family or the *karkhanadar* to become traders. Partly because technical options and knowledge had expanded, and partly because markets were larger and had induced the division of labour and specialization, in some industries there existed economies of scale. These could be large enough to force the production unit itself to enlarge. There were instances of rich Hindu

[68] Sources on Benares *karkhanadari*, cited in note 58 above, illustrate these features especially well.

artisan families adding equipment, sending women and children back to the interior of the house and hiring labour; or rich *ustads* turning into merchant-coordinators, factory-owners, labour-contractors. But these tendencies became universal in a craft town only when external conditions were added, for example, the mass migration of artisans, the extension of public utilities, the infusion of foreign capital, or the evolution of an efficient informal credit market. The most dramatic form these movements could take was the 'factory'.

Factories

Factories arose in these contexts out of two classic tendencies: small producers expanding scale, often after some engagement with trade; and merchants turning producers. The former tendency, in turn, can be subdivided into two types: the family expanding the scale of production, or the north Indian master becoming a *karkhanadar*. The former movement was conspicuous in urban handloom weaving of interwar western India. Venkatraman described it as follows:

A weaver working for ... a merchant desires to become an employer himself. Without giving up his work under his employer, he gathers together two or three persons who cannot otherwise find employment and secures work for himself as well as for his men from his merchant-employer ... He also provides his workers with looms and other requisites and sometimes their lodgings.[69]

The latter movement has not been so clearly described, but it can be inferred from sources in interwar Benares and other craft towns of northern India, where *karkhanadars* were becoming more powerful. The case of handloom weaving in western India has been dealt with in detail in recent textile history scholarship.[70]

The two best illustrations of the other route, the merchant turning factor, were tanning and carpet. These two examples were, however, quite different. The tannery centralized the process of raw or semi-processed hides. It was usually owned by an export merchant, or by one of his agents or suppliers. The operatives were mainly immigrant rural tanners. There are perhaps three reasons why in tanning the urban factory eventually replaced the spot market in country-tanned leather. First, while there was probably no degradation of country tanning, its

[69] K. S. Venkatraman, 'The Economic Conditions of Handloom Weavers', *Journal of the University of Bombay*, 11, Part I, January and July (1942), 85.

[70] For example, Douglas Haynes, 'The Logic of the Artisan Firm in a Capitalist Economy: Handloom Weavers and Technological Change in Western India, 1880–1947' in Burton Stein and Sanjay Subrahmanyam (eds.), *Institutions and Economic Change in South Asia* (Delhi, 1996); and Roy, *Artisans and Industrialization*, chapter 3.

quality was variable and poor. Secondly, there were some economies of scale in tanning, the process being intensive in space and in chemicals that were cheaper when dealt in bulk. Thirdly, great migrations of tanners, socially constrained to be labourers rather than capitalists, favoured large-scale production.

The carpet factory was an extreme form of the northern *karkhanadari*. In size and looks, a nineteenth-century carpet factory was probably not very different from its precolonial ancestors. But it *was* different in that it was owned by, or controlled by, export merchants of usually foreign origin. These merchants were familiar with the idea of the modern factory. They needed to contract on a large scale, and also control the quality of their goods by means of proximity to the production site. Often quality control demanded investment in processes, such as dyeing of wool, which tended to expand the workshop size. Inside the factory, two dissimilar contracts joined together, a piece-rate product contract between the merchant and the master, and a wage contract or income-sharing contract, or even a simple commitment to teach, between the master and the artisans. Credit and apprenticeship secured the foundation of trust and reciprocal support, based on which the triple exchange could function smoothly. Generally, intricate craftsmanship tended to involve closer master–disciple bonding. This triple contract can be seen almost wherever the term *karkhanadari* was applied. Between the seventeenth century and the twentieth, the *karkhana* had one element in common: the middleman was not a simple labour contractor, but a 'master', a guarantor of quality. In one era, this feature served conspicuous consumption; in another, it served long-distance trade.

Triple contract as such is not a north Indian invention. It has a useful logic which was also utilized in southern and western India, but with a difference. In the two best-known examples of triple contract in cotton handlooms, the *mungani* in the southern Andhra districts,[71] and the contract mediated by the *assami* in Sholapur, the number of principals and agents was always three. But the parties, the terms, and the regularity of the contract were not well defined. In *mungani*, the master was often a factory owner engaging labourers, but the merchant–master transaction was a contract in a very loose sense, and left a large element of spot sale in the exchanges of yarn or cloth. In Sholapur again, there was a trinity at work, but the *assami* was usually a mediator, and not a factory owner. In both situations, the degree of intervention by the middleman was not a permanent feature of the transaction, but varied

---

[71] The semi-arid region on the northwestern boundary of the Madras Presidency, also called the Ceded Districts in the sources, presently the southern part of Andhra Pradesh.

according to demand. And, in either case, there was no essential connection between the mediator and levels of skill. The middleman could be anyone, hailing from the craft or outside; in the latter case, he will be called a *dalal* or *paikar* in northern India. But in north Indian cities, the triple contract had a less contingent character, the middleman was often an *ustad*, and only in north India did the triple contract join with factories. This contract could lean more towards putting-out, or more towards factory. Carpet was an example of the latter form.

The factory, after all, was a rare occurrence. Usually, commercialization did not induce dramatic changes in the work site, though it did induce slow and impalpable changes in the nature of contracts, as mentioned above. And it induced specialization. Specialization involved people and tasks, as well as places. The next two sections deal with these aspects.

Division of labour and technical change

At the production process, tasks tended to become separate. In leather, flaying, tanning, and leather manufacture separated. In almost all metalwork, the making of sheets, bars, and rods separated from forging-casting, with associated changes in furnace size, type, and usage. Here was at least one source of the growth and diffusion of general engineering. In plain woollens, competition from urban weaving and the depletion of pastures brought about a separation between spinning, weaving and the rearing of sheep, which tasks not too long ago united in the person of the nomadic shepherd almost throughout the country. Within crafts that already functioned under a fairly well-developed division of labour, such as metal engraving, or wire drawing, there are many instances of small changes in processes, which can be seen as a pressure to specialize. In cotton handloom, weaving and processing separated.

The division of labour increased in rural industry in another sense, one that referred to the *person* rather than the *product*. The world market in leather broke up the unity of coarse crafts and agrarian labour. Any demand for leather arising out of peasant communities created a condition for servile relationships to loosen up. Formerly, it was the urban leather crafts where one could see specialist artisans at work. The export demand for hides expanded this sphere, and brought it within reach of the rural tanners. Industry and agriculture bifurcated in a vital way in and through leather.

In a more subdued way, a similar change characterized two other important rural professions: pottery and smithy. The north Indian *Lohar* shared with the tanner, not his abject status, but the overwhelming commitment to perform cultivation and agricultural labour, for himself and for others. When his caste occupation was threatened by products of the town foundry, the specialized and the non-specialized artisan became more sharply distinguished, the former coming out as 'a smarter man'. During the interwar period, many blacksmiths entered the flourishing factory enterprise in cutlery, metal tools, machine parts, and durable consumer goods, though the movement was never as dramatic as in leather. The *Kumhars*, likewise committed to rural labour, were reportedly affected by the growing preference for metal utensils, the unremarkable character of their pottery, and the difficulty of long-distance trade in the average articles. The vessels of mass consumption were flimsily made, given the force of a custom that frowned upon reusage of earthenware. The only segment where some 'evolutionary progress' could be seen were the objects of art, made by specialized town potters, whose output needed more expensive kilns.[72] Towards the end of the period under study, this sector diversified into ceramic tools and components, which is now one of its major outputs.

As specialization increased, there were incremental changes in tools and processes. Tanning saw some changes in chemical processes, the most important of which was the replacement of lesser-known tannins with those of well-known properties, and of vegetable tannin with chromium salts. Brassware saw innovations on the plating-polishing side. *Jari* saw the replacement of hand by power in the plating of wires; it was this process more than anything else that had defined the better finish of imported thread. The most well-documented records of accretional changes come from the main branches of textiles. The three most important changes were the substitution of vegetable dyes, the fly-shuttle, and the warping mill.[73]

Most innovations, thus, merely modified the original tools, for instance replacing a manual wire-drawing apparatus with few spools by one with several. This character of accretion makes it hard to identify the immediate impact of technological change on productivity or organi-

---

[72] Chatterjee, *Notes on Industries*, 130; and E. Maconochie, *A Monograph on the Pottery and Glass Industries of the Bombay Presidency* (Bombay, 1900?), 2.

[73] Two studies on conditions leading to technical change in handloom weaving are Haynes, 'The Logic of the Artisan Firm'; and Tirthankar Roy, 'Acceptance of Innovations in Early Twentieth Century Indian Weaving', conference on Cloth, the Artisans and the World Economy, Dartmouth College, New Hampshire, 1993. The focus of the former essay is on the importance of the nature of the firm for choice of techniques and innovation. The focus of the latter essay is on the importance of the ability of artisan groups to form collectives and share information on techniques and innovation.

zation. In the short run, the change in the capital–labour ratio was minimal, and the impact was almost invisible. In the long run, however, the effects could go deeper. Over several decades, accretions could lead to three sorts of development: changes in age and gender relations within the family work unit; change in skill composition making migration easier; and, more subtly, an erosion in the artisans' identification with specific manual skills, transforming them from 'masters' of a process into generic 'employees'. There are examples of the first in cotton textile processing, a sphere in which labour-saving innovations were somewhat successful. *Jari* is a case of the second: the innovations at Surat did concur with increasing physical mobility of labour in the industry. The third is more difficult to pinpoint, but indistinct signs were present in a range of northern crafts.

The few dramatic cases of the employment of machinery occurred when an input needed to be mass-produced. Thus, metal rolling allied to brass or *jari*, the spinning of wool, and the processing of cotton yarn tended to separate from the performance of the final tasks, and evolved into capital-intensive sectors supplying raw material to the artisans. These branches retained their bond with the artisans for a long time, but were also equipped to serve a diverse clientele, or invest in the production of the final good. An example comes from glass-making. A crude glass industry began primarily from bangle-manufacture based on indigenous material and small furnaces. A part of the same sector moved into sheet glass during the First World War, and eventually invested in final output and diversified to meet the wider and newer demand for glass articles.

Relocation and clustering

Stories of the migration of artisans, and the growth of some manufacturing towns in place of dispersed rural or semi-rural industry, are central in each of the case studies. Handloom weaving in western India offers examples of the rapid urbanization of textiles fed by steady movements of capital and labour from northern and southern India.[74] In leather, the port towns grew by drawing tanners from the interior. In brassware, Moradabad increasingly overshadowed other towns with the passage of the twentieth century. In *jari*, Surat and Benares similarly dominate. These similarities are neither accidental nor confined to history. Small firms, even today, universally tend to be more dependent

---

[74] See Douglas Haynes and Tirthankar Roy, 'Conceiving Mobility: Weavers' Migrations in Colonial and Precolonial India', *Indian Economic and Social History Review*, 36, 1 (1999).

than large firms on resource-sharing, especially such shareable common resources as infrastructure and information.[75] Dispersion is often the state in which one meets small firms. But the dispersed state implies a local market, when the need for such resources remains limited. Once markets begin to be mainly non-local, clustering is inevitable. It starts with production of the final good and ends with factors of production.

At one level, the urbanization of industry reflected the decline of an entire rural or quasi-rural industrial system. Irfan Habib proposed that the most important and visible precolonial industry could be classified either as a situation where *both* production and consumption were primarily rural, or as one where *both* were primarily urban.[76] The former set corresponds to a range of industries and services which carry one or more of these attributes: (i) production for subsistence (of the producing household, community or village); (ii) primarily barter, grain-based exchange; (iii) peasantry-dominated social relations of production; and (iv) narrow or non-diversified markets and skills. Examples include leather, coarse woollens, and utility metals. The latter set, which would consist of many medieval administrative and garrison towns with factories, seem to display (i) the presence of diversified markets and skills, and, therefore, merchants engaged in long-distance trade, though the place remained the royal domain; (ii) cash economy; and (iii) production for non-subsistence consumption. Examples include silks, carpets, and engraved metals. Commercialization in the nineteenth century can be said to have upset the former network by altering the structure of production and transactions costs as well as tastes. For example, demand for relatively standardized subsistence goods is likely to be price-elastic, such that expanded commerce and the presence of new goods can imply more intense competition for the *rural* producer, typically forcing him to migrate towards points of trade. In the new competition, the rural producer was already handicapped by the near-absence of a division of labour. Expanded cash transactions may drive participants out of barter. The persistence of restrictive social relations in the villages can have a similarly migratory effect, when much improved communications and a less hierarchical society in the towns increased the opportunity costs of staying on in the village.

[75] Recent literature on small-scale industry has given shape to the idea that the natural inclination of small firms is to congregate rather than stay dispersed. See for a representative selection of writings, *IDS Bulletin*, 23, 3 (1992), and especially the essay by H. Schmitz, 'On the Clustering of Small Firms'.

[76] The two other possibilities – rural industries with primarily urban demand, and urban industries with rural demand – do not have many examples. Irfan Habib, 'Potentials for Capitalistic Development in the Economy of Mughal India', *Journal of Economic History*, 29, 1 (1969).

The trading cities, therefore, were well placed, more than in the previous several centuries, to receive craftsmen, to diversify occupations, to utilize old skills in new ways, but also to compete more fiercely between themselves. The fortunes of many eighteenth and nineteenth-century towns, and the history of manufactures are closely bound up. The commercialization literature refers to the growth of new 'market towns' dealing in cash crops in the nineteenth century. There was, in fact, a parallel movement in industry. It was not merely as if general urbanization happened to coincide with urbanization in the crafts, but the former happened *because of* the latter. To illustrate with a small sample, the growth of Sholapur in western India or Salem in the south derives from the weaving of cotton cloth on handlooms; that of Benares or Madura from silk; Surat from lace and gold thread; Moradabad from engraved brass; Madras, Kanpur, and Agra from leather; Mirzapur and Warangal from carpets; Saharanpur from wood-carving; and Firozabad from the enterprise in glass bangles.[77] Amritsar's rise as a trading and manufacturing town derived from two raw materials: wool and silk.[78] There were contrasts as well. Masulipatnam is a great precolonial craft town that did not industrialize to a similar extent. But this experience is outweighed by that of many others. In either case, the nineteenth-century history of these cities is intricately connected with craftsmen movements.

Craftsmen movements, indeed, represent a great historical force which, until very recently, has been active in creating and animating cities all over the world. In early stages of industrialization in Europe and East Asia, it has been seen to play a productive role. Such a role was present in South Asia as well, with the important difference that, in this region, the productive role of artisans did not connect strongly with rapid economic development. We are, then, led to a question in comparative history: what elements were general and what elements specific, in the story so far outlined in this chapter?

[77] To lend more substance to the point, see Table XXV in India, *Report of the Fact-Finding Committee (Handloom and Mills)*, Commerce Department (Calcutta, 1942), 66. The table shows the proportion of population dependent on handloom weaving in the population of major textile towns. These were, to select only towns with populations over 100,000 in 1931: 41 per cent in Sholapur; 29 per cent in Surat; 10 per cent in Nagpur; 25 per cent in Benares; 30 per cent in Madura; 38 per cent in Salem; and 25 per cent in Coimbatore.

[78] Of Amritsar, R. H. Davies wrote in 1864: 'This rising city ... monopolizes the import of raw silk ... is the principal mart in the Punjab for the cotton fabrics ... the gold thread ... metal utensils ... sugar ... and the seat of shawl and silk manufacturers, ... advancing yearly in wealth and population'. *The Trade of Central Asia* (London, 1864), 32.

Comparisons

The comparisons selected are early modern Europe and late-nine-teenth-century East Asia. The purpose of what follows is analytical, and not a narrative history of episodes. The discussion, therefore, will focus on concepts of organizational change, rather than on evolutionary models. First, parallels between India and these cases will be pointed out, and on that basis, an attempt will be made to suggest what might have made the Indian trajectory a special one.

Europe

This period in South Asia can be shown to belong within conventional accounts of the advent of industrial capitalism. The gradual concentration of creative energy in artisanal activities in western Europe is now the subject of an extensive and growing literature and many intersecting controversies. One of these relates to the question whether the history of artisan enterprise in early modern Britain or Europe suggests typical models. The absence of a model, however, need not frustrate comparative history, for the literature agrees that certain movements did dominate early industrialization. What is questioned are their primacy or sequence in specific historical contexts. Comparisons can proceed by abstracting these movements from such context-bound debates.

It is convenient to distinguish two broad constituent processes. The first consists of changes that can be directly attributed to the creation of supraregional markets for industrial goods made in new towns, in old industrial cities, and by peasant producers. No matter where and how production takes place, long-distance trade has certain effects: specialization and division of labour at the production site; and the coming into being of new exchange contracts in place of old at the level of inter-mediation. The dynamics of industrial transition, however, cannot be completely explained by supraregional markets, but must consider who supplied that demand and how; that is, explain the 'genesis' of *industrial* capital, labour, and organization. This, the second of the two constituent processes, is a terrain that has been contested, partly by theories, and partly, by variable local experiences, including those of the towns as opposed to those of the countryside.

Industrialization implies the release of surplus labour tied to non-industrial sectors for industrial uses. Who are these workers, and by what process do they become available? The shared premise in European history is that industrialization utilized and reinforced the alienation between land and labour initiated by the decline of feudalism.

But, who was the first *industrial* producer? One influential method in discussing this question owes to Franklin Mendels, and the literature on 'proto-industrialization', which stemmed from his writings.[79] The focus falls on domestic production in the countryside. In Mendels' own description, the process has three basic features: long-distance trade, peasant artisans who represent the source of labour surplus; and the symbiotic development of commercial agriculture and rural industry. Mendels further suggested that commercial production could induce high-fertility demographic regimes, a thesis developed in later research.[80] The concept also implied a definition of the roles of 'town' and 'country'. There were instances of manufacture shifting from the town to the country; but, perhaps more generally, the town specialized in skilled tasks, in trade and finance, leaving labour-intensive industry to flourish in the country.[81] In principle, the entire process can be seen as a precondition for full-blown industrial capitalism. It might have enabled increased population growth, accumulation by merchants, and commercial agriculture. Later research and debates, however, qualify the claim. Proto-industrialization is a dynamic process which shaped the transition to industrial society, but neither in denial of other processes – like the rise of manufacture in the towns – nor as a uniform, linear, irreversible trajectory. As a conception of organizational change, it is a special case and an example of putting-out.

Proto-industrialization, directly or indirectly, implicates the merchant engaged in rural industry as the 'pioneer' industrial capitalist. The debate on the pioneer, however, is a much older one, in which the progressive role of the merchant has been defended or disputed.[82] Hindsight, and a much enlarged literature, have not only blurred the

---

[79] S. C. Ogilvie and M. Cerman (eds.), *European Proto-industrialization* (Cambridge, 1996).

[80] See Hans Medick, 'The Proto-industrial Family Economy: The Structural Function of Household and Family during the Transition from Peasant Society to Industrial Capitalism', *Social History*, 1, (1976); and P. Kriedte, H. Medick, and J. Schlumbohm, *Industrialization before Industrialization. Rural Industry in the Genesis of Capitalism*, trans. Beate Schempp (Cambridge, 1981).

[81] J. Schlumbohm, 'Proto-industrialization as a Research Strategy and a Historical Period – A Balance Sheet', in Ogilvie and Cerman, *European Proto-industrialization*.

[82] Important figures in the German Historical School, Lujo Brentano and Adolf Held, are associated with the view that the merchant evolved into industrial capitalist. For a survey of this position and the contrary evidence from eminent works in British industrial history, see H. Otsuka, *The Spirit of Capitalism, the Max Weber Thesis in an Economic Historical Perspective* (Tokyo, 1982). The position that the merchant, as opposed to the master who accumulates capital in production and trade, is a passive if not regressive force originates in Marx. It has been influential in Maurice Dobb's treatment of the subject in *Studies in the Development of Capitalism* (London, 1946), and in the Marxist 'transitions' debate of the 1950s, see the essays in Paul Sweezy et al., *The Transition from Feudalism to Capitalism* (London and New York, 1992).

merchant–producer distinction, but also revealed how perspectives in this debate can be influenced by which region of Europe one looks at. Even in Britain, where 'merchant capital' has not found many advocates, a rich corpus on the sources of industrial capital suggests a complex genealogy for the 'vanguard' industrialist and the modern factory. Several eminent works described accumulation by small masters, which remains an important hypothesis because of the ubiquity of profit-financed fixed investments.[83] However, as Pat Hudson argued recently, the relevance of mercantile operations derives from the network of credits, especially working capital credits, which influenced larger investment decisions. The most numerous direct pioneers were neither 'merchants', the largest among whom maintained a distance from industry but tended to move into crucial tertiary activities, nor the ordinary working person. Rather, they came from what François Crouzet has called 'the middle classes', with backgrounds such as 'bankers, merchants, large retailers, manufacturers and industrialists', and the 'lower middle classes – shopkeepers, managers and other non-manual employees, self-employed craftsmen, cultivators of all kinds, with or without industrial pursuits, coalmasters, etc.'.[84] In the cotton industry, many pioneers among the 'middle classes' were merchant manufacturers, in turn, artisan farmers ('yeoman manufacturers') by parental occupation.

New organization is conventionally seen as the outcome of two movements, not necessarily sequential: from market transactions[85] to putting-out, and from putting-out to factory. Together, they completed the reduction of the 'independent' artisan, the seller of wares, into wage labourer. The basic putting-out contract left production in the cottages, the techniques unchanged, and the producer in possession of the skills and the tools. But it divested him or her of marketing functions, which now concentrated in the trader (of artisan or outsider origin), who supplied input and received back output. The producer sold labour, not wares. Being engaged on piece-rates, he or she sold labour in quantities changeable at each turnover. The trader hired only such labour for which there was demand, giving rise, in principle, to a perfectly smooth quantity-clearing market for product and labour. In an analytical sense, there is one circumstance critical for the existence of a system like this: labour surplus, and, relative to labour, scarcity of capital and informa-

---

[83] A survey of this large literature can be found in Pat Hudson, *The Genesis of Industrial Capital. A Study of the West Riding Wool Textile Industry, c. 1750–1850* (Cambridge, 1986), chapter 1.

[84] François Crouzet, *The First Industrialists. The Problem of Origins* (Cambridge, 1985).

[85] The German term *kaufsystem* is occasionally used to refer to a combination of artisanal workshops, merchants, and primarily spot-sale.

tion. Labour surplus ensures the continued operation of a piece-rate system and a quantity-clearing market. Relative capital scarcity ensures barriers to entry in trade and technological stasis.

Putting-out does not explain, and does not need, the *family* as the production unit. The family survives where domestic workers are in surplus because their opportunity costs are small, and/or when the costs of extra-family training are high. When these conditions become weak, putting-out may continue without the family, and with a kind of unit for which S. D. Chapman has the useful expression, 'proto-factory'.[86] This is typically a unit slightly larger than a family industrial unit and often evolves out of a family unit. It trains young inexperienced recruits on the job, and tends to arise in a situation where product demand is rapidly expanding, such that the existing units have to hire in labour from outside the domestic group. In continental Europe, early stages of industrialization, that is the period from the middle of the eighteenth to the middle of the nineteenth centuries, saw the development of this kind of workshop in the urban economy of a number of countries. A notable example is France, where 'the small-scale, crafts, workshop industry was much larger than the centralized, capital-intensive sector' in this period.[87] A significant example of such growth induced by long-distance trade was Lyons, which city played a major indirect role in the story of Indian *jari*, as we shall see.

In acknowledgment of the fact that such 'dualism' has endured rather than disappeared in industrial regions, recent scholarship has pointed out that historical 'alternatives' to mass production in the large-scale factory can, in an analytical sense, exist.[88] Berg elaborates on this theme in her 'cooperative structures'.[89] The notion of codes of conduct, which in principle can substitute formal hierarchy but serve the functions of hierarchy, has gained currency in studies on small-scale industry world-wide. In India, caste associations often served a similar role in stabilizing the transition from local to distant markets. Such forms, along with

[86] S. D. Chapman, *The Early Factory Masters: The Transition to the Factory System in the Midlands Textile Industry* (Newton Abbot, 1967).

[87] François Crouzet, 'France', in M. Teich and R. Porter (eds.), *The Industrial Revolution in National Context. Europe and the USA* (Cambridge, 1996), 54.

[88] The idea is central in the multidisciplinary discourse on small-scale enterprise in contemporary industrialized and developing worlds. A core theme is the ability of the small entrepreneur to 'flexibly specialize'. This broad characterization would hold for most artisanal industry engaged in consumer goods. In markets where ease of diversification matters more than costs, it can be a competitive strategy. For a wide-ranging survey with cases, see the essays in *IDS Bulletin*, 23, 3 (1992).

[89] Maxine Berg, *The Age of Manufactures: 1700–1820. Industry, Innovation and Work in Britain*, second edition (London and New York, 1994).

putting-out and the factory, represent an organizational option that has many examples in the Indian material.[90]

East Asia

Between late and early industrializations, there is a visible contrast in the initial effect of exposure to trade. The destructive effect of exposure is magnified in the former, precisely because exposure is delayed. In this respect, India is comparable to Japan and China. The entry of Lancashire in Chinese markets witnessed a rapid decline in the hand-spinning of cotton yarn. But in handloom weaving, not only was competition muted, the most visible effects were a many-sided reorganization. This included the separation of weaving from cotton cultivation, the long-distance trade in cloth, and the growth of putting-out and weaving factories.[91] The early years of Japan's economic exposure saw the rapid decline and dislocation of older crafts for reasons very similar to India's, the decline of the old hierarchy and entry of cheap imports. These included ordinary crafts like cotton spinning, sugar refining, and rapeseed oils, practised in peasant farms; as well as those dependent on the consumption of the lords and especially the Shogunate at Yedo. On the other hand, these early years also witnessed a surge in exports of artisanal goods. Raw silk was the principal exportable, along with a range of traditional goods like pottery, fans, papers, lacquer and bronze-

[90] Another strand, one that does not concern this study directly, in the literature on organizational change pertains to the rise of the factory in place of putting-out, especially in nineteenth-century Britain. Why was the factory more productive? What made the productivity gain realizable now and not earlier? There are three approaches to these questions, which focus on machinery, the management of workers, and the lower transactions costs of hierarchical organization. On machinery, disciplining, and the rationale of the factory, an insightful survey can be found in G. N. von Tunzelmann, *Technology and Industrial Progress* (Aldershot and Brookfield, 1995), chapter 4. On the view that the factory is an intrinsically superior form on account of transactions costs, see O. E. Williamson, 'The Organization of Work: A Comparative Institutional Assessment', *Journal of Economic Behaviour and Organization*, 1 (1980). The 1982 and 1989 issues of the same journal contain further discussions on this theme. The basic idea behind transactions costs is that it is costly for a producer or trader to obtain the knowledge required to organize resources through the market. If this knowledge happens to be asymmetrically distributed, either between consumers and traders or between traders and producers, there is scope for cheating. If these 'transactions' costs become large relative to the 'governance' costs of a system of production by command, command systems will tend to replace price-directed buy-and-sell systems. For a general reference on this framework and the related literature, see O. E. Williamson and S. G. Winter (eds.), *The Nature of the Firm. Origins, Evolution, and Development* (New York and Oxford, 1991).

[91] See Linda Grove, 'Rural Manufacture in China's Cotton Industry, 1890–1990', in conference on Cotton as Prime Mover in Global Industrialization, 1600–1990, Manchester, 1997.

ware. Traditional techniques could not compete in intermediate goods, such as cotton spinning or dye manufacture. But at least five factors ensured the continuance of small-scale and labour-intensive techniques in consumption goods: surplus labour, the diversity of preferences in the home market, inherited artisanal skills especially in textiles, low economies of scale, and the mass production of intermediate goods. This element of continuity in small-scale manufacture gave Japan's industrialization an enduring 'dualistic' character.[92] The small-scale producers were distinct from the segment more central to the government's economic programme, consisting of initiatives such as model factories, financial innovations, institution-building and the import of technology. But the former is the segment which defined and sustained Japan's comparative advantage until the 'new economy' could take over, and continued to be important as a supplier to the home market.

The term 'dualism' tends to underplay the adaptability of small-scale industry. In fact, in the second and third decades of the twentieth century, when average productivity was rising rapidly, both the modern and the traditional industry contributed to the rise.[93] Exports induced a number of changes in organization. One example is the partial relocation of silk-reeling and spinning from peasant farms to specialist reelers and filatures. These new types of enterprise, set up by merchants and on occasions by lords, were more closely involved with the export trade, and were capitalized by the latter in a condition where banking had limited reach.[94] In cloth production, handlooms were displaced by factories using the powerloom in the interwar period. Along with a change in capital intensity, there was also an extension of wage labour, and where weaving was de-integrated from finishing, a factorization and improvement in the allied processes.[95] In terms of the origins of industrial capital, it has been suggested that, while the new enterprise did involve entrepreneurs previously unconnected with industry or trade, accumulation by 'capitalists of traditional industry scattered

---

[92] On the co-existence of traditional and modern industry, see H. Rosovsky and Kazushi Ohkawa, 'The Indigenous Components in the Modern Japanese Economy', University of California, Institute of International Studies (Berkeley, 1961); and Kazushi Ohkawa and Mutsuo Tajima, 'Small–Medium Scale Manufacturing Industry: A Comparative Study of Japan and Developing Nations', International Development Center of Japan (Tokyo, 1976).

[93] On the quantitative dimensions of the 'take-off' in Japan, see W. Lockwood, *The Economic Development of Japan* (Princeton, 1954), chapter 3.

[94] Raw silk exports also witnessed successful state intervention to ensure quality.

[95] Takeshi Abe, 'The Japanese Cotton Industry: A Study of the Cotton Spinning Enterprise during the Interwar Period', in conference on Cotton as Prime Mover in Global Industrialization, 1600–1990, Manchester, 1997.

throughout the various regions' played a role that cannot be over-looked.[96]

India

Between India and cases of late industrialization, the violence of the shock of exposure is a shared feature. But so are the persistence of comparative advantage in major artisanal activities, commercialization, changes in organization in response, and a dualistic character of industrialization. In no case did the shock become regressive.

In the effects of supraregional markets on organization, India and Europe are not dissimilar cases either. Long-distance trade required working capital, information and risk-taking. These resources were not easily available to the average producer. Trade also enabled some substitution of local by imported inputs. All of these led to a transition from spot-sale to putting-out arrangements under merchants, many of whom were of relatively new origin. Under certain conditions, mer-chants and producers could converge, either because merchants needed to make fixed investments to stay in business, or producers could take up trade relatively easily. Examples of the former are leather and carpets. An example of the latter is high-quality weaving. In skilled weaving, such as south Indian silks or Sholapur cotton, producers were in possession of collective institutions and scarce information on processes, and were thus better able to take up trade. In towns where the scale of activity grew, industrial organization tended to change from traditional employment arrangements towards greater hiring-in of labour in small workshops and factories. Labour for such hiring came from various sources: rural servants no longer able or willing to stay in the village; migration from depressed regions and segments; domestic workers; or intra-community surplus labour whose recruitment and mobility were regulated by apprenticeship. In the skilled crafts, the merchants often took close control of the production process and the production site. The need arose from 'agency' costs that arose frequently in dealings between skilled artisans and foreign merchants. In this respect, the transactions costs literature on the birth of the factory has an affinity with some of the Indian material dealing with contractual changes, where opportunistic behaviour can be seen.

On certain points of institutional detail, India contrasts with early modern Europe and East Asia. Excepting carpet weavers in one region, the peasant artisan was entirely exceptional in India, which makes

[96] On this debate and the view cited, see Takafusa Nakamura, *Economic Growth in Prewar Japan*, trans. R. A. Feldman (New Haven, 1983), Appendix to chapter 3.

'proto-industrialization' – as a theory of the growth of *rural* industry, and as a theory of specialization and interpenetration between the city and the countryside – largely incompatible with Indian material. The Indian literature on commercial agriculture is justifiably silent on the artisan. Similarly, it is justified to leave the peasantry out of a narrative on industry. The only completely agricultural figure we deal with is the leather-worker, but he was not really an artisan at all. No other example involves part-time peasants in a serious way. Ownership of land, indeed a certain amount of cultivation, was not unknown for a rural weaver, and might have influenced the decision of city merchants to put out work. Cases like these are not absent, but sufficiently atypical for agrarian structure to be treated as a minor factor in industrial change.

The most plausible hypothesis about transactions between the city and the countryside must consider the substantial *discontinuity* between the two spheres. It is, however, debatable exactly what this discontinuity means. Does it suggest that caste created a separation, fundamental if not static, between land and industry? Or, that the power of the city guild, which in Europe often induced capital to look for rural producers, has no counterpart in India? Or, that a fundamental separation between town and country operated at the level of consumption? Or, even, the infrastructural and informational gap between town and country ruled out symbiotic developments? We do not know the answer yet.

But, if the peasant family has no counterpart in Indian data, the family firm has. The European literature focuses on the low implicit costs of domestic labour, and surprisingly neglects the other reason why families exist and do well, the economy in intra-family training. Neither benefit is easily observable, but it seems justified to stress the latter somewhat more, for most of the examples in this work are skilled crafts. The demographic consequence, if any, of the participation of households in commercial production is a theme on which the Indian data appear weak, but one on which future research may suggest patterns comparable with other parts of the world. Broadly, the history of the family needs to be more explicitly integrated within the economic processes described in this book. At the moment, the connections are obscure.

Differences

Finally, what was different between India and successful industrialization? Before answering this question, it is necessary to define the term 'successful' industrialization. In this context, it means several things usually thought of as basic attributes of the 'Industrial Revolution'.

These are the relatively high rates of growth of industrial employment, high rates of growth in labour productivity, changes in industrial organization which enables productivity to accelerate, and sectoral shifts in employment and incomes. It is reasonable to believe that the growth rate of employment in informal industry has been relatively high in India. Although aggregate employment has grown slowly at all times in the twentieth century, the aggregate trend is misleading being a summation of two contrary tendencies, the decline of domestic workers and the rise in wage employment. A measure of the growth of wage employment is available from the post-independence censuses, 1961–91. In these years, employment in India's informal sector factories grew at possibly 3.3 per cent annually, a remarkable performance by any international standard.[97] A large segment of these factories owe their origin to the transition described in the book. Leather and textiles are important examples.

Measured in terms of any of the other indices, however, the Indian transition was a weak one. Average income rose much too slowly in colonial or post-colonial India. So did, by implication, labour productivity in industry and agriculture. Industrial organization did change, as the displacement of domestic labour by wage labour suggests. But, it did not change enough. The myriad 'proto-factories' did not become myriad real factories. The revolution, which widespread adoption of machinery can induce in both productivity and organization, was weak in India. Neither in employment nor in incomes was there a structural change. Even in 1991, the share of industry in total employment was only about 10 per cent, not much different from what it was in 1891. Among other indices of structural change, urbanization increased by about 4 per cent in the century spanning the beginning of Crown rule (1858) and independence.[98] The ratio of industrial investment to GNP remained stable at around 2–3 per cent in any period before independence.[99] Measured in terms of share in world trade or manufactures, colonial India is a story of steady and significant relative decline.[100] In

[97] Male employment in manufacturing industry grew at 1.4 per cent in the UK between 1841 and 1911, 1.5 per cent in the Netherlands (1849–1909), 1.9 per cent in Germany (1882–1907), 0.9 per cent in France (1856–1906) and 3.3 per cent in the US (1870–1910, both sexes together). B. R. Mitchell, *International Historical Statistics. Europe 1750–1988* (New York, 1992); and, in the same series, the volume on *The Americas* (New York, 1993).

[98] Leela Visaria and Pravin Visaria, 'Population (1757–1947)' in Dharma Kumar (ed.), *The Cambridge Economic History of India*, vol. II, *c.1757–c.1970* (Cambridge, 1983), 519.

[99] Raymond W. Goldsmith, *The Financial Development of India, 1860–1977* (New Haven and London, 1983), 20, 80.

[100] P. Bairoch, 'International Industrialization Levels from 1750 to 1980', *European Journal of Economic History*, 11, 2 (1982).

other words, India did industrialize in the limited sense of expanding wage employment in industries intensive in manual labour, but did not experience significant structural change or economic development.

There are several features which set colonial India and successful industrialization apart. Industrialization requires sustained and rapid growth of markets for industrial goods. A common feature of successful industrialization is a rise in agricultural productivity, raising internal demand and initiating, in a number of senses, a rural industrialization.[101] This precondition was weak in much of South Asia for a long time. The absence of proto-industrialization in India may not have been structural, but a result of poorly growing rural (not necessarily local) demand for industry.[102] Clear signs of a rapidly expanding home market, in India's case inevitably of agrarian origin, cannot be seen in most regions. Rising agrarian demand, especially from 'the landholding and cultivating classes', did play a role in those regions where cash crop production flourished over long periods of time under relatively tranquil weather conditions, and significant government investment in water. [103]

[101] Peter Mathias has compared the nature of the interdependence in industrializing Britain with that in postwar developing economies. In the former, agriculture not only supplied labour, but was a significant source of enterprise, savings, cheap food, and demand for industry, all of this sustained by organizational change and significant productivity gains. Peter Mathias, *The First Industrial Nation: An Economic History of Britain, 1700–1914* (London, 1969), chapters 3 and 12. See also, for an assessment of the role of agricultural growth and productivity in the industrialization of Japan, Kaoru Sugihara, 'Agriculture and Industrialization: The Japanese Experience' in Peter Mathias and John A. Davis (eds.), *Agriculture and Industrialization* (Oxford and Cambridge, MA, 1996).

[102] National income and productivity estimates prove beyond doubt the fact of an agricultural stasis in India in the period of this study. This 'stylized fact' has not yet been adequately explained. In an interpretive essay, David Washbrook explains it in terms of 'metropolitan and industrial capital' exploiting the Indian peasant, David Washbrook, 'Agriculture and Industrialization in Colonial India' in Mathias and Davis (eds.), *Agriculture and Industrialization*. Such 'logic of development' is unlikely to work without the unstated assumptions of high population growth and continuous addition to surplus labour.

[103] The term 'landholding and cultivating classes' is from the 1898 Famine Commission. The context was the degree of hardship in a famine. The full passage is worth citing, for a broad but not unrealistic way of looking at the rural economy in the course of commercialization:

> [I]t may be said of India as a whole that of late years owing to high prices there has been a considerable increase in the incomes of the landholding and cultivating classes, and that their standard of comfort and of expenditure has also risen. With a rise in the transfer value of their tenure, their credit has also expanded. During the recent famine, these classes, as a rule, have therefore shown greater power of resisting famine, either by drawing on savings, or by borrowing, or by reduction of expenditure, than in any previous period of scarcity of like severity.

The report goes on to say that 'skilled artizans' and 'the poorer professional classes' both faced hardships, but needed little official relief. It was 'the day-labourers and

The indirect signs of agrarian prosperity were increased consumption, activated credit markets, savings, and investment.[104] They were, nevertheless, rather exceptions than the rule. Compared with India, exports were a more powerful impetus on Japanese industry, a condition which forced a faster pace of change in Japan, and also connected small-scale industry to modern infrastructure more closely.[105] In several cases of late industrialization, protection was used as a temporary instrument to stimulate the home market.[106] In India, the instrument was used late and insufficiently.

On the supply side, successful industrialization requires conditions that can transform craft-based enterprise into enterprise using machinery, or replace the former by the latter. These conditions include changes in factor-endowment, the development of credit markets and financial intermediation, and education and training in scientific knowledge, etc. The latter two, in turn, usually require an activist State and a propensity for private funding of public goods. South Asia's demographic trend has been a powerful factor slowing down industrial maturity. Levels of fertility in the region have few parallels in the world. From the middle of the nineteenth century, birth rates in industrializing Europe were falling steadily. By 1900, most of Europe had a birth rate below 30 per 1,000 per year. In India, the rate towards the end of the nineteenth century was near 50, and remained almost stable between 1891 and 1931. It declined only slowly thereafter, even as the death rate dropped sharply. It took India until 1991 to cross 30.[107] Both India and Japan faced surplus labour in the nineteenth century, but Japan had unusually low population growth rates, whereas India's accelerated in the course of the colonial period. No region in the world, which experienced successful industrialization, had to deal with such sustained

---

least-skilled artizans' who were the most vulnerable, and returned highest mortality during famines, and that was because the rise in food prices usually outstripped rise in money wages. India, *Report of the Indian Famine Commission*, 363.

[104] Two examples are Punjab and coastal Andhra. See Malcolm Darling, 'Prosperity and Debt' in Sugata Bose (ed.), *Credit, Markets and the Agrarian Economy of Colonial India* (Delhi, 1994); G. N. Rao, 'Changing Conditions and Growth of Agricultural Economy in the Kistna and Godavari Districts 1840–90', PhD dissertation, Andhra University (Waltair, 1975); and A. Satyanarayana, 'Expansion of Commodity Production and Agrarian Markets' in David Ludden (ed.), *Agricultural Production and Indian History* (Delhi, 1994). None of these studies deals directly with consumption.

[105] Exports as a proportion of domestic product hovered around 30 per cent between 1907 and 1936; it was less than 10 per cent in the first phase of economic reforms. In India, the ratio averaged 9–11 per cent in the interwar period.

[106] See, for example, J. L. van Zanden, 'Industrialization in the Netherlands' in Teich and Porter (eds.), *The Industrial Revolution in National Context*.

[107] Mitchell, *International Historical Statistics, Europe 1750–1988*; Visaria and Visaria, 'Population', Table 5.16, 509.

imbalance between demand for and supply of labour. [108] Many cases of early industrialization utilized surplus labour and artisanal labour. But, aided by a decline in population growth rates, sooner or later they reached a point where labour began to become scarce, and entrepreneurs were encouraged to innovate and invest in fixed capital. In India, a high population growth and a sustained excess supply of labour has delayed that outcome. The resultant industrialization can generate growth in employment, but cannot generate growth in average income.

The mounting surplus of labour was reinforced by poor efforts by public and private institutions towards enhancing human and non-human capital. [109] The history of public investment in colonial India is a history of unrelentingly conservative fiscalism. Despite the sustained pressure of opinion and examples of other countries urging a more activist State, there are few instances in which the government made unorthodox long-term expenditure commitments, and carried them through by innovations in the budget. The result was, except in pockets, supplementary inputs to an industrialization process – chiefly formal credit and education – changed sluggishly. It is now well known that, in independent India, despite the usage of public investment as a tool of development and politics, no fundamental break with the past occurred in prioritizing social development. In successful industrialization, government guarantees and institution-building played a major role in financial development. In British India, this role was marginal in contrast with Britain itself.[110] While labour was forever cheaply available, institutional credit was scarce. The condition eased in the case of rapid accumulation, and in towns like Surat where trust-based credit networks had developed to enable limited investments by families. But, by and large, the transition from own to borrowed capital in financing fixed investments took a long time. Local accumulation of capital fed by small profits could not become an accumulation fed by conversion of assets into liabilities on a large scale.

[108] Interestingly, the idea of the autonomy of high fertility seems to be regaining popularity in South Asian economic history. See, V. Kaiwar, 'Property Structures, Demography and the Crisis of the Agrarian Economy of Colonial Bombay Presidency', in David Ludden (ed.), *Agricultural Production and Indian History* (Delhi, 1994). An antecedent is Eric Stokes: see his article 'Dynamics and Enervation in North Indian Agriculture: The Historical Dimension', reprinted in the same volume.
[109] The view that late development tends to involve a more activist State owes its origin to A. Gerschenkron, *Economic Backwardness in Historical Perspective* (Cambridge MA, 1962). The focus on public goods, and especially on education, is a relatively recent trend and influenced by the post-war growth of East Asia. For example, Amsden, *Asia's Next Giant*, chapter 9.
[110] For the British case, see Phyllis Deane, 'The British Industrial Revolution' in Teich and Porter, *The Industrial Revolution in National Context*, 22–3.

There is reason to infer that a similar kind of immobility gripped the private funding of public welfare in the region. Colonial India began with a crippling initial condition that changed too slowly. By and large, precolonial Hindu society had no notion of literacy or scientific knowledge as a commonly shareable resource. Notions of welfare were not intrinsic in the caste-divided society, a priority neither for the literate castes, nor of the colonial State. Every village in India had tanners. But only a small percentage among them could become merchants or industrialists. For, there were social barriers to their taking up capitalist roles. The conversion of craft skills into industrial and innovative capacity required an induced social revolution in India, the conditions for which were not created.[111]

What the book describes is a powerful impetus in artisanal industry, one common to industrialization in general – the creation of commodities, the extension of trade, and changes in industrial and mercantile organization. It gave rise to capitalists who were often of different origin from their counterparts in earlier periods, were mobile and innovative, and worked in collectives, partnerships, and networks. And yet, all that did not lead either to rapid growth in average income, or to a new managerial, technological or financial paradigm in India. For, essentially, this industrialization was driven by traditional resources: informal training, informal credit, and plenty of low-quality labour. Accumulation involved large masses, but failed to pull the average along rapidly enough.

Having finished with the generalizations, it is now time to explain from what ingredients these were assembled. Handloom weaving is the natural starting point because of its scale, complexity, and long continuance. Weaving also best illustrates the effects of competitive imports, and the conditions for the co-existence of machinery and tools in the same industry.

---

[111] The role of 'values' in industrial development has been widely discussed in India since Max Weber speculated that the Hindu world-view was not suited to the spirit of capitalism. See, for a selection of works on this theme, Morris D. Morris, 'Values as an Obstacle to Economic Growth in South Asia: An Historical Survey', *Journal of Economic History*, 27, 4 (1967); Dwijendra Tripathi, 'Indian Entrepreneurship in Historical Perspective: A Re-interpretation', *Economic and Political Weekly*, 7 (1971); and Jack Goody, *The East in the West* (Cambridge, 1996). 'Values' in this context can have two aspects. The first, the motivation driving the prospective entrepreneur, has received the most attention. Weber dealt with this aspect, and much of recent scholarship disputes his thesis. The second aspect follows from the hierarchical nature of Indian society and concerns whether social hierarchy restricted occupational choices, exit, and entry. Some examples from this book would suggest that they did so systematically. If this is generalizable, social or cultural backwardness in this sense did contribute to economic backwardness in India.

3   Handloom weaving

Any general account of the history of the Indian artisan in the nineteenth and twentieth centuries must begin with textile production. In the 1911–31 censuses, a quarter of the workers in industry were employed in textiles, and in mainly artisanal textiles. The share of textiles in employment was probably higher about 100 years previously, but it declined only to stabilize at a percentage that still made it the largest industry by far. Textiles has unique historiographic significance. Its importance reflected the fact that cloth, unlike the other products dealt with in this book, was a mass-consumed good. Its history is bound up with the histories of inland trade and patterns of consumption. Textile history is a particularly good example with which these changes can be understood. Further, cotton textiles is the most important example of a craft threatened by steam-powered technology, or of premodern industry threatened by the Industrial Revolution, or even of Indian livelihood threatened by industrializing Britain. The threat came from Lancashire until the prewar decade, and from Bombay in the interwar period. Despite the unequal nature of the contest, handloom weaving in India did not succumb. The market-share of handloom cotton cloth was roughly stable between the 1890s and the 1930s, and no overall decline in loomage can be established from the periodic loom censuses. One must examine how the handlooms adapted to competition, and the answer to that question might suggest an answer to a more general one, how artisans adapted to big changes in their market.

Exposure to foreign trade and commercialization transformed Indian textiles in basic ways. Commercial hand-spinning of cotton became extinct due to competition from British and Indian machine-spun yarn. On a more limited scale, several other inputs began to be mass-produced and imported. Mineral dyes, *jari* and raw silk are examples. Upon cloth, the effects of machinery, or the powerloom, were more ambiguous. While there were reports of a decline in the production of many types of cloth, in the twentieth century handloom cloth production experienced overall growth and reorganization. The production of cotton cloth

61

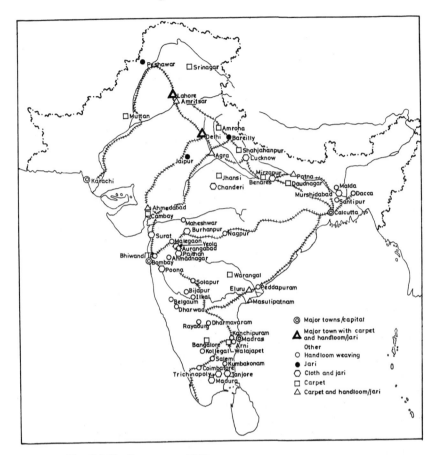

Map 3.1 Textile centres, *c*.1940

expanded by about 30 per cent between 1900 and 1939. Market shares were stable. And productivity increased, for loomage does not seem to have deviated much from the long-term average of 2 million during the period 1900–47. New investments were made. New tools and processes, such as the fly shuttle and beam-warping, were adopted on a large scale. In southern and western India, handlooms urbanized to give rise to large textile towns. And wage labour expanded in place of family labour.[1] What made growth and reorganization possible? The domestic

[1] On the chronology of decline, survival, or growth in major weaving regions, see Sumit Guha, 'The Handloom Industry of Central India: 1825–1950', *Indian Economic and Social History Review*, 26, 3 (1989); Konrad Specker, 'Madras Handlooms in the Nineteenth Century', *Indian Economic and Social History Review*, 26, 2 (1989); and

market as a whole was growing. Handloom weavers benefited from the availability of inputs that were cheaper or easier to handle than before, though these savings are not directly measurable. The reorganization derived largely from changes in the fortunes of labour and capital in weaving. The colonial period saw the ruin of many types of weaver, or their reduction into a state of extreme vulnerability. Some of them continued in the industry, but increasingly as labourers, or under putting-out contracts. On the other hand, new trades provided other groups of weavers with opportunities for capital accumulation. Long-distance trade in yarn, dyes, silk and *jari* did exist before the railways and steamships, but was not as extensive or as organized as they became from the 1870s. Cloth for internal consumption was being traded over longer distances after the advent of the railways. These trades saw the entry of new mercantile classes, the participation of artisan groups in the material and cloth trade, and a general decay of systems of spot-sale such as hawking or fairs in favour of permanent markets and contractual sale in textile towns.

How far is this picture of dynamism compatible with the image of a violent and regressive exposure to trade the Marxist thesis (chapter 2) speaks of? Undeniably, both elements were present, and they together constitute the outcome of commercialization in handloom weaving. In the interwar period, surveys of the industry, produced in the course of the Tariff Board enquiries (during the period 1926–40 for textiles), or the making of the *Fact-Finding Committee* report on textiles (1942), create a mixed impression. The industry had parts that were in depression, and parts that were doing well. The former offered smaller or more

Haruka Yanagisawa, 'The Handloom Industry and its Market Structure: The Case of the Madras Presidency in the First Half of the Twentieth Century', *Indian Economic and Social History Review*, 30, 1 (1993). These three essays have been reprinted in Tirthankar Roy (ed.), *Cloth and Commerce: Textiles in Colonial India* (New Delhi, 1996). See also Peter Harnetty, 'Deindustrialisation Revisited: The Handloom Weavers of the Central Provinces of India, c.1800–1947', *Modern Asian Studies*, 25, 3 (1991); Ruma Chatterjee, 'Cotton Handloom Manufactures of Bengal, 1870–1921', *Economic and Political Weekly*, 22, 25 (1987); and Christopher Baker, *An Indian Rural Economy: The Tamilnad Countryside* (Delhi, 1984), 393–414. On aggregate trends in size and organizational change, see Tirthankar Roy, *Artisans and Industrialization: Indian Weaving in the Twentieth Century* (Delhi, 1993). For a detailed study of industrial organization in western India, see Douglas Haynes, 'The Logic of the Artisan Firm in a Capitalist Economy: Handloom Weavers and Technological Change in Western India, 1880–1947', in Burton Stein and Sanjay Subrahmanyam (eds.), *Institutions and Economic Change in South Asia* (Delhi, 1996). For a study of an urban weaving community in relation to economic changes, see Tirthankar Roy, 'Capitalism and Community: A Study of the Madurai Sourashtras' in *Indian Economic and Social History Review*, 34, 4 (1997). An earlier brief discussion of some of these changes and the possible reasons therefor can be found in A. K. Bagchi, *Private Investment in India* (Cambridge, 1972), section 7.1.

uncertain incomes, the latter higher or stable incomes. The generic coarse cloth *garha* belonged in the former economy; the gold-bordered silk *sari* in the latter. With some types of cloth, weavers could pull out of a depressed segment and diversify or migrate into a dynamic one. But with other cloths, there were limits to such a strategy, and the weavers either worked harder for less income, or tended to fall out of weaving altogether. These segments were distinct not merely in terms of cloth. They represented different configurations of product, region, even caste and community of weavers engaged. These differences, or inequalities, were not static: segmentation changed; segments overlapped; and there were limited movements of capital and labour between segments. But without recognizing the existence of depressed and dynamic spaces within the same industry, it is impossible to talk coherently about the industry at all.

Until recently, textile history either ignored these diversities and inequalities, or simplified them, or was not quite clear what they meant. The 'de-industrialization' literature, for example, by and large talked about the experience of 'the weaver', and debated what this mythical figure wove and how much he earned.[2] But, from about the middle of the 1980s, scholars began to pay closer attention to the divisions within the industry. Three broad hypotheses on the survival of handloom weaving seem to emerge from this concern with detail. First, the existence of segmented markets for cloth, and the advantage of the handloom over the powerloom in making certain types of cloth, enabled some weavers to continue, even prosper, in the colonial period.[3] Secondly, segmented markets imply that, quite apart from powerloom competition, there was another force at work on the weaving industry, namely, changes in consumption.[4] Thirdly, the surviving segments experienced organizational change. The impetus came from several sources: long-distance trade induced the accumulation of capital by producers; competition among handloom weavers for markets induced an increase in scale or the adoption of new methods; and local circumstances such as migration created large pools of hireable labour.[5]

[2] See, for example, references to wages earned by 'the weaver' in Deepak Lal, *The Hindu Equilibrium*, vol. I, *Cultural Stability and Economic Stagnation: India 1500BC–1980* (Oxford, 1988), 186.

[3] Identification of survival and decline with specific products is a theme in Yanagisawa, 'The Handloom Industry'; Specker, 'Madras Handlooms'; Baker, *An Indian Rural Economy*; and Roy, *Artisans and Industrialization*.

[4] The point is explored, in different ways, by Yanagisawa, 'The Handloom Industry'; and Haynes, 'The Logic of the Artisan Firm'.

[5] Organization is a central theme in Haynes, 'The Logic of the Artisan Firm'. The broad contours of organizational change in Tamil Nadu are described in Baker, 'An Indian Rural Economy'.

The concern of the new scholarship with market segments is indeed a productive one. But, it needs to be taken further. Two things in particular need to be noted. The question of which markets and cloths were not competing with the powerloom, or competing only indirectly, is subject to some speculation. The literature has tried to identify these cloths mainly with regional and local data. There is scope to generalize from these and other data, and create a broader picture of the non-competing market segment. Secondly, while scholars have noted the existence of *market* segments, they have overlooked the existence of segmentation among *producers*. These two differences were associated. The central Indian village weaver making coarse cloth for the peasant employer was a vastly different figure from the well-off and educated Sourashtra weaver in Madura town: the two were as unlike as their outputs and clientele were. These inequalities played a role in the changes in industrial organization, which is yet to be fully understood.

Against this outline of where textile scholarship stands today, it is now possible to state the purpose of this chapter. It does not attempt a detailed narrative of the industry in the colonial period. Recent regional and aggregate studies have already addressed such a task.[6] The aim of this chapter is more specific. It recreates and fills up the notion of *differentiation* within the handloom industry. It draws together, on the one hand, facts about decline and depression, and, on the other hand, facts about survival and reorganization. Two types of profile emerge therefrom. One describes the typical products, people, and places in decline, whether due to competition from machinery or to changes in preference. And the other describes the product, people, and places that faced markets not threatened by machinery, but did see changes in tastes and increasing long-distance trade. There is no suggestion of a 'dualism' in this project. Rather, the attempt is to illustrate the point that the history of handloom weaving consisted of contradictory experiences.

The chapter proceeds in the following sequence: an illustration of inequality; a profile of the depressed segment; and a profile of the dynamic segment.

Images of inequality

There are two types of data on the inequality and divisions among handloom weavers in the early twentieth century: economic and ethnographic. The former consists of incomes and wages collected by various

---

[6] See notes 1–5 above.

governmental surveys. The latter consists of information on how specific groups of weavers were situated in relation to their neighbours in the local society, and sometimes in relation to other groups of weavers. The two types of information overlap, when a clear association between income and social situations seems to exist. This section will study the broad nature of the inequality that emerges from both sets of data. The sections that follow will partly draw upon this information and point out associations where they are evident.

Provincial surveys of the industry collected a great deal of data on wages and earnings of weavers in the first half of the twentieth century, for each of the major regions, for several locations, and by types of work. They arise from non-random samples. But the samples were often quite large, and collected by scholars who knew the industry closely. They can be taken to be a reliable picture. The figures are mostly piece-rates, which was the usual system of payment. But, on rare occasions, evidently with workers employed in factories and workshops, time wages were reported. Piece-rates can be converted into reasonably accurate monthly earnings, because productivity and prices for major types of cloth are also available from the same sources. Table 3.1 presents a collection of such figures for the middle of the 1920s. Since prices were usually quite volatile, years must be compared cautiously. From this point of view, 1925–28 is a normal period.

The table shows that, with few exceptions, the weaver handling silk or very fine cotton cloth had incomes between three and five times that of a weaver making cloths variously called 'coarse', 'ordinary', '16s–20s' or '20s *dhoti*', etc. *Dhoti* and *sari* were generic men's and women's wear respectively. For the time being, this class of cloths will be referred as 'coarse weaving', but the term will be defined more precisely further on. The range in the original piece-rate wages is somewhat narrower, but silk offered greater continuity of work. Coarse weaving wages varied relatively little between regions, though they seem to have been low on average in the Andhra regions. There are two monthly time rates reported in this set of figures, one from Sholapur town and the other from Madura. Both towns developed, in the interwar period, quite extensive wage employment in local textiles.[7] Both wages are higher than the minimum income of non-factory weaver (in coarse cotton) in these regions, but considerably lower than the maximum incomes (in silk). A range of money wage such as Rs. 6–15, in which most coarse weavers belong, is comparable to what a field labourer or unskilled non-

---

[7] See Haynes, 'The Logic of the Artisan Firm' on Sholapur; and Roy, 'Capitalism and Community' on Madura.

Table 3.1. *Approximate monthly earnings of weavers, 1925–1927*

Region	Place	Cloth	Rs. per month
Bengal	Dacca, rural	16s–20s *sari/dhoti*	11–12
	Rajbalhat	≥60s *sari/dhoti*	40–50
	Dacca, rural	≥60s *sari/dhoti*	18–20
Bombay	General impression	coarse cotton	11–15
	General impression	silk	23–28
	Sholapur, factory wage	8-yard cotton *sari*,	
		coarse–medium	15
Coastal Andhra	Eluru	20s *dhoti*	6–9
	Pedana, Palakol	exportable *kaily/rumal*	18
	Palakol	fine *sari*	21
	Ponduru	120s *sari*	33
Tamil Nadu	Jayankondam, Thoraiyur	ordinary cotton	11–12
	Madura, Coimbatore	fine cotton or silk turban	26–30
	Madura, wage-earner	silk	15–20
	Madura, owner of 5–10		
	looms	silk	40–80
Southern Andhra	Bellary-Kurnool wages	coarse cotton	7–15
	Bellary-Kurnool, owner		
	of 3 looms	coarse-medium cotton	40
	Bellary	20s–40s *sari*	14
	Bellary	silk-bordered *sari*	22–30
	Pullampet	silk	12–23

Sources: Bengal, *Report on the Survey of Cottage Industries in Bengal,* second edition (Calcutta, 1929); S. V. Telang, *Report on Handloom Weaving Industry in the Bombay Presidency* (Bombay, 1932); N. G. Ranga, *The Economics of Handlooms* (Bombay, 1930); K. S. Venkatraman, 'The Handloom Industry in South India', *Journal of the University of Bombay,* 7, 1 (1935) and 8, 1 (1936); and D. Narayana Rao, *Report of the Survey of Cottage Industries in Madras Presidency,* Bellary District (Madras, 1925).

agricultural labourer would earn in a month in these years, though employment intensity may vary considerably between weavers and field labourers.[8] But a range such as Rs. 40–80, in which the south Indian silk weavers belong, is decidedly above standards in agriculture. Rs. 40 was an income an experienced carpenter or blacksmith in a northern town might expect to earn. Rs. 80 was closer to what a qualified engineer could get in a modern factory.[9] Income inequality among handloom weavers, in other words, corresponded to the distance

[8] S. Sivasubramonian, 'Income from the Secondary Sector in India 1900–47', *Indian Economic and Social History Review,* 14, 4 (1977), Table 17.
[9] The compared figures are from Harish C. Sharma, *Artisans of the Punjab* (Delhi, 1996), 97.

between an agricultural labourer and a member of the urban middle class.

To convert these earnings into a time series, such that long movements in real wages can be inferred, is a difficult task. A time series is rarely available for any closely defined type of cloth. Further, whereas estimates for several locations at a point in time come from a relatively small number of surveys, a time series must pull together many surveys, making comparability more difficult.[10] Finally, direct data on the less visible and less commercialized coarse weaver are always scanty.

We do, however, have impressions of how levels of living had been changing for specific groups. For example, a 1908–9 report on central India recalled the recent history of ordinary weaving in the province:

The only alternative [of exit] for the indigenous weavers was to reduce the price of their goods to compete with the foreign goods, till at last it was brought to a level which left a margin of two annas per diem for the maintenance of their entire families.[11]

Alfred Chatterton, Director of Industries in Madras, wrote of the coarse weaver: 'the majority of them have to work harder to make a bare living.'[12] Both these statements suggest that coarser cotton weaving suffered a decline in real wages, possibly in the last quarter of the nineteenth century. More examples of depression in coarse weaving will be discussed further on. Information on earnings of the more skilled and market-oriented weavers is richer. Earnings from silk, fine cotton, and exportable goods from the eastern coast can be compared relatively easily over different pairs of years in the long span of 1880–1940. With adjustments made for price movements, none suggests a fall, and most suggest a rise. Three specific cases of increase in real earnings are: Santipur fine cotton weavers between 1890 and 1941; *kaily* weavers of the Andhra coast between 1912 and 1927; and Surat silk weavers

[10] Clusters of earnings similar to 1925–28 can be created for three other time points: the 1880s based on district gazetteers and two reports on Bengal and the Central Provinces; 1898–1900 based on a series of monographs on the artisans prepared by the provincial governments; and 1906–7 when again a number of provincial government surveys of northern India coincide. But these clusters have problems. The first one is limited in coverage, whereas the other two witnessed unusual price movements. They are not comparable between themselves, but the earnings within each can be compared. Such comparisons do not contradict the basic conclusion of Table 3.1. A yet fourth year for which a wage data set might be possible to reconstruct is 1941–2 when a few provincial reports and the important source, India, *Report of the Fact-Finding Committee (Handlooms and Mills)*, Commerce Department (Delhi, 1942), were published. But the Committee was far too brief on wages, though very rich on prices and costs.

[11] Central Provinces and Berar, *Report of the Industrial Survey of Central Provinces and Berar* (Nagpur, 1908–9), 21.

[12] Cited by H. Maxwell-Lefroy and E. C. Ansorge, *Report on an Inquiry into the Silk Industry in India* (Calcutta, 1917), vol. II, 54.

between 1900 and 1927.[13] It is, therefore, possible to conclude not only that average levels of living were much higher in silk and fine cotton than in coarse cotton weaving, but also that *levels* and *trends* in earnings were correlated. Why these inequalities increased is a question the following sections will try to answer.

A further stylization derives from ethnographic data compiled in the castes and tribes anthologies prepared around the turn of the century for the major provinces. They suggest that the nature of weaving and social status were associated. Parallel to the hierarchy in earnings, there was a hierarchy of earners. These two hierarchies were correlated. Brief descriptions of four major social orders – the services castes, the Muslim weavers of north India, the Hindu cotton weavers, and the Hindu silk weavers – illustrate this point.

Rural coarse weaving was performed largely by part-time agricultural labourers. In western and central India, coarse weaving was practised by groups of people defined and seen as labourers, but who wove on the side, even as a form of labour. Such people can be called the 'services castes', because their identity as makers and sellers of cloth was dependent on and secondary to their labouring status. Their occupation was almost entirely confined to the least skilled weaving. The Mahars (Dheds) and Gandas of central India, the Malas of Andhra coast, the Chamars of Punjab and United Provinces, who were primarily tanners, were known to practise weaving along with agricultural labour. Western India also had some settled tribal weavers who were occupationally not very different from the castes mentioned above. The coarse weaving castes of the Gangetic plains, the Tatwas of Bihar, the Tantis of Orissa, and the Koris and Kolis of United Provinces, were somewhat more of specialist weavers. But they experienced continual infiltration into their rank by the menial castes, weaving being 'the highest occupation ordinarily open to the outcast section of the community'.[14] In this segment, the connection between tanning and weaving was especially close. The Chamars (hereditary tanners) of Punjab were known to weave as freely as the Mahars tanned hides. None was an especially skilled occupation, and all were off-season employment for people whose primary duty was agricultural labour. In the colonial period, migration, monetization, and reform movements weakened the practice

---

[13] Venkatraman, 'The Handloom Industry of South India'; Ranga, *The Economics of Handlooms*; S. M. Edwardes, *A Monograph upon the Silk Fabrics of the Bombay Presidency* (Bombay, 1900); Telang, *Report on Handloom Weaving*; and Bengal, *Handloom Cotton Weaving Industry in Bengal*, Department of Industries (Calcutta, 1941).

[14] Ibbetson, *Panjab Castes* (Lahore, 1916), 302.

of customary services,[15] whereas markets for cloth were expanding beyond the boundaries of the village. Thus, towards the end of the nineteenth century, the industrial towns employed large numbers of erstwhile 'menials' in diverse 'lowly' services and industrial jobs. In striking contrast, the main networks of textile production and trade that emerged in the middle of the twentieth century from the mass migration of artisans rarely involved the services castes. That they did not is hardly surprising. The rural coarse weaver did not command great craftsmanship. Nor did he have access to entrepreneurial resources such as business organization or credit. And there were explicit prohibitions as well, for example one on Mahars from dyeing cloth.[16]

The northern plains possessed a large body of Muslim weavers, the Julahas, the most numerous of the Muslim castes in northern India. Weavers, indeed, are believed to be the first Hindu occupational group to convert to Islam. They were spread from Punjab to Bengal, and migrated southward with the spread of Muslim power. In the nineteenth century, many came to central India, to the Khandesh weaving towns of Malegaon and Ahmadnagar, and to Bhiwandi near Bombay, where they gave leadership to a 'powerloom' revolution from the 1940s.[17] Further south, in the Deccan, Muslim weavers became rarer, and, though called Julahas or, more often, 'Deccani Momins', they were mainly converted local Hindus speaking the local tongue. The Julahas were a heterogeneous group. In the villages, they were lowly placed like all coarse weavers. They tended to be degraded by their peasant customers and occasionally by employers. The name 'Julaha' became a symbol of rusticity.[18] But they were also present in the silk industry of the Awadh, and settled by a patronizing court in Ahmadnagar. The town Julahas tended to claim high descent, and formed powerful associations.[19] In

---

[15] For a general discussion, see the section 'Social control and the "Market"' in C. A. Bayly, *Rulers, Townsmen and Bazaars: North Indian Society in the Age of British Expansion, 1770–1870* (Cambridge, 1983), 315–19. For a specific industry example, see chapter 6 below.

[16] See R. V. Russell and Hira Lal, *The Tribes and Castes of the Central Provinces and Berar* (London, 1916), 'Mahar'; E. A. Hobson, *Cotton in Berar* (Nagpur, 1887), 4–5 on the prohibition on dyeing, and 11 on Mahars finding employment as millhands and railway workers and in other factories, after the cotton famine (1865–70) in central India. See also M. Stevenson, *Without the Pale, the Life Story of an Outcaste* (Calcutta, 1930).

[17] For a definition of 'powerlooms', see chapter 1. See, on this theme, Douglas Haynes, 'Weavers' Capital and the Origins of the Powerlooms: Technological Transformation and Structural Change Among Handloom Producers in Western India, 1920–1950', annual meeting of the Association of Asian Studies, Washington DC, 1996.

[18] 'The physique of the Jolaha ... is generally inferior to that of the village craftsmen, and he is the butt of his neighbours who lead a healthy life out of doors, and understand crops and cattle'. W. Crooke, *Races of North India* (London, 1907), 137.

[19] G. Ansari, *Muslim Caste in Uttar Pradesh* (Lucknow, 1960), 44.

eastern parts of the United Provinces, they acquired the curious notoriety of being a 'turbulent race'. Gyanendra Pandey has attributed this image to long depression in the craft, and its subjection to Hindu traders.[20] This explanation can be questioned, for silk in the long run was not a depressed industry and this reputation of the Julahas had a local character. Another probable factor behind the image is that the silk weaver among the Julahas carried a pronounced sense of hierarchy and self-respect, which needed to be aggressively asserted, being at odds with the image of the Julaha based on the figure of the rural semi-skilled weaver. The latter image is reflected in numerous Punjabi Hindu proverbs.[21]

The services castes were rare in the deep south, and weaving tended to specialize in the hands of four great castes who identified weaving as their traditional occupation, and all of whom enjoyed, by 'cleanliness' standards, a higher social position than the coarse weavers of northern or central India.[22] The predominant Telugu-speaking weaver caste is the Padmasalis, the cotton-weaving branch of the broader category of Sali. They occur mainly in the present territory of Andhra Pradesh, from where a large number migrated into the Deccan towns such as Sholapur, to work in the mills, and supply capital and labour in handloom factories in the early twentieth century. The bilingual Kannada-Tamil Devangas occurred somewhat further south, in southern Andhra, Mysore, and northern Tamil Nadu.[23] Devangas dominated industry and trade in Salem, and in textile towns of the region of Tamil Nadu locally known as Kongunad. Neither caste-group was identifiable with specific products. But their main concentrations, such as Sholapur or Salem, did specialize. Sholapur was known for cotton *saris* and jacquard sheets, and Salem for fine cotton. Both groups migrated a great deal and such migrations splintered homogeneous communities into classes and subcastes in the

---

[20] Gyanendra Pandey, 'The Bigoted Julaha', in *The Construction of Communalism in Colonial North India* (Delhi, 1991).

[21] Ibbetson, *Panjab Castes*; H. Risley, *The People of India* (Calcutta, 1908).

[22] Technologically, cotton weaving in the south and the north were different. In the north, harsh winters necessitated thick handspun cloths. Also, early-modern European trade had created a tradition in superfine cotton in the north. The cotton weaving in the south was more in the middle counts. Possibly as a result, in the north, coarse and fine weavers were often distinct and hierarchized. But the major southern weaving castes were not associated with grades of cotton, nor placed unequally between themselves, and had no explicit internal hierarchy.

[23] Salis and Devangas were similar in many ways. They had a similar origin myth. In Tamil Nadu, one was a 'left hand' and the other a 'right hand' caste. Yet, the Devangas had a curious custom whereby once in twelve years a Devanga made a ritual request to be readmitted as a Sali, which probably suggests a common origin, but perhaps a subsequent separation as one became Saivites and the other Vaishnavites. Edgar Thurston, *Tribes and Castes of Southern India* (Madras, 1909), 'Devanga'.

towns to which they came.[24] Yet, they maintained a strong sense of identity, at the core of which prevailed the sense of being a *skilled* artisan. The other great cotton-weaving caste in the deep south was the Kaikkolar, spread over a smaller area, less mobile, more rural, and more rarely the dominant economic group in major textile towns. But they did share with the other weaver castes the existence of social organizations.[25]

The sense of a special kind of collective found outward expression in caste associations, far more visible as institutions in the textile towns of southern and western India than in the north. Less visible, but present, were guild-like barriers to entry into the craft that arose from the close association between critical skills and membership of informal collectives. Textile history now recognizes these collectives as an important feature of the strategy of migrant weavers to establish themselves economically and redefine themselves socially.[26] Attempts to recreate a community and regenerate roots characterized the Julahas of Bhiwandi, the Padmasalis of Sholapur, and the Sourashtras of Madura, among others. There were several mutually reinforcing elements in such attempts: these weavers possessed unique and valuable skills (something the rural coarse weaver did not); they were migrants and needed to stick together; and they faced a contradictory need to collaborate and yet compete between themselves. The social associations enabled collaboration of various kinds, while they also tried, via investment in common good, to preserve fellow feeling despite rising economic inequality.

Silk weavers almost everywhere enjoyed the status of the urban middle-class. As they transacted exclusively with urban elites, whether merchants or consumers, they were often in positions of power, and, where power derived from religion, claimed Brahmanhood or the warrior (*Kshatriya*) status. In the twentieth century, silk weavers usually controlled a part of the trade in cloth and raw material. In cotton,

---

[24] In Poona, the Salis who hailed from Narayanpeth, and those from Paithan, both major Hyderabad weaving towns, were virtually separate subcastes. In Sholapur, there were more than twenty such divisions. They arose because the groups migrated at different dates, under different leaders to whom each owed allegiance: R. G. Kakade, *A Socio-economic Survey of the Weaving Communities in Sholapur*, Gokhale Institute of Politics and Economics (Poona, 1947). But, neither group 'admit outsiders [non-weavers] into the caste': H. V. Nanjundayya and L. K. A. Aiyar, *The Mysore Tribes and Castes* (Mysore, 1931), 567.

[25] K. R. R. Sastry, *South Indian Gilds* (Madras, 1925), 29, 36; Thurston, *Tribes and Castes*, 'Kaikolar'. Mattison Mines's study of the Kaikkolars argues that this organization was based on territories of state rather than on kinship, a feature other Tamil artisan castes shared. In recent times, the cooperative took over some of the functions of caste associations: *The Warrior Merchants: Textiles, Trade and Territory in South India* (Cambridge, 1984).

[26] See Douglas Haynes, 'Weavers' Capital and the Origins of the Powerlooms'; and Roy, 'Capitalism and Community'.

foreign trade in cloth and yarn had introduced many types of non-artisanal groups in long-distance trade. In silk, such entry was rarer.[27] In some places known for their dyeing, silk weavers owned dye-houses. The Hindu silk weaver in all his glory is best seen in the deep south. The main silk product of the southern town, the bordered *sari*, was especially skill-intensive and had stable, almost mass demand. The Julaha penetration did not go much further southward of Bombay city, and, even in Khandesh and Gujarat, the Julahas rarely took up silk, or managed to break into the Hindu monopoly in silk.

In Madura, the Sourashtras dominated the silk and cotton industries. They began as producers, but controlled trade in the twentieth century. They formed a small and relatively homogeneous group. Occupationally, almost two-thirds of the 'actual workers' in 1921 were engaged in textile trade and production. As with silk weavers elsewhere, Sourashtras carried a strong sense of identity. In their case, this sense was dominated by the memory of a migration from western India through Vijayanagar to Madurai, spanning several centuries and involved with the rise and decline of major regimes of south India. In Madura, they claimed high status, and were partially successful in resisting Brahman opposition to the claim. Consistent with the claim, the Sourashtras also invested a large part of their business profits in basic education. In the twentieth century, the community was economically differentiated, the main division being that between the traders and the weavers. And yet, there was remarkable stability of contractual relations and explicit or implicit cooperation on dealing with common problems.[28]

Some of these features – the claim to status, the accent on education, cooperation, and the ownership of both fixed and working capital – can be found in other silk-weaving groups. Thus, Saliyans, a caste settled in Tanjore, made Brahmanic claims as they prospered in textile business. They were probably a breakaway from the Salis, and, if so, show how a group pursuing a distinct and superior kind of weaving can crystallize into a caste. The Patwegars of the Deccan were an 'honest and thrifty people' whose children attended school till they were old enough to weave. The Koshtis of Khandesh, Sholapur, and Poona had customs similar to those of the Salis, but were ranked above them. 'There are exceptional cases in which he has educated his children to a higher standard than his own.'[29] The Bombay Gazetteers of the 1880s located

---

[27] With the possible exception of Bengal where the silk trade was controlled by urban merchants, remnants of a decaying but old export trade in Bengal silk.

[28] Roy, 'Capitalism and Community', and sources cited therein.

[29] Thurston, *Tribes and Castes* (see under specific names); and Edwardes, *Monograph on Silk*, 51–3.

the Ahmadnagar Khatris, silk weavers, between the Brahman and the main peasant castes in wealth and power. The 'rich work both as weavers and moneylenders, and many are landholders.'[30] The Khatris of Hyderabad State were distinctly wealthier than Padmasalis, the cotton weavers.[31]

The basic hierarchies influenced how groups of weavers responded to the long reversal in fortunes. The services castes and rural cotton weavers usually left the industry for general labour and semi-skilled services. Between the 1911 and 1931 censuses, the proportion of Mahars and Gandas engaged in weaving declined sharply in central India. When they left the village, they tended to be employed as factory hands. Groups mainly rural or mainly engaged in cotton weaving tended to leave weaving more frequently. Thus, instances of Kaikkolars giving up weaving were more common than that of the Salis or the Devangas. The average Kaikkolar family abandoned weaving to become 'coolies', a term that connoted general labour, including labour in handloom factories. The urban communities and silk weavers responded differently. When the silk weavers had to leave weaving, they tended to shift to skilled professions and trade rather than labour. The silk-weaving Salis of the Andhra coast, for example, dominated the tobacco trade when supply of the fine handspun yarn they used to weave dried up.[32] In general, among silk weavers and the major weaving castes in northern or southern India, the percentages engaged in weaving were usually higher than that in the services castes, and, while the percentages did decline, they declined more slowly.[33] They diversified, and innovated within weaving. They migrated from depressed regions and resettled as weavers at points of flourishing handloom trade.

In the course of such developments, Sholapur emerged as a major handloom centre led by Padmasali weavers. The number of looms expanded from 2–3,000 in the 1890s to over 20,000 in 1950.

---

[30] *Bombay District Gazetteer*, Ahmadnagar District (Bombay, 1884), 110.

[31] 'It is only those who have some capital that make silk fabrics.' Raghbir Sahai, *Report on the Survey of the Handloom Weaving and Dyeing Industries in HEH Nizam's Dominion* (Hyderabad, 1933), 16.

[32] See Thurston, *Tribes and Castes*, 'Sali'.

[33] In 1921, the percentage was about 40 per cent for the Julahas of United Provinces, the Jugis, Julahas, and the Tantis of Bengal. In Madras, the average for the three main cotton-weaving castes was over 50 per cent. For the Sourashtras, it was 70 per cent. These results derive from census tables which calculated the proportion of members of a caste engaged in hereditary occupation. Between censuses, the tables are not perfectly comparable. Apart from the censuses, examples of occupational shifts in this and the following passages have been drawn from Harnetty, 'Deindustrialization Revisited', 497; Russell and Hira Lal, *Tribes and Castes*, 27; Edwardes, *Monograph upon Silk Fabrics*, 49; and Thurston, *Tribes and Castes*, 'Kaikolar' and 'Pattusale'.

Employment in textiles expanded correspondingly. A growth of equally impressive order occurred in Madura, led by the Sourashtras, and in Salem, led by Devangas and Kaikkolars. There are other examples of similar growth in handlooms and the handloom trade from western and southern India. The weavers in these towns became artisanal as well as mercantile. Their engagement in trade was a relatively recent affair, as were the trades themselves. Market and technological information were available in these towns relatively easily, because many weavers interacted between themselves. Sometimes, such interactions took place in the associations. The information and the money accumulated in trade were invested in industry.

Technological change within the handloom industry accelerated as a result. The general direction of change was towards a separation of weaving, processing and dyeing on the one hand, and, on the other hand, towards a sustained improvement in quality and speed of each process. Originally, the three tasks tended to coalesce either in the family firm, or under various forms of communal pooling of labour. As the male migrant in Sholapur joined the weaver proletariat, the women and the aged became available to perform sizing and warping in a separate workshop. Small lots of warping on sticks or pegs gave way to beams. This was a universal tendency. The first Sholapur factories were pioneers in the use of the fly-shuttle slay. From the end of the interwar period, and accelerating after independence, there was a noticeable diffusion of looms mounted on frames rather than on pits dug in the ground, and fitted with overhead attachments that made woven designs much easier to implement. An important example of innovation in dyeing comes from Madura. In the middle of the nineteenth century, German and Belgian mineral dyes began to replace the Indian vegetable colours on account of cheapness and facility. But few Indian weavers knew how to handle these materials well. The result was a widespread decline in quality of colour usage. Pre-eminent among the few places which made the transition successfully was Madura. But here, the transition meant a growth of workshops owned and worked by Sourashtras in a quasi-guild situation.

To conclude, the depressed space in handloom weaving consisted of artisans who had the following features: they were engaged in cotton cloth as opposed to silk; in coarser and plainer type of weaving as opposed to skilled decorative weaving; were mainly rural; and included a large number of artisan-cum-labourers or members of menial castes. This type of weaving was not always depressed, but became so. How did it become depressed? The question leads to forces acting on the market for handloom cotton cloth in the nineteenth century.

Figure 3.1 Pit Loom in western India, *c.* 1950

Figure 3.2 Frame loom in western India, *c*.1950

Locating decline

The composition of handloom cotton cloth output changed dramatically in the course of the nineteenth century. The simplest way to describe how it changed is by means of cotton counts. In a convention started probably by Raoji Patel in 1906, 'coarse' cloth referred to cloths made of 6s–16s counts of warp yarn, 'coarse–medium' to 20s–26s, 'medium' to 31s–40s, and 'fine' cloth meant those made of above 40s warp yarn. Weft yarn was usually finer than warp yarn, but its fineness progressed with that of the warp. Subsequently in government reports, standard class-intervals changed somewhat, making the 1906 figures not exactly comparable with those of the 1920s or the 1940s. However, these changes do not vitally affect the analysis to follow.

Consider that at a date like 1815, handlooms had a 100 per cent market share in all four classes of cloth, though the exclusive usage of handspun yarn might mean somewhat different composition of yarn counts available. By 1900, Lancashire cloth induced the handlooms to specialize differently. After 1900, the presence of Lancashire cloth declined rapidly in the Indian market, from 66 per cent (in quantity) in

Table 3.2 *Segmentation of handlooms by fineness of cotton yarn*

	Handloom share in total yarn consumption (percentage)		Share of yarn group in handloom production, 1906 (percentage)	Market size, 1940 (billion lbs yarn consumption)	Share of yarn group (percentage) 1940
	1906	1937–40			
1s–20s	41	28	55	0.71	55
21s–30s	6	24	9	0.30	19
31s–40s	26	33	27	0.15	14
41s+	23	49	9	0.09	12

Notes: 1906 classifications are different: 6s–16s, 20s–26s, 30s–40s, and above 40s. Therefore, the 1906 and 1940 figures are only roughly comparable.
Sources: Raoji B. Patel, 'Handloom Weaving in India', in *Proceedings of the Industrial Conference at Baroda* (Madras, 1906); and India, *Report of the Fact-Finding Committee (Handloom and Mills)*, Commerce Department (Calcutta, 1942).

1900 to 10 per cent in 1939. The war provided the capital and opportunity for the Indian mills rapidly to expand cloth production. From the middle of the 1920s, cotton cloth received increased protection, the benefit of which was shared by handlooms and Indian mills. This new competition necessitated further adjustments in specialization of handlooms.

The composition of cloth by warp counts for two benchmark dates, 1906 and 1940, are shown in Table 3.2. In 1906, in coarse cloth, handlooms had a share probably equal to or greater than that of Lancashire. In medium and fine cloth, the handloom share was significant, probably around one-third. In coarse–medium cloth, on the other hand, handlooms were a much smaller player. Between 1815 and 1906, a retreat occurred across all types of cloth, but handlooms held on relatively well in coarse cloths, fairly well in medium and fine cloth, and poorly in coarse–medium cloth. The 1940 'coarse–medium' cloth is a more inclusive class than its counterpart in 1906, which partly explains its larger share. But it continued to be the sphere where the handloom share was the smallest. Between 1906 and 1940, both Indian mills and handlooms gained from the retreat of British cloth from the Indian market, hence the rise in the handloom share in three out of four classes. But the rise was of unequal extent between the classes, reflecting the new competition. Handlooms were successful in defending market shares against the mills in fine cotton cloth. In coarse cloth, on the other hand, they were almost certainly supplying a smaller share than in 1906. In coarse–medium and medium cloth, the handlooms gained, but the mills gained much more. This pattern was a result of the concentration of the Indian mills in spinning coarser and medium counts of yarn. Import-substitution in cloth by the mills favoured these classes, whereas import-substitution by handlooms favoured the finer classes.

In more general terms, competition with Lancashire in the nineteenth century had forced a bipolar specialization on the handlooms: coarse and fine cloths were their forte; coarse–medium cloth decidedly was not. This bipolarity survived a long time, and became the basis for contemporary analysis of the industry. In the twentieth century, both handlooms and mills gained from the substitution of imports by domestic supplies. As a result, the bipolarity weakened. But handlooms substituted imports more actively only in fine cotton. In all other classes, mills gained far more.

The bipolarity can be understood with reference to attributes of cloth and those of the techniques in question. The basic advantage of a powerloom over a handloom is in weaving cloths where value is added mainly by the *speed* of weaving. The basic advantage of a handloom over a powerloom is in weaving cloths where value is added mainly by *thread manipulation*, which slows down the pace of weaving. Plain cloths in medium or coarse–medium yarn tend to belong to the former class. But cloths that involve designs woven on the loom tend to fall into the latter class. Examples were coloured, bordered or striped *saris, dhoties, turbans* (in which class belonged the important southern product *rumal*), and some shirting and suiting made in the factories of Punjab and Malabar. These were not necessarily made of fine cotton, but had a bias towards fine cotton. Rarely were yarns of 24s or less used in garments. Also in the second group belonged cloths of very coarse yarn, made from inferior cotton, which could not be woven on the powerloom unless heavily sized. Examples are the generic grey or bleached cotton cloths made in the north – the *garha, gazi, khaddar* or *khes*. Rarely were yarn counts below 20s coloured. Presumably, the consumers of coarse cloth could not afford to pay for the colour. In counts like 22s, 24s and 26s, a fair amount of colour was used and/or yarn dyeing was practised. In 40s+, yarn was as a rule coloured.[34] The vast space in between these two extremes – very coarse plain cotton cloth and coloured fine cotton typically with woven designs – witnessed the most intense competition between the handloom and the powerloom. It is here that the handloom was least able to defend itself, with the exception of markets which retained a conventional preference for handloom.

In the interwar period, with the expansion of Indian mills in cloth production, handlooms continually retreated from the coarse–medium

[34] This generalization is based on the custom in Bengal, *The Report on the Survey of Handloom Weaving Industry in Bengal* (Calcutta, 1937), 68.

coloured cloths. In 20s–30s coloured garments, some mills aggressively tried to break into the preserves of handlooms. The pressure was intense in western India, especially in the handloom centres of Bombay, Central Provinces, and Hyderabad. These regions were well within the marketing hinterland of the newer mill centres in Bombay–Deccan, chiefly Sholapur, where mills paid wages not much more than what a weaver would receive in a handloom factory about 1935. The wage parity enabled them to expand operations into well-known Deccani *sari* brands. Witnesses at the Tariff Board enquiries observed that the keenest competition with the Indian mills was being faced in the range 16s–24s, very severely in Bombay and Hyderabad, more mildly in Madras, Bengal, and Punjab.[35] In 1939, a Central Provinces report found that the handlooms weaving mill yarn were 'in a desperate state', barring 'limited spheres'.[36] In 1940, the *Fact-Finding Committee* found that, in the previous decade, competition had extended from the 20s to the 31s+ in Bombay and Bengal.[37] This competition, limited as it was to few types of cloth and few mills, did not lead to a quick obsolescence of handlooms. But it probably underscored that the powerloom could occupy these spheres once wage-disparity narrowed.

Coarse weaving had a regional character. It was far more extensive in northern India – Bihar, United Provinces, the Punjab, and parts of Central Provinces and Berar – than Bombay, Bengal, Madras (Table 3.3), or Hyderabad. Within Madras, which had the largest number of handlooms, it was customary to distinguish three fairly homogeneous weaving complexes: the Andhra coast; southern Andhra; and the Tamil-speaking region, the territory of the present-day Tamil Nadu state. The 11s–20s class was mainly used in the coast, where about 20,000 looms were engaged in 16s–20s in the middle of the 1930s. Bihar weavers used

---

[35] Indian Tariff Board, *Cotton Textile Industry Enquiry*, vol. III (Calcutta, 1927), 92, evidence of the Director of Industries, Bombay, on this province. The competition between mill and handloom was intense in 16s–20s, and up to 24s. Such cloths included plainer stuffs. Interestingly enough, the statement does not refer to production costs, except the saving the mills obtained from using own yarn, but does mention processing costs and quality. Mill yarn is machine-sized, whereas hand-sizing is very laborious. To avoid sizing, weavers tended to use doubled yarn (for example, 32s doubled where 16s sized yarn could be used), which turned out expensive. Mills could calender the cloths to give them a better appearance, etc. Competition weakened in coarser and finer counts, the latter including bordered *saris*, *dhoties* and *turbans*. In Madras, Amalsad observed increasing mill competition in coarse cloths in rural markets: *ibid.*, 95. Competition with medium-count weaving was reported in Punjab by the Director of Industries, Punjab: *ibid.*, 11. See also Indian Tariff Board, *Cotton Textile Industry*, Report (Calcutta, 1934), 105 (Bengal), 108 (Hyderabad).

[36] Central Provinces and Berar, *Report of the Industrial Survey Committee*, Part I, vol. I (Nagpur, 1939), 19.

[37] India, *Fact-Finding Committee*, 170.

Table 3.3 *Distribution of coarse weaving, 1940*

	Percentages of estimated quantity of yarn used			
	1s–10s	11s–20s	21s–30s	31s+
Punjab	64	26	4	6
Bihar	36	57	5	2
United Provinces	29	55	8	7
Central Provinces and Berar	12	60	16	13
Orissa	3	39	29	28
Madras	7	35	17	40
Bengal	1.5	8.5	50	40
Bombay	6	10	32	52

Source: India, *Report of the Fact-Finding Committee (Handloom and Mills)*, Commerce Department (Calcutta, 1942), 160.

mainly 7s–16s, those in United Provinces 10s–20s in bulk; in Central Provinces and Berar, more than 90 per cent of yarn used went into 16s–20s 'ordinary *saris*', and 10s–16s *dhoties*. On the other hand, the bulk of Bombay and Hyderabad's products belonged in 20s–30s coloured *saris*.[38] In Table 3.3, Bengal would appear to specialize in fine weaving. However, Bengal fine cotton tended to be relatively devoid of colour compared to the western Indian. Besides, the proportion of the more highly valued *non-cotton* weaving was many times higher in Bombay, Madras, and United Provinces, than in Bengal.[39]

The steady decline of coarse–medium and medium-count weaving in handlooms, a feature of the nineteenth century, seemingly continued in the twentieth century in one major region, Bengal. The fine cotton weavers in this province were well off, but a large number of coarse-medium and medium count weavers had become vulnerable. The censuses reveal a continuous decline in numbers in Bengal in the twentieth century. While criticizing the census data, a detailed survey in 1937 agreed that, 'during the last 40 years ... there has been a steady decline in the number of workers following the hand-loom industry'.[40] Those who followed weaving as a part-time occupation generally earned

[38] Indian Tariff Board, *Cotton Textile Industry* (1934), 21, 41, 69, 98.
[39] The Indian Tariff Board's data suggest that the annual value of silk good produced in 1934 were about Rs. 22.9 million in Bombay, Rs. 17 million in Madras, Rs. 12.5 million in United Provinces, Rs. 4.8 million in Mysore, around Rs. 3.5 million in Central Provinces and Berar and Hyderabad State each, Rs. 2.6 million in Punjab, and Rs. 1.8 million in Bengal. Indian Tariff Board, *Report of the Indian Tariff Board Regarding the Grant of Protection to the Sericultural Industry* (Delhi, 1934), 104.
[40] Bengal, *Report on Survey of Handloom Weaving*, 29.

somewhat better incomes than the specialist weaver, the same survey found. This leads to a hypothesis about the survival of weaving in Bengal. The decline of coarse–medium and medium-count weaving in this large province was delayed or drawn out by two circumstances: one was its reputation in plain cotton weaving, a reputation inherited from Bengal's role in early-modern trade. And the other was the greater possibility of integrating agriculture with handlooms. Peasant weavers were considerably more numerous in eastern India, including Bengal, than anywhere else in India. On the strength of these two factors, Bengal may have been a rather special case.

In India as a whole, the real coarse cloths, 6s–16s, were relatively less affected by competition. But nor was it a field which offered opportunities for growth and high incomes. The reason was that, its market was mainly local and dependent on subsistence demand. Coarse cloths were consumed, and therefore largely produced, in the villages. 'The Madras weavers', wrote J. B. Clark, the textile expert in the Government of Bihar and Orissa, 'cater for the urban middle classes, while the weavers of Bihar and Orissa meet the demand of the ryots.'[41] All the samples of coarse cloths described in a 1908–9 industrial survey of the Central Provinces represented the 'general wear of the labourer and small farmer. The classes who weave them are the poorest and most backward among the weaving castes, and not infrequently combine weaving with agriculture. The work is of the simplest.'[42] The coarse cloth market was not necessarily in crisis. Four positive influences on its demand were: (i) a strong cultural preference for handwoven cloth, as in the northeastern regions; (ii) agricultural prosperity; (iii) a demand for coarse cotton as winter wear (northern India); and (iv) sheer remoteness. The second of these is worth some comment, because that factor alone might account for the *growth* of coarse weaving. A possible example of this influence was coastal Andhra, a major beneficiary of agrarian commercialization, where weaving expanded and levels of living were above average in the interwar period.[43]

But, by and large, real coarse weaving was subject to a stagnant

---

[41] Cited in Venkatraman, 'The Handloom Industry in South India', 185.

[42] Central Provinces and Berar, *Report of the Industrial Survey*, 32.

[43] N. G. Ranga drew stark contrasts between the coast and southern Andhra, the two main cotton-weaving regions in Andhra which did similar work, were peopled by the same weaver castes, had equal access to spinning mills, but differed markedly in the fortunes of weaving. The interior, extremely susceptible to famine and bad harvests, saw a steady depopulation of its weavers, whereas the coast showed signs of growth. These signs included wages, stability of contracts, security of employment, levels of living, levels of turbulence, likelihood of emigration, and contentment of the weavers' womenfolk. Ranga, *Economics of Handlooms*, 114. This region is discussed further below.

market and limited opportunities. This was apparently a field where competition was subdued. But, in fact, at the lower end of cotton counts, there were really few kinds that the mills could not use at all. If they did not use them, the reason was extremely low profitability in coarse cloths, their buyers being the poorest people. In general, fabrics for the poor were woven by the poorest of weavers. In Hyderabad, for example, they were woven by 'the poor Mohammadans or low-caste Hindus, such as Kolli or Chamar. They are unskilled weavers.'[44] Being unskilled, they either continued with such weaving even when the returns were too low, or simply left weaving. Even if free from competition directly, the coarse weaver was nevertheless constrained from raising prices because mills competed fiercely at the next grade.[45] In the twentieth century, it was in yarns like the 10s, 12s, and below that exit and self-exploitation occurred most frequently. The censuses consistently reported exit from weaving of the castes that handled the coarsest yarn. All reports on the industry mention their very low levels of living. In 1907, a rural weaver in United provinces earned less than an 'unskilled earthwork labourer', and 'a good many have found other means of livelihood'.[46] Fly-shuttle slays, the most important new tool popularized in the twentieth century, were rare in rural weaving; the weaving castes who used the coarsest or handspun cotton did not normally have the means to invest in even such a cheap tool as the fly-shuttle, not to mention beams or powerlooms. If coarse weaving survived, it did so by using surplus labour of the family firm. They held on despite being uncompetitive at market-wages. A. C. Chatterjee, the author of a classic industrial survey of northern India, wrote of the ordinary weaver of the United Provinces:

The hand-weaver often combines the industry with other occupations ... Moreover, working at home in the midst of his family, he is generally willing to, and does, work much longer hours than an operative at a factory does. The women of the family ... afford a great deal of assistance ... If hand-weaving were altogether to disappear, only a very small proportion of such women would be engaged in any other industrial employment. These circumstances interfere with the operation ... of the ordinary economic law of wages.[47]

The essential factors behind survival despite uncompetitive costs were, in this view, the availability of part-time work, an invisible return to labour, and the zero opportunity cost of family labour.

The extreme vulnerability of the rural coarse weaver is best illustrated

[44] Sahai, *Report on the Survey of Handloom Weaving*, 40.
[45] Central Provinces and Berar, *Report of Industrial Survey*, 32.
[46] A. C. Chatterjee, *Notes on the Industries of the United Provinces* (Allahabad, 1908), 13, Meerut Division, and 15, Rohilkhand.
[47] Chatterjee, *Notes on Industries*, 13.

in records of the famines in the last quarter of the nineteenth century. These documents made two distinctions which overlap to some extent: between coarse cloth weavers and fine cotton or silk weavers; and between specialized and non-specialized weavers. This differentiation was incorporated in famine policy in the separation of special relief from ordinary relief.[48] The former employed weavers on a contract for making cloth; the latter included weavers employed in general manual labour, usually construction. For an example of the former type of distinction, the report of the Madras famine in 1896–7 may be quoted:

According to the fineness and kind of fabrics turned out by the weavers, they may be divided into fine cloth weavers and silk weavers, and weavers of coarse cloths. It is the coarse cloth weavers that would be affected with the first appearance of distress. The consumers of their manufactures are the poorer classes, and, with the appearance of scarcity and high prices, the demand for the coarser kinds of cloths would cease. Such was actually the case at the beginning of the recent distress.[49]

For an example of the latter type of difference, we have an almost contemporary statement:

It is important to differentiate between two different classes of weavers. Many, especially in the rural tracts such as the Pariahs of Madras and the Dhers and Mahars of the Central Provinces, combine ordinary labour with weaving as a subsidiary occupation; others by caste and occupation are solely weavers, usually occupied in weaving of a special or superior character. For the former class, and for scattered members of the latter class, the ordinary methods of relief alone are necessary or practicable ... the latter class are generally met with in communities, as a rule in considerable towns; their habits are generally sedentary, and they are unable to work in the sun.[50]

The non-specialized groups, or 'services castes', have already been introduced. They were usually of the lowest castes, came to the relief camps the earliest, and suffered the heaviest mortality and malnutrition.[51] They were necessarily coarse weavers. Coarse weaving also involved many members of specialized weaver castes. All such people

---

[48] Implicit in special relief was the expectation that cloths made by skilled weavers had niche markets which would survive famines. One could not be sure of that with the cloths made by the Paraiyans and Mahars. For more discussion on the special relief in Bombay, and the implementation of the scheme in Sholapur, see Douglas Haynes, 'Urban Weavers and Rural Famines in Western India, 1870–1900', mimeo, 1996.

[49] Madras, *Report of Famine in the Madras Presidency, 1896–97*, cited in Thurston, *Castes and Tribes*, vol. VI, 275.

[50] India, *Report of the Indian Famine Commission* (Calcutta, 1901), 78.

[51] 'Those who received relief mainly belonged to the humbler castes of the Hindu community, and to the class of field labourers, of rude artisans, and of village menials.' William Digby, *The Famine Campaign in Southern India*, vol. I (London, 1878), 369, which refers to Bombay. Other contemporary records mention part-time weavers as the main constituent of the class of 'rude artisans'.

were constrained by the nature of their markets, as the former quotation suggests. That is, their customers were themselves vulnerable to agricultural fluctuations.

At the other end, silk weavers, bordered cloth weavers, those in towns, and those members of the weaver castes who did finer work, served customers who were better off and felt the famine less intensely than labourers and small peasants. Also, as a class, such weavers could themselves fall back, to a greater extent than the former groups, on private and social resources during famines. The upper castes tended to consider the relief camp as polluting, and so did some silk weavers with claims to high status. The southern silk weavers were known never to come to the ordinary relief works.[52] Much private charity, even public relief, centred in or near the towns. The upper caste weavers had their own organization providing limited relief. For example, Salem silk weavers organized, and survived the 1876 famine on the strength of private charity.[53] In Sholapur, the work of a 'guild' was observed and commented on in administrative circles in the first decade of this century, following the experience of a minor scarcity and plague outbreak in 1906–7. The key point was the impact the guild had in moderating terms of credit. By the turn of the century, special relief, which again had urban orientation, had taken shape, though they involved a rather small proportion of weavers.

It was not as if calamities such as famines left the specialist weavers untouched. But they did differ in the degree of vulnerability, and in the search for alternatives. The coarse and non-specialized weavers tended to enter general labour. That option was not absent among specialized weavers. But many among them tended to seek work *within* weaving: they moved to other towns, or villages, where weaving work was available.

There were, then, two types of weaver in the early twentieth century who can be called depressed: those engaged in coarse–medium cloths and facing competition from the powerloom in increasing intensity; and those engaged in rural coarse weaving who stayed poor and vulnerable because of dependence on local markets. There was exit from both spheres. But the former class tended to look for alternative options within weaving. The latter tended to leave weaving when alternatives, usually casual labour of various kinds, became available. Quite in contrast with either, there stood the skilled artisan. This figure operated in both fine cotton and silk. Since silk never faced competition from

[52] Sir Richard Temple, cited in Digby, *Famine Campaign*, vol. II, 357, with reference to Madras.
[53] Digby, *Famine Campaign*, vol. II, 357.

machinery in a serious way, it demonstrates the effects of other factors shaping the textile market, factors that were earlier categorized under 'commercialization'.

The dynamic segment

The *Fact-Finding Committee* stated that silk weaving in India was 'little affected by the Industrial Revolution and the cheap imports from Lancashire'.[54] Evidence contrary to this statement exists, but is rare. Cases of cotton weavers shifting to silk were more frequent than the reverse. N. G. Ranga observed that in major silk towns the former kind of shift could raise incomes by as much as a factor of four.[55] The silk industry, however, was far from stagnant in the colonial period. Critical long-term changes involved consumption, the cloth trade, and the import of raw silk and silk cloth.

Consumption

Silk, as far as one can gather, had been mainly commercial, mainly urban, and frequently traded over long distances, in the precolonial period. A form of patronage did exist, in that silk weavers were often settled directly by those in power. But, unlike carpets, silk was not consumed mainly inside palaces. It was not a luxury in that narrow a sense, but a durable good consumed by 'the higher classes', broadly defined.[56] This demand, arising from 'the rajahs, courtiers and zamindars', probably declined from the middle of the nineteenth century. An external trade in Bengal, nurtured by the East India Company, was also on the wane from somewhat earlier. The 'bourgeoisie' who could afford to compensate for these losses, tended to have quite different tastes.[57] But there was still a large ritual usage of pure silk garments. The demand for cloths for ordinary use which utilized silk, such as silk-bordered fine cotton saris, or silk-weft cloths like *himroo* or *mushroo*, was also quite stable, and probably even expanded.

Nevertheless, tastes were changing. The *Fact-Finding Committee* reported that, for certain occasions, a change of fashion had been taking place from heavy silk garments towards shorter, lighter, more cotton-

[54] India, *Fact-Finding Committee*, 18.
[55] Ranga, *Economics of Handlooms*, 78, regarding Dharmabharam. But very rarely would one see shifts between coarse cotton and silk-based fabrics. These were woven by distinct producers who maintained the distinction.
[56] George Watt and Percy Brown, *Arts and Crafts of India* (Delhi, 1904), 310.
[57] See, for one reference to this transition, D. R. Gadgil, *Industrial Evolution in India in the Recent Times* (Delhi, 1971), 45.

based ones in most parts of India.[58] Such a trend might mean a smaller demand for pure silk, but a greater demand for bordered cloths. In the sources discussed here, the term 'silk weavers' usually referred to weavers making any silk-based cloth. Pure silk weavers often did take up bordered cloths. This shift towards lighter designs coincided with a weakness for European patterns. Around 1900, all established silk towns followed, or at least greatly revered, sample books of English wallpaper designs, setting aside the dusty old mica sheets that contained etchings of the uniquely Indian ones. The illustrated trade catalogue from Europe veritably overran the practice of skilled crafts in India. This 'monstrous degeneration' was apparent in all classes of designed goods, but most clearly in textiles. Silk was no exception.[59]

Relocation and reorganization

A series of monographs prepared in the 1890s by provincial governments suggest that around that time, the production and trade of silk-based cloth had been relocating. Some old weaving towns and regional complexes were in decay, whereas other towns attracted trade and expanded production. In some instances, the relocation was attributed to the railways; in most cases, the role of the railways is a plausible inference. The late 1890s also witnessed a devastating famine, followed by an epidemic of plague, and the monographs suggest how these events added to the effect of the railways. All famines temporarily destroyed the links between local production and local consumption, as consumers stopped buying anything other than food, and producers left the occupation or the place. Usually, the end of the famine witnessed a hesitant reconvergence. But, apparently, the 1890s delayed or disrupted that pattern of recovery. The railways enabled supplies of cloth to come in from more distant parts while local supplies were yet to recover.

Several examples of relocation come from south India. Silk weaving was widely spread here in the middle of the nineteenth century, owing to the existence of sericulture in the Kollegal area of Mysore. The raw silk trade was located in Mysore, Bangalore, and Kollegal towns, fanning out to several distinct weaving complexes. The most important were Bellary-Kurnool (which had a local demand, as well as a fair amount of trade with Hyderabad, Bombay–Deccan, Mysore, and the deep south), Anantapur (Dharmavaram town, whose cloths were traded mainly in Bangalore), North Arcot (Gudiyatam town, trading within the south), and a cluster of towns in the Tamil country (Tanjore, Madura,

[58] India, *Fact-Finding Committee*, 18.
[59] Watt and Brown, *Arts and Crafts*, 336–7.

Kumbakonam, and Kanchipuram), where silks existed for a long time primarily for local usage, and vastly expanded in the early twentieth century. The proximity to another source of raw silk, Bengal, also supported a minor tradition in coastal Andhra (Godavari and Krishna districts, where demand was mainly local).

In Madras Presidency, the main decline seems to have occurred in the southern Andhra region. 'A tree-less plain of black clay', this vast and sparsely populated area was 'never long free from the possibility of distress' arising from harvest fluctuations.[60] This region was devastated by the 1876–8 and 1896–8 famines. Possibly due to its proximity to Vijayanagar and to patronage from smaller local principalities in the precolonial period, several towns of this region had developed into centres of cotton, silk and even wool weaving in the early 1800s. However, after the railways connected it to Bombay–Deccan in the northwest, and the Tamil region in the south, it began to regress steadily towards obscurity in the twentieth century. The censuses of 1901–31 are witness to the role this large region, along with parts of Hyderabad State, played as a source of migrant labourers for plantations and industry elsewhere in India, and even beyond. Many migrants were former weavers. Ranga recorded the unsettled conditions.[61] From his account, and sporadically that of others, it would appear that, from about the 1890s, the region was gradually moving away from cotton and silk that competed with products of mills as well as handlooms elsewhere in southern India. Silk cloth came from two sides, the Tamil country in the south, and Bombay–Deccan, chiefly Poona. In Bellary district, 'formerly the cloths of Kampli, Bellary, and Adoni were extensively used'. But the local 'better classes' preferred the southern product once they began to come in more easily after the railways. 'For about a year', reported Edgar Thurston, 'the weavers have been trying to weave cloths like those manufactured in the south', with partial success.[62] Similar examples come from coastal Andhra, and from Kurnool district, where one of the few silk carpet locations in India, Ayyampet, declined in the latter part of the nineteenth century.

Where did the industry thrive? In the cluster of towns in the Tamil country it grew – evidently in Kanchipuram and Madura, and possibly in Tanjore and Kumbakonam as well. On a smaller scale, Arni and Kollegal also attracted new business. In Madura, for example, many

---

[60] Madras, *Report of the Madras Famine Code Revision Committee, 1938*, vol. I, *Report* (Madras, 1940), 3.
[61] Ranga, *The Economics of Handlooms*, 114 and *passim*.
[62] Edgar Thurston, *Monograph on the Silk Fabrics of the Madras Presidency* (Madras, 1899), 7.

weavers formerly engaged in fine cotton shifted to silk.[63] Much of the products made in the deep south were pure silk *saris* with borders of *jari*, the type known as 'Kornad', a garment whose demand has proven remarkably stable in the long run. Within southern Andhra, survival was restricted to the small artisanal trading town, Dharmavaram. There were also a few successful silk factories, in coastal and southern Andhra, started by cloth merchants shortly before the First World War. Ventures in Uppada, Peddapuram, and in Rayadurg in Bellary are the main examples.[64]

Somewhat similar in nature, but less documented, is the effect of Bombay and Madras products on the weavers of Hyderabad State. The state had apparently become a net importer of handloom cloth in the interwar period. Cotton and silk cloths were both imported, by one estimate in 1935 to the extent of about 12 per cent of the value of local production and import.[65] Local cotton and silk weaving had to live with competition from the far south, which became more intense over time.[66] The reason for the popularity of imports was their better quality and standardization. The competition was fierce and caused much alarm among the officers of the state dealing with industry. And yet, the impact was not entirely destructive on silk. The silk weavers of Hyderabad had both specific markets and specific skills. Examples of the former are the mixed cotton-silk cloths popular with the Muslims (*himroo* and *mushroo*) and brocades, both woven in Aurangabad. Examples of the latter are *saris* woven in Paithan town, and reasonably good quality *pitambar*, a Hindu dining and ritual robe. In these segments, the Hyderabadi weaver seemingly expanded long-distance trade, and the scale of production. One sign of such changes was the factory owned by rich silk weavers who traded, and at the same time contracted out part of their orders. By 1942, 40 per cent of the 100,000 weavers in the state were employed in such establishments.

Western India witnessed another local contest. In the middle of the nineteenth century, silk weaving here was in existence not only in the former capital Poona, and in major trading and manufacturing towns like Surat, Yeola, and Ahmedabad, but in fact in 'most of the places in this Presidency, which contain hand-loom'. The last type of location produced a small quantity of cloths, which 'never voyages further' than the local market, and which flourished or decayed according to 'the

---

[63] Ranga, *Economics of Handlooms*, 154.

[64] D. Narayana Rao, *Report of Survey of Cottage Industries in Madras Presidency* (Madras, 1925), Bellary District, 5; and Ranga, *Economics of Handlooms*, 51–2.

[65] Indian Tariff Board, *Written Evidence Recorded During Enquiry on the Grant of Protection to the Sericultural Industry*, vol. I (Delhi, 1935), 320–1.

[66] On condition in the1930s, see Sahai, *Report on the Survey of Handloom Weaving*, 76.

personal wealth of the local residents'.[67] Of the four major centres, Surat and Ahmedabad specialized in *jari*-based silk cloths. In the twentieth century, Surat developed and greatly expanded industries in *jari*, lace, silks, and 'art silk'. Yeola and Poona, along with many towns in the Dharwar, Belgaum, and Bijapur districts, made traditional garments of the Hindus. These consisted of *pitambar*, and silk-bordered cotton *saris* with distinct border designs identified with Ilkal, Maheshwar, Nipani, and Paithan towns. Edwardes, writing in 1900, suggested that, in the last quarter of the nineteenth century, the smaller centres withdrew from these cloths. Prominent cases where silk weavers gave up silk – in rare cases for fine cotton, but more often for trade and services – were Thane, and the Ahmadnagar-Bhingar complex.

In 1900, Poona and Yeola were both well off. Weavers in neither 'had reasons to complain'. But in reports of the 1930s a further shift seemed to be occurring. In both towns, silk had a similar origin, eighteenth-century royal monopolies granted to Muslim weavers in Poona, and to Gujarati traders in Yeola, who settled a group of migrants from Paithan. Weaving and trade grew in both places in the course of the nineteenth century, but the clientele differed. Yeola supplied a mainly rural, peasant demand from vast areas of central India. Its goods were sold in the great annual fairs, Maheji and Nagarnath. Yeola's prosperity was attributed to that of the cotton growers.[68] Poona goods, in contrast, had more of an urban demand. In the interwar period, Poona's industry declined in competition with cloths from Surat, Benares, south India, and East Asia. The decline in Yeola, which remained a rather small and specialized industry, was related to unstable demand for cotton in the 1920s. Like coarse cotton weaving, Yeola displayed the vulnerability of dependence on agrarian demand. Peasant demand offered a certain security, being local, visible, and conventional. But this security could work against innovation and adaptation in the long run.[69] During the Great Depression, wages were in general decline, but they fell in Yeola and Poona much more than they did in Surat, where in fact minimum wages were remarkably high even in the worst years.[70]

Ahmedabad's decline occurred around the prewar decade, as a result of three factors: Surat's competition; demand for weavers by cotton mills; and the decline of brocades. Surat, at the same time, more than doubled its looms from 2,000 to 5,000 between 1896 and 1914. Surat

[67] Edwardes, *Monograph upon the Silk Fabrics*, 26.
[68] This is a point suggested by N. M. Joshi, *Urban Handicrafts of Bombay Deccan*, Gokhale Institute of Politics and Economics (Poona, 1936), 75.
[69] *Ibid.*, 93, 120.
[70] Indian Tariff Board, *Report of the Indian Tariff Board Regarding the Grant of Protection to the Sericultural Industry* (Delhi, 1934), 114.

had a highly diversified textile industry. It relied not only on traditional markets in the interior of the province where Surat goods competed with those from Poona and Yeola, but also on an export trade to Burma, and on the cosmopolitan western coastal demands. The Parsi women who loved *jari*, and the Muslims who consumed a lot of mixed cloths as well as brocades, were buyers of Surat cloth.[71] 'The lesson', of Surat's growth amidst many cases of localized decline, was 'clear enough', wrote Maxwell-Lefroy and Ansorge: 'there was no lack of markets for Indian silk manufactures.'[72] It was, in other words, a question of efficient supplies.

In northern India in the nineteenth century, silk was woven almost wherever Bengal raw silk could be transported. Of these locations, Benares grew almost continuously in the twentieth century, and its '*karkhanadars* grew rich by the trade'.[73] But, close by, the Azamgarh area was seemingly in persistent crisis, which was the reason why relatively well-off Julahas from these parts migrated steadily to western India from the end of the nineteenth century.[74] Some old silk centres, like Amritsar, were also in 'serious decline' about 1918. The ordinary Punjab silks were plain sheets, and not complex enough work to compete with cheaper imports, the 'finer qualities being all supplied from other provinces or foreign countries'.[75]

In Bengal, silk culture and weaving had once flourished due to the patronage of the East India Company. The diversity of cloths then produced in Bengal is impressive, judging by an 1805–9 order book recovered about a century later.[76] In the course of the nineteenth century, the industry had not only shrunk, but also had to reorient itself to local and home demand. Local demand in Bengal meant a large proportion of *korah* or undyed silk, and *matka*, or the coarse cloth made from pierced cocoon converted into thread. The work carried such low returns that it was usually performed by the poorest and least employable of domestic labour, generally widows. In other words, the industry had also suffered a de-skilling and narrowed its capability. Thus, in

---

[71] Edwardes, *Monograph upon Silk*, 58, has references to local demand; and Maxwell-Lefroy and Ansorge, *Report on an Enquiry into Silk*, vol. II, 31–4, has references to Surat's success.

[72] Maxwell-Lefroy and Ansorge, *Report on an Enquiry into Silk*, vol. II, 34.

[73] United Provinces, *Industrial Survey of the United Provinces* (Allahabad, 1922–4), Benares District, 9.

[74] Chatterjee, *Notes on Industries*, 42. The depression was attributed to plague and a series of bad seasons. Steady migration of weavers from these eastern districts of the United Provinces to Surat, Bombay, Malegaon, Ahmadnagar, and elsewhere is reported in sources on these towns. Census migration figures are inferential evidence.

[75] Maxwell-Lefroy and Ansorge, *Report on an Enquiry into Silk*, vol. II, 67.

[76] Watt and Brown, *Arts and Crafts*, 303–5.

1900, the Bengal industry was considerably smaller, less skilled, and more rural than major silk-weaving complexes in other regions. No wonder that Benares' rise adversely affected the prospects of Bengal products. In Bengal, 'a Hindu lady who can afford to wear a Benares *sari* will not look at even a high-class Baluchar' from Murshidabad.[77] There was decline in smaller centres such as in Hooghly, Burdwan, Birbhum, and Bankura districts. The weaving industry came to be concentrated in Murshidabad district (Baluchar, Mirzapur, Khagra, and Islampur villages), owing to local sericulture. But, even here, the scale of trade was small, not only compared to Surat or Benares, but even compared to an average year in a relatively small town like Yeola.[78]

What constrained the smaller centre? It seems that three adverse factors were at work. First, long-distance trade in silk created barriers to entry into the trade in silk cloth and yarn. The need for capital, especially working capital, was greater than before. Risks increased, because of proliferation of principals and agents, and because the traded goods in silk were expensive. Silk, for all these reasons, required capital and information. These were easier to obtain in large agglomerations.[79] Secondly, as in the case of several decorated crafts, quality was a factor in the competitive success of brands. In silks, quality mattered crucially in respect of dyeing, and, to cite K. S. Venkatraman in reference to Madura, 'dyeing requires more skill than weaving'. Bigger towns had better infrastructure and common facilities such as dyehouses. Thirdly, the consumer faced a choice between numerous local decorative styles, all traditional and closely similar to each other, and a new type of decorative capability which could, simultaneously, simplify old designs, standardize them into fewer ones, and create new designs. That there was indeed such a choice, and that preferences shifted from the former to the latter, was noted by the *Fact-Finding Committee*.[80] Integrated trade at first caused the disappearance of many locational names for *sari* borders in southern India. A few remained. But these few later began to innovate and branch out on the foundation of a core decorative style with which the town was identified. As these towns grew in scale and reputation, trade information such as the European pattern books began

---

[77] N. G. Mukherji, *A Monograph on the Silk Fabrics of Bengal* (Calcutta, 1903), 51.

[78] S. V. Telang estimated the average daily trade in silk cloths in Yeola at Rs. 10,000, and in Surat at Rs. 15,000, in 1932: *Report on Handloom Weaving*, 8. In 1941, when prices were much higher, Murshidabad district's trade was placed at Rs. 2.2 million a year, or Rs. 6,000 per day, including cotton and silk. The latter figure comes from Bengal, *Handloom Cotton Weaving*, 13.

[79] See, on the implications of becoming a capitalist in silk, the impressively detailed report by R. Balakrishna, *Survey of Handloom Industry in Madras State, 1955–6* (Bombay, 1959), 115.

[80] India, *Fact-Finding Committee*, 127.

to gravitate towards them. Thus it happened that the most famous of silk towns were often the leaders in what Watt and Brown called 'decadence of taste'. Benares brocade is an example.[81]

In the successful agglomerations, the nature of the production contract was changing in the interwar period. Ranga observed in the middle of the 1920s, that the requirements to succeed in trade made not only 'wage earning the rule' in silk (Madura), but encouraged factories, because capitalists 'do not trust their silk, gold and silver thread to weavers working in their own homes'.[82] 'Few could have imagined at the beginning of the century', wrote R. Balakrishna about the Madras state in the 1950s, 'that such enormous capital could be raised and invested in handloom factories.'[83] In fact, in Madras, factories were more exceptional, accounting for roughly 10 per cent of loomage in the middle of the 1950s, whereas in Bombay and Hyderabad, nearly half the number of weavers operated in factories in 1942.[84] Factories handled both cotton and silk. Many of the Hyderabad ones, for example, made cotton and silk-bordered cotton *saris* simultaneously.[85] But, whereas in pure cotton weaving, the factory was an exception, in silk and silk-cotton weaving, the factory was more of a norm.

The factory had its costs, which became visible in the 1950s. Of Madras, it was written: 'in the present *milieu* of socialist pattern, strident demand for higher wages, more closed days, less output, more labour and welfare legislation and consequent rising overheads, the prospect of the continuance as capitalistic concerns is not easy.'[86] Factories, always 'extremely chameleon-like' in the backdrop of the older quarters of an

---

[81] Watt and Brown, *Arts and Crafts*, 336.
[82] Ranga, *Economics of Handlooms*, 132.
[83] Balakrishna, *Survey of Handloom Industry*, 129.
[84] India, *Fact-Finding Committee*, 71.
[85] The Indian Tariff Board, *Written Evidence . . . Sericultural Industry*, 328–36, printed the results of a survey of 218 such factories with 5,132 looms conducted by the Hyderabad government. The following are some of the salient features. Their main products were silk-bordered cotton *saris*, pure cotton goods, and pure silk goods, in that order; 43 per cent of the looms were owned by the main Hindu weaving castes, Khatri (silk) and Salis/Padmasalis (cotton); 18 per cent by Muslim weavers or Momins; and another 14 per cent by miscellaneous castes identifiable as textile producers. The average size of these factories was about twenty-four looms per unit. The size became larger for pure silk and silk-cotton weaving, smaller for pure cotton. The modal sizes of the factory were two, eleven to twenty looms per factory, and more than forty per factory. It is not clear how this bimodal distribution arose. About 10–20 per cent of the units in any size contracted out part of their work. Those that did, in fact, 'controlled' or 'distributed' many more looms than they directly owned. In other words, such indirect and direct productions were seemingly two alternatives. The average wage paid was higher in the larger factories, which wove mainly silk and silk-cotton. Size, value-added, wage, and skill intensity were, thus, correlated.
[86] Balakrishna, *Survey of Handloom Industry*, 135.

industrial city, probably retreated irreversibly after independence because of threats from the Labour Inspector and the amateur trade unionist.

With or without factories, the main mercantile contract in silk was putting-out. The factory was either a larger version of the home workshop, or a centralized form of putting-out, where workers continued to work on piece-rate wages not too different from the piece-rates received by households. The growth of factories of the latter type reflected the increase in scale of operation of the average silk cloth trader. N. G. Mukherji's account of central Bengal suggests one possible pattern of mobility. A 'rich' weaver, regarded in the community as patriarch, occasionally collected a bundle of his own and others' produce to sell to the merchants. This was a commonly agreed system of intermediation via someone who commanded greater influence on the collective than did the merchant in long-distance trade.[87] Another pattern is supplied by the owner of a small workshop in Benares who 'grew rich by trade'.[88] Even the owner of one or two silk looms could expand scale, by optimally utilizing family and hired labour. Ranga deduced this from his data on profitability in Andhra, which show that net incomes of weavers tended to rise more than proportionately to the number of looms.[89] Elsewhere, such weaving 'families' with exceptional dynamic prospects have been called 'large households'.[90]

Import trade

From the end of the nineteenth century, the silk market also saw great expansion of the import trade, in materials and in silk cloth. In the interwar period, this trade began to shape institutional and locational changes.

From about the third quarter of the nineteenth century, Indian, especially Bengali, sericulture entered a crisis of persistently poor quality and high prices. The problem was an old one, but exposed after East Asian silks entered India having first captured a major part of the European market. From Japan and Hong Kong, and to a smaller extent Europe, came coarser silks for weft-yarn or embroidery, and from China came 'weaving silk' or warp yarn, the main trade item. Where were the

---

[87] Mukherji, *Monograph on Silk*, 54.

[88] United Provinces, *Industrial Survey*, Benares District, 9. Chatterjee, *Notes on Industries*, 45, identifies this class with *kinkhab* weaving.

[89] Ranga, *Economics of Handlooms*, 134. A similar tendency was noted by Ranga with respect to fine cotton weaving of Salem town: a link between a concentration of trade, an increasing per capita turnover, and upwardly-mobile weavers.

[90] Roy, *Artisans and Industrialization*, chapter 3.

inputs being used? In Punjab, where there was an extensive embroidery tradition, spun silk found a major market. In Benares, Poona and Surat, spun silk for weft, and Chinese silk for warp was a fairly common combination shortly before the war. Only in the deep south were imported silks, even Chinese silks, emphatically rejected on the ground that they interfered with conventional standards.[91]

With the home advantage in inputs threatened, that in cloth became threatened too. Competition could be restrained to the extent weavers could use cheaper imported inputs to produce specialized garments. Yet, large increases in manufactured imports did take place. Much of it, however, happened in new types of garment. These new markets testify to the effectiveness of Japanese marketing skills, the untiring labour of Japanese manufacturing agents and importers in studying local tastes, flexibly adapting to tastes, and developing collaborations with Indian trade. In the case of both raw silk and silk cloth, the Indian retreat was an instance of poor organization rather than poor technology. What triumphed in its place was a trade network with coordinated supply, better access to information, and a will to use this information creatively. All this was based on close contacts between Japan and major Bombay-based import firms in silk (such as Chinai, Gobhai, Currimbhoy Ibrahim, and Tata). This system prevailed over a decentralized, fragmented, and chaotic system of supply.[92] A broad picture of the import trade in silk and silk-substitutes in the relevant period of the twentieth century is given in Table 3.4.

In clothing, the successful imported cloth was quite different from a marriage or ceremonial garment. It created a new use for silk as an elevated daily wear. Imports consisted of flowered silks, satins, damasks, gauze, *paj*, and crepe. Much of it was meant to be used in stitched garments such as shirts or blouses, but some could be used as a radically redefined *sari*. The main markets for these goods were Bombay and Punjab. They touched Bengal marginally, and Madras not at all. The import of pure silk cloths dwindled away from the middle of the 1930s under fairly stiff protection granted to local industry. But by then it had created a market for simple, non-ritual, experiment-minded silk garments, and that effect lasted. From the 1920s, art silk (rayon) entered the production of cheap silk-like *saris*, and it ended by snatching away part of the traditional demand for silk or fine cotton *saris*. These new cloths did not necessarily define themselves by borders, that is, by the

---

[91] Maxwell-Lefroy and Ansorge, *Report on an Enquiry into Silk*, vol. II, 18–19. This remains the best source on the crisis, and the rise of trade: see vol. I on sericulture, and the first few pages of vol. II on trade.

[92] *Ibid.*, 25.

Table 3.4 *Import of silk yarn and cloth, 1901–1938*

	Raw silk	Silk yarn	Silk cloth	Art silk yarn	Art silk cloth
1901–5	8.82	4.61	104	–	–
1906–10	10.09	3.88	128	–	–
1911–15	12.92	5.29	155	–	–
1916–20	9.43	2.94	118	–	–
1921–5	7.54	4.54	82	4.50	43
1926–30	10.39	7.99	117	35.43	253
1931–5	11.54	11.19	204	60.29	62
1936–8	6.75	6.87	80	66.47	33

Notes: Raw silk and yarn in million lbs, cloth in million yards. Silk cloth and art silk cloths included mixed cotton and silk, which represented a genuine demand as well as a means to avoid duty on pure silk. The raw silk trade figures ignore land frontier trade, which was a small source.

Source: India, *Annual Statement of the Sea-Borne Trade of British India with the British Empire and Foreign Countries*, vol. I, Calcutta, various years.

principle of thread manipulation. They could, therefore, be taken over by high-speed weaving systems.

How did these goods affect the weaver? Where garment preferences were somewhat flexible, the weavers invariably adapted either the cloth or the raw material, or both. The main instances of the use of imported raw silk come from western India. The proximity to import houses and the ports was the reason why the coastal weaving towns, such as Surat, did better in silk than most places in the interior. Surat and Bhiwandi were heavy users of imported silks and imported *jari*.[93] These towns were not too specialized in any specific cloth. They used silk as a raw material in traditional bordered cotton *saris*, but shifted between garments often. 'If there is a demand for a particular cloth, they convert themselves at once.'[94]

More significantly, powerlooms to weave pure silk and rayon began to be set up. Between 1934 and 1939, the years of publication of successive Tariff Board reports on silk, there was a massive expansion in the number of silk mills, working both on pure silk and on rayon, and equally, a 'marked increase' in the number of handloom weavers who used rayon. A whole range of entrepreneurs, including these weavers and handloom merchants, seized the new opportunity in setting up rayon powerlooms in Bombay and Punjab. In Aurangabad, similarly,

[93] Indian Tariff Board, *Written Evidence . . . Sericultural Industry*, vol. I, 466–7, evidence of Jamiatul Momin, Bhiwandi.
[94] Indian Tariff Board, *Oral Evidence recorded during Enquiry on the Grant of Protection to the Sericultural Industry* (Delhi, 1939), 359.

powerlooms were set up to weave *himroo* and *mushroo*. Initially, the cotton mills supplied the equipment and the organizational model. The silk and rayon importers and cloth merchants, along with capitalists among the handloom weavers, supplied the capital. But as powerlooms spread beyond silk into cotton, the role of merchant capital tended to decline in favour of what Haynes has called 'weavers' capital'. Eventually, in each major powerloom town, three factors coincided: the presence of handloom weavers; proximity to mills and/or ports, and therefore, inputs and process shops; and the presence of capitalists among weavers, as traders, *karkhanadars*, or moneylenders.[95] The seeds of a veritable revolution led by the small weaving factory had thus been laid.

Conclusion

Three points explored in this chapter may be restated. First, the forces acting on the textile market in the colonial period were broader and more complex than competition from foreign textiles. Competition with machinery was intense in coarse–medium cotton cloth in the nineteenth century. In the sources used in this book, this competition can be inferred, and not be directly seen, to happen. Coarse cloth was sustained by local and rural demand, but this was a stagnant, low-profit and slowly decaying market in the twentieth century. The dominant forces on silk, on the other hand, were quite different. They were changes in tastes, the integration of trade, the import of raw material, and experiments with new goods. The second point follows from the first. There were great asymmetries in the way the exogenous forces affected textile production, because cloth had segmented markets. Thirdly, just as cloths were segmented, so were weavers. Coarse weaving, rural weaving, and non-specialized weavers tended to coincide. Not only did their cloths offer limited opportunities, the communities who wove them had limited access to resources needed to diversify or innovate. Coarse–medium cotton, fine cotton, and silk, on the other hand, were woven by

[95] See, for example, the description in India, *Report of the Powerloom Enquiry Commission*, Ministry of Industry (New Delhi, 1964), chapter 1. The Indian Tariff Board reports on sericulture also observed the tendency at its inception. See *Oral Evidence recorded during Enquiry on the Grant of Protection to the Sericultural Industry*, vol. II (Delhi, 1935), on the first powerlooms in Sholapur and Surat. These were set up by 'the sowkers among weavers' who knew the weavers and knew the cloth trade, 278, evidence of P. B. Advani, the Director of Industries, Bombay. See also, Sahai, *Report on the Survey of Handloom Weaving*, 75; *Written Evidence . . . Sericultural Industry*, 301, on Aurangabad. Two recent studies on the powerloom industry are, Haynes, 'Weavers' Capital and the Origins of Powerlooms', and Tirthankar Roy, 'Development or Distortion? Powerlooms in India, 1950–97', *Economic and Political weekly*, 33, 16 (1998).

specialized groups. Members of these groups became capitalists using new opportunities opened by the extension of long-distance trade. The adaptations and innovations in handloom towns such as Sholapur and Madura testify to the productive use of such capital.

The discussion 'images of inequality' drew a correlation between the levels and trends in earnings, which imply increasing inequality in the industry. It is now possible to state why it arose. On the one hand, different cloths faced different market prospects. And, on the other hand, different groups of weavers faced variable capacity to diversify and innovate. This capacity was not innate, but shaped by their position in society. As a result of such constraints, coarse weavers remained coarse weavers despite low and falling real incomes, whereas silk weavers adapted to new market trends.

This account dealt with cloth. But it has already introduced *jari*, an essential input in the making of handloom cloth, and the subject of the next chapter. Like most manufactured raw material, *jari* was a relatively standardizable product, and allowed economies of scale. The Indian *jari*, therefore, had to face competition from cheaper imports made by partially mechanized processes. On the other hand, *jari* in India entered a highly differentiated end use that was itself undergoing complex changes. The need to standardize, and yet to serve a differentiated market, constitute the story of *jari*.

4   Gold thread (*jari*)

'The European manufacturer who may have attempted the introduction of metal into his fabrics, will all the more readily comprehend and admire the results obtained by the Indian weaver.' With these words, John Forbes Watson, the author of a classic catalogue of Indian fabrics, began the section on a uniquely Indian and singularly complex class of textiles, 'loom-embroidery' with gold and silver.[1] Forbes Watson was familiarizing his intended readers, British cloth-makers, with Indian tastes, and declared that this class of cloths 'is destined yet to occupy a somewhat important place amongst the list of manufactured articles exported from India to this and other European countries'.[2] He was primarily interested in trade and comparative advantages, and omitted the importance 'loom-embroidery' in metals had in the domestic market. In fact, this continued to be one preserve of handloom weaving which the powerloom did not touch at all.

Forbes Watson was aware that the accumulated skills in the manufacture of the metal thread itself contributed to this advantage. *Jari*, or twisted silver thread with a golden shine, was a widely used material on the borders or surface of decorated cloths. It was woven on cotton or silk, or embroidered by hand. No other major industry was so closely associated with silk and, occasionally, with cotton weaving. At the same time, none of the textile-related occupations specialized into an independent craft to the same extent. And yet, the making of *jari* itself, *jari* being a more standardizable product than the garments that used it, was vulnerable to changes in tools and processes. To write the history of *jari* is to attempt to understand the product in terms of its bonds with textiles, and, simultaneously, to see it as a particular kind of metal craft which survived foreign competition. As we shall see, the two towns that came to dominate what used to be quite a dispersed industry before the

---

[1] John Forbes Watson, *The Textile Manufactures and the Costumes of the People of India* (London, 1866), 109.
[2] *Ibid.*, p. 114.

twentieth century, Benares in northern India and Surat in western India, represent this duality about *jari* in contrasting ways.

The two singular features about *jari*, which help us explain its history, were, its status as an input, and the distinction of being the only purely craft product to receive fiscal protection in the 1930s. Being an input like yarn, *jari* was more homogeneous than cloth. Although economies of scale were generally weak, the possibility of using power for some of the operations did exist. Western Europe utilized these options earlier, and exposed the Indian *jari* to competition, not so severe in cost but intense in quality. The industry adapted to this competition primarily by three means: endogenous technical change; relocation and regional specialization; and protective tariffs. The experience with tariffs can be seen as a validation of the 'infant industry' argument, to a degree not very common in contemporary Indian history.

This chapter has five parts. The first describes the consumption of *jari*. It describes the cloths that used *jari*, and their fate in the nineteenth and twentieth centuries. The section also discusses competitive imports, and features of the cloth which made the impact of competition uneven between towns producing *jari*. The four sections that follow deal with various responses to these changes in consumption and competitiveness. The spheres of change are: location; tariffs and import-substitution; technology; and the nature of contracts.

The product and its market

Jari, in a form usable in textiles, was the outcome of four processes: drawing silver wire from bars; flattening the wire; spinning the flattened wire on silk or cotton; and gold-plating this thread. In the first two stages, silver was melted, then the bar-shaped metal drawn through a perforated metal plate, and the wire flattened by hammering it on an anvil to produce *lametta*. The tasks were skilled, arduous, and, therefore, specialized. Wire-drawing, by having to maintain a furnace, required a certain investment and usually functioned in workshops. The holes on a drawing plate were of successively narrower dimension. The process was completed when a standard weight of 180 grams (one *tola*) was reduced to 600 to 1,200 yards of wire. In recorded history, gold bar is not known to be so transformed, mainly on account of the easier pliability of silver. But until the middle of the twentieth century, the silver bar was often plated with a thin gold leaf which imparted a shine to the wire. In that case, the furnace performed a separate stage, the melting of gold. The output of this process, disc-shaped gold plates, were hammered into thin leaves. The entire operation of the furnace, whether in gold or

Figure 4.1 Tinsel workers, undated (possibly 1920s)

silver, required a great deal of judgment on the extent of heating necessary to yield a ductile, hard, and yet not brittle piece of metal. With the development of the final stage, electro-plating of the finished wire, the gold leaf could be dispensed with. In the final stage, the *lametta* was twisted manually. The spinner suspended a silk thread from a hook in the ceiling by a spindle, and then gave the spindle a sharp twist to revolve fast, while the lametta or flattened wire was made to touch delicately on the spinning thread. The outcome was *jari*. Apart from *jari*, silver thread was also used in the making of 'tinsel'. Tinsel is hard to define, as it used to refer to a wide range of bright, metallic, but non-durable ornaments. One common example was garlands made of metal foil. But certain kinds of tinsel, usually made by flattening silver wire singly or after winding it around another wire, had uses in textiles, especially in embroidery.

The four principal woven stuffs that used *jari* in its finished or semi-finished state were, lace or *gota* in north Indian terms; hand-embroidered cloth or the technique known as *zardozi*; cloth studded with wire or metal leaf, or *kamdani*; and, most importantly, cloth with *jari* woven onto it. The northern variant of weaving *jari* in a regular loom was usually called *kamkhwab*, itself a heterogeneous product. Although uses of *jari* for any or all of these were very widely dispersed, manufacture of *jari* had become more or less extinct in south India by the end of the nineteenth century, and it was primarily a north Indian industry.

Embroidery with gold or silver wire is believed to be an essentially Asian craft: 'India is doubtless its home.'[3] An earlier source cited in Forbes Watson, however, traced the ancestry of the craft (in Dacca, or Dhaka) to the near east, and it flourished in Dacca with the Muslim merchants who settled in the city to conduct a trade with Busra and Jeddah, 'the great marts for the embroidered goods in Bengal'.[4] The craft itself did not spread far, for the fine cotton cloth needed the humid climate of Bengal. The climate was recreated, with a similar cloth that came from Chanderi in central India, in underground workshops. This long concentration ensured that the kind of craftsmanship with which the Indian towns became identified, became uniquely their own creations. Loom-embroidery with metals (*kamkhwab*), hand-embroidery with metals (*zardozi*), and hand-embroidery with cotton or silk threads (*chikan, kashidah,* and *phulkari*) were overlapping crafts, but not identical. Dacca, for instance, seems to have begun with metals as well as fibres, but by the late nineteenth century specialized only in fibres embroidered on muslins, a kind of work in which two distinct reputations fused into one. In Lucknow, *zardozi* and *chikan* were co-existent, but more or less in parallel. Benares was chiefly known for its loomwork.

The recorded history of embroidery is replete with instances of the patronage the craft received from the later sultans, and early mughals. These initiatives, the specific cloths with which the craft came to be associated, and its kinship with Asia Minor and the Arab world had turned Indian embroidery into more or less a north Indian craft. In northern India, embroidery was more than a commercial skill: it was part of the education of girls in Muslim families, rich or not-so-rich.[5] The highest stages of its development, as a commercial craft and as styles, can be seen in the towns of the United Provinces, of which Agra and Lucknow were probably the most important. In the predominantly

---

[3] C. W. Gwynne, *Monograph on the Manufacture of Wire and Tinsel in the United Provinces* (Allahabad, 1910), 1.

[4] Watson, *Textile Manufactures*, 114.

[5] The craft monographs prepared around 1900 supply some instances of home-made articles. One example comes from Fanny Parks' accounts of the customs of the north Indian home, such as the visit in about 1840 to Hyatulnisa Begum, a princess of Delhi: 'Four trays, filled with fruit and sweetmeats were presented to me; two necklaces of jasmine flowers, fresh gathered, and strung with tinsel, were put round my neck; and the princess gave me a little embroidered bag filled with spices. It is one of the amusements of the young girls in a zenana to embroider little bags, which they do very beautifully.' *Wanderings of a Pilgrim in Search of the Picturesque* (London, 1850, reprinted Karachi, 1975), 215.

Hindu south, embroidery existed to the extent north Indian traditions were carried into the smaller urban Muslim settlements. Hadaway described the 'characteristic family collection' of a wealthy Muslim household (in Tamil Nadu) to consist of men's caps and waistcoats dotted with tinsel, 'richly and heavily' embroidered on the pockets and the arm bands; head coverings, jackets, trousers and skirts for women, embroidered on the bands around the feet; large embroidered handkerchiefs and headdresses, not to mention the 'great use . . . made of small embroidered articles at weddings and other festive occasions'.[6] All of Forbes Watson's eleven samples in *zardozi* on silk or cotton, collected about 1850, were purchased in Madras, Tiruchirapalli, and Hyderabad. This is no proof that the craft was even more frequent in the south, for all his samples had a great deal of acknowledged randomness. But it does show that the craft was familiar enough in the south in the middle of the century.

Hand embroidery was an occupation that did not visibly flourish at any time in the twentieth century. The Muslim nobility's reduced state in British India affected the demand for embroidered cloth, and the loss was never compensated by the 'Indians of education', the vehicle of European fashion.[7] Products like palanquin covers, saddle cloths, embroidered bangles, tinsel on garlands, decorations on the bridal carriage and *pandals* at weddings were, in 1900, relics from an earlier time. Contemporary descriptions suggest, in blurry outline, the following changes in north Indian embroidery: the number of specialized craftsmen declined; embroidery retreated into the hands of domestic workers, and inside relatively depressed Muslim middle-class homes; and smaller and less well-known centres were in decline. 'The extensive series of *zardozi* work [at the Indian Art Exhibition at Delhi, 1903(?), had] come from every province.'[8] But, by the middle of the twentieth century, no such dispersion was in evidence. Even in Benares, one of the most important points of manufacture, it was practically dead and its remains were subject to the high seasonality of an occasion-specific demand.[9] In Lucknow, the *chikan* work suffered a de-skilling in its design content while trying to copy Swiss embroidery.[10] Other survivals

---

[6] W. S. Hadaway, *Monograph on Tinsel and Wire in the Madras Presidency* (Madras, 1909), 8–10.

[7] Gwynne, *Monograph on the Manufacture*, 3.

[8] George Watt and Percy Brown, *Indian Arts and Crafts*, Official Catalogue of the Indian Art Exhibition (Delhi, 1904), 420. See also the description in Class VIII.

[9] India, *Report on the Jari Industry at Important Centres*, All India Handicrafts Board (Delhi, 1961), 8.

[10] W. G. Raffé, 'Industrial Art Education', *Journal of Indian Industries and Labour*, 3, 1 (1923), 13.

were distinctly smaller than they once were: Jaipur with about 1,000 workers, and Delhi, Agra, and Bareilly with 500 to 700 each, many of whom were domestic workers. A degradation of quality in essence similar to what can be seen time and again in the decorative crafts beset embroidery. In a labour-intensive industry in decline, the struggle to survive often led to the utilization of less experienced women workers from depressed families, which tended to degrade the product. A long-term shift in decorated wares from everyday use to occasion-specific use also tended to degrade quality.[11]

Finally, there followed a strenuous adjustment to the very different standards demanded by the Europeans, 'the more considered purchaser' of the better classes of north Indian embroidery at the turn of the century. The Europeans wanted articles, such as curtains, screens, or table-covers, which needed much lighter use of embroidery than, say, on a cloth used to drape royal elephants on parade. There was, thus, a shift towards silk-embroidery away from metals. There was also the difficulty of communication when the artisans were in *purdah*. The Indian mediator either blatantly exploited the situation, or, at the least, was mistrusted by the buyer.[12] There were other, more structural reasons why imperfect contact could affect embroidery very badly. Embroidery involved a rather free and irregular system of designs, unlike, say, bordered *saris* or carpets, on which traditional motifs and the geometric framework imparted a basic continuity. Embroidery, in other words, had to adapt somewhat cautiously to what the customer wanted. But the kind of contact that could ensure this was rare. The embroiderer, who 'thoroughly understood' the usual combinations and the 'correct artistic quantity in which [gold] is used' for Indian work, in trying to guess the European's predilections, cast aside conventions.[13] Where the contact did develop, most notably in Agra, the effect was not only a welcome simplification of designs, but a probable dilution of individuality, stemming from 'a tendency to forget the purely Oriental features of the art, and to . . . copy European designs'.[14] The tendency might have been

---

[11] Gifts at marriages are 'not as carefully made as pieces intended for more permanent use': Hadaway, *Monograph on Tinsel and Wire*, 9.

[12] A. Tellery, 'Embroidery, Braiding, Lace, etc.', *Report of the Fourth Industrial Conference of the United Provinces Held at Benares* (Benares, 1910), 148–9. Tellery was a textile exporter with a major presence in north India. See also on the European purchase of northern *jari* embroidery, in Gwynne, *Monograph on the Manufacture*, 2–3, and G. D. Ganguli, 'The Art Industries of the United Provinces', in *Report of the First Indian Industrial Conference (Benares, 1905)* (Allahabad, 1906), 350.

[13] Hadaway, *Monograph on Tinsel and Wire*, 15.

[14] Gwynne, *Monograph on the Manufacture*, 2. See the same source on the decline of embroidery in Benares and the smaller centres.

reinforced by later developments in embroidery wherein the non-textile, specially leather-based, applications expanded.

The *jari-woven* cloth, on the other hand, was much more dispersed. It found distinctive modes of expression almost wherever bordered garments like the *saris* were woven extensively. The main northern example of *jari*-woven cloth in this century was Benares, whereas the southern examples would include the silk *saris* of Madura, Kanchipuram, Tanjore, and Kumbakonam, and men's upper cloth or *angavastrams* of Salem. There was an important contrast between the northern and the southern styles of weaving *jari*. Benares products were typically more intensive in *jari*, used the threads on the border and the body of the cloth, that is, not necessarily to highlight the border, and being more expensive on average, had occasion-specific usage. In the south, on the other hand, *jari* was usually a manner of executing borders, and the products that utilized the material belonged, in looks and in price, to a wider tradition of bordered garments which were neither purely occasion-bound nor luxuries.

Lace was a woven product, but came off a loom of narrow width and frame-mounted, quite different from the loom the cloth weavers generally used. The practice of stitching a lace border on a garment was common in western India, and a traditional occupation of Surat. The distinction between a *sari* with a woven border, and a detachable lace one corresponded somewhat to 'the difference between a Hindu and a Parsee'.[15] Laces for different sorts of garment were made in northern India as well, and served a widely dispersed market, from cheap coats and caps, to saddle cloths and curtains. On the whole, lace was both a minor art in the range of *jari*-based textiles, and, with the exception of some forms of garment, probably a declining one. In more recent times, pure border weaving on lace looms survived in Surat, and as a very minor offshoot of brocades in Benares, under persistent threat from Surat.

The three manners of applying *jari* on cloth implied an important difference in the quality of the thread demanded, and, in turn, a difference in the manner of producing *jari*. When the thread is embroidered, the quality and thickness of the thread matters relatively less. A deft hand can compensate for a heavier or coarser thread. Where the thread is woven separately as lace, the variations in quality can again be somewhat ignored. For, a detachable lace is itself an intermediate good, and not a finished one. If the lace happens to be an indelicate one, an

---

[15] Indian Tariff Board, *Evidence Recorded During Enquiry Regarding Gold Thread Industry* (Calcutta, 1931), 110, evidence of W. M. Martin, representative of the Bombay Chamber of Commerce.

indelicate cloth can be found for which it is appropriate. Besides, the loom for weaving lace is of a distinct kind and adapts itself to weaving *jari*.

But when the thread is woven on a loom meant for silk or cotton, the quality of the *jari* becomes crucial. First, the garment with a woven border is a composite product of fibres and metals. An indelicate border is out of the question if the cloth is already a delicate one. Where the metal is expensive, it makes sense to weave it on fabrics that add value on the metal. Silk is the natural choice; its rare usage and inherent strength define it as a durable. Now, a coarse *jari* woven on fine silk can tear up the fabric. A *jari* loosely wound can come unstuck. And *jari* wound with fibres that are coloured with fugitive dyes can impair the look of the cloth every time the cloth is washed. The costlier the cloth, the more its resale value mattered. The latter depended on the content and quality of the *jari*. A typical bordered *sari* with good *jari* could fetch 5 per cent of its constant purchase price even after twenty years of use.[16]

The diversity of regional styles, combined with these input preferences, meant that the bordered silk *saris* of southern India emerged as *the* users of the best quality *jari* the market, and expressed a certain rigidity in this preference. Quality options were more flexible elsewhere. The use of coarser thread was far more common in the north or the west. Much of northern Indian embroidery, and lace weaving at various places, could be satisfied with 'imitation' *jari*, whereas in bordered weaving its use was unknown. Cotton was acceptable as a foundation for the thread consumed in the north, but never in the south.[17]

It was this attitude to quality, and the manner in which the various products absorbed *jari*, that determined the course of the competition between the Indian thread and the imported ones. The imports came mainly from Lyons in France, and steadily increased from the late nineteenth century, possibly because the prior decline of brocades in French fashions, and the consequent decline of Lyons 'fancy' silk weaving during the Second Empire forced the local thread industry to look for markets overseas.[18] In India, the competition was on quality. Because of the variation in preferred quality in India, the foreign *jari* had a very uneven impact on the producers of *jari* in different regions and on the weavers who used them. To understand the diverse impact, a clearer

---

[16] *Ibid.*, 125, P. B. Advani, Director of Industries, Bombay; and *ibid.*, 178, Behram Karanjia, Vice-President of Indian Chamber of Commerce.

[17] *Ibid.*, 89, 91, A. T. Palanpurwala, importer at Bombay; *ibid.*, 74, E. G. Cornet, probably importer at Pondicherry.

[18] On changes in tastes, see George J. Sheridan, Jr., *The Social and Economic Foundations of Association Among the Silk Weavers of Lyons, 1852–1870* (New York, 1981), vol. I, chapter II.

idea of the differences between the Indian and the imported threads is necessary.

Jari involved three basic processes: drawing of silver wire from bars; spinning it on silk or cotton; and gold-plating this thread (more details of the manufacturing process will be given below). In 1930, each of these could be done either by hand or by machine. Mechanization could proceed unevenly, since the processes did not need to be integrated. It was rare, even in the relatively capital-intensive industries of Lyons, Nuremberg, and Milan, to have a single firm perform all the processes. Besides, in some of the processes, rarely was a firm engaged in textile-related usage alone. Wire factories used their machines on a variety of metals and for various purposes. Hot-plating was the outcome of a process that, likewise, had diverse applications. The relatively low over-head of a diversified industry was surely one of advantages of the French thread in India. Yet, costs constituted a small advantage, narrow enough to be wiped out by a moderate revenue tariff. The competition was one on quality.

Of the three operations, wire-drawing was the most highly developed in India relative to Europe. Artisans, with the help of simple and adaptable tools, could draw silver wire to a thinness much exceeding that of the average French thread. They were, in other words, well able to satisfy the weavers of the finest silk garments. In this skill, in terms of cost and quality of labour, Benares seems to have enjoyed an advantage over Surat. The impact of competition from imported thread reflected this advantage. Surat altered its product composition, tended to move into installation of power-driven machinery, and for finely drawn wires depended partially on the Benares artisans. Similarly, the Indian Gold Thread Mills of Madras, a pioneering attempt to reproduce the Lyons manufacturing process, found it cheaper to dispense with mechanized wire-drawing, and purchase the wire from Benares.[19]

The quality gap between the manual Indian, especially Surati, thread and imported thread arose mainly in spinning and gilding. In the French thread, the silver and silk threads were first spun, then electro-plated to give the golden shine. In the Indian thread, gold plating *preceded* spinning. That is, in the latter process, gold-plated silver was spun with silk, such that some of the lustre of gold was lost. That was not the only difference. The Indians were good at making thin wire. For that thinness to stand the strain of weaving, or washing, the silk–metal twist needed to be very fast. The French could achieve fast twist on a machine that

---

[19] Indian Tariff Board, *Evidence Recorded*, 15, N. R. Rangachari, manager of the firm.

exerted greater pressure on the yarn. The machine could be used in India, but it would not have reproduced the particular efficiency the 'Lyons workgirls' had acquired in this task. On the closeness of the twist, Benares was inferior to Surat, and Surat was inferior to imported thread. But the Madras venture which copied Lyons processes was apparently more successful.[20]

A further difference arose from the silk. If the flattened silver wire or *lametta* was relatively thick, as anywhere other than Benares, the fineness and evenness of the *jari* depended on the silk yarn. The usual Mysore silk yarn did not answer very well to these standards. Kashmir silk possibly could, but its use in *jari* was as yet rare and costlier. Given the twist, and the silk itself, the Indian *jari* imparted to the cloth a feel of irregularity.[21] Moreover, the colour on the silk yarn was not guaranteed fast, and it ran when the twisted thread was subjected to the gilding process. The Madras factory, moreover, found that the extent of physical manipulation of the thread during that process left, in a climate like Madras', a residue of dirt on the thread, robbing it of lustre. Probably for similar reasons, another integrated factory at Surat withdrew from *jari*, and concentrated on wire-drawing at the height of the competition.[22]

Competition began in the 1880s, following the decade when agents of German and Lyonnaise firms are believed to have first collected samples of north Indian *jari*.[23] By the last years of the century, imports were a recognized threat. They had more or less decimated *jari* manufacture wherever it was allied to lace or embroidery, which would include much of the north Indian industry. Imports were a less serious hazard to that part of *jari* feeding into *kamkhwab*.[24] In Lucknow, the weavers' guild (Panchayat) forbade the use of French thread in weaving.[25] In Benares, it made the artisans 'very guarded to talk about their methods, fearing that the stranger will copy it in machines'.[26] By 1910, the entire

---

[20] *Ibid.*, 34–5, B. J. G. Shastri of Surat Gold Thread Merchants' Association, and a pioneer in technical experiments.

[21] With the sensibility of a previous generation, Hadaway believed that precisely this quality made an Indian cloth or embroidery 'a much more human and interesting article altogether': *Monograph on Tinsel and Wire*, 2.

[22] Indian Tariff Board, *Evidence Recorded*, 25, B. J. G. Sastri.

[23] For two instances, see B. M. Ray, *A Monograph on Wire and Tinsel Industry in Bengal* (Calcutta, 1900?) 6, and V. N. Mehta, *Gilt Wire and Tinsel Industry*, Bulletin of Indian Industries and Labour No. 25 (Bombay, 1922), 17.

[24] Implied in Mehta, *Gilt Wire and Tinsel*.

[25] Ardhendu Bhattacharya, 'Extracts from a Survey of the Small Urban Industries of Lucknow', in United Provinces, *The United Provinces Provincial Banking Enquiry Committee*, vol. II of Evidence (Lucknow, 1930), 415.

[26] Gwynne, *Monograph on the Mnufacture*, 3.

southern industry had switched over to imports, and nearly two-thirds of the French thread arrived at Madras.[27]

These changes in consumption and import led first of all to a decline in *jari*-producing towns.

Relocation

Jari in the middle of the nineteenth century was mainly an urban industry for several reasons. First, the products that used *jari* heavily were consumed by the relatively affluent. Secondly, there were also towns where *jari* was manufactured for distant markets. It was generally performed as a specialized occupation. In some cases, the distant market was export. For example, Surat had an ancient trade in the near east for its gold and silver thread. Thirdly, the raw material being too expensive to be carried over hazardous roads, there was a tendency to congregate near points where silver was traded. Thus, the advantage of Burhanpur, Lahore, Poona, or Lucknow partly consisted in the organization of their silver trades. The continued supremacy of Surat must be attributed partly to its proximity to Bombay, which was Asia's premier bullion exchange in the 1920s. Raw material trade influenced location in yet another way, and one parallel to brassware. The makers of *jari* recycled silver from old garments quite extensively, in part from considerations of purity of metal, and in part for reasons of cost.[28] This trade was performed by itinerant hawkers. Until as recently as the 1970s, roving groups of women based in Benares, exchanging new brassware for old *jari* clothes or old brassware, were a familiar sight in middle-class localities in north India. The exchange often involved, where the cloth was threadbare, carefully tearing the border off. To minimize the costs of this expensive trade, the industry which was to use this material needed to be concentrated, and needed to have such large silver dealers who could afford the cost.

Though urban, *jari* in the middle of the nineteenth century was more dispersed than it became in 1930. About 1870, the *jari*-consuming and producing towns in India could be classified in the following groups:

1. Towns with a reputation in *jari-woven* cloth, but which made *jari* to a *small* extent. These included Poona, Tanjore, Trichinopoly (Tiruchchirappalli), Madura, Yeola, Jaipur, Chanderi, Peshawar, Lahore, Aurangabad, Paithan, and Nawanagar (Bombay).

---

[27] Hadaway, *Monograph on Tinsel and Wire*, 3.
[28] There is a brief reference to this trade in J. Nissim, *A Monograph on Wire and Tinsel in the Bombay Presidency* (Bombay, 1910), 2.

2. Towns with a reputation in *embroidery*, but which made *jari* to a *small* extent, such as Lucknow and other smaller towns in the United Provinces, Patna, Calcutta, Ahmedabad, Delhi, and Murshidabad.
3. Towns with a reputation in *weaving*, and which also had a *large* presence in production of *jari* itself: Burhanpur, Surat and Benares.
4. Towns with a reputation in *embroidery*, and making thread in *large* quantities: Agra and Bareilly.

These classes are of course approximate, because there were overlaps. Towns such as Poona or Yeola had, in fact, a very diversified cloth output, from lace to embroidered *turbans* to bordered *saris*, all using local *jari* in different styles. But, textile towns did differ in the source of their reputation, and the distinction between embroidery and loom-woven *jari* is a relevant one in identifying this source.

Competition between *jari* towns and between local and imported thread in the late nineteenth century had an adverse effect mainly on those towns where the industry was on a small scale, that is, classes 1 and 2 above.[29] In the fourth class, competition probably de-skilled the making of *jari*, and even weakened the embroidery tradition itself, but did not destroy *jari*. Bareilly is an example. The third category was the most stable, where the industry was large and strong enough to actively adapt. Burhanpur did decline, but did so because of exogenous reasons. One of its key advantages, its location on the old trade route between Agra and western India, had been eliminated by the railways.[30] This left only Surat and Benares.

Most examples of decline come from the first two classes. In southern India, Madura was probably the most important town. Some of the mid-nineteenth-century district manuals mentioned local *jari* manufacture at Madura and Arcot.[31] By 1909, Hadaway observed that the surviving *jari* industry was a curiosity in the south. It consisted of scarce itinerant artisan teams, said to be Sourashtras. Whether they were from Madura, the main centre of Sourashtra enterprise in textiles, is not

---

[29] See Mehta, *Gilt Wire and Tinsel*, 29, on Lahore and Amritsar, and 28–9, on Burhanpur and Chanderi; V. R. Chitra and V. Tekumalla (eds.), *Cottage Industries of India (Guidebook and Symposium)* (Madras, 1948), Section II, 202, on Paithan; Gwynne, *Monograph on the Manufacture*, 4–5, on Delhi, Meerut, Amroha, and Karra yielding to Benares; Bengal, *Report on the Survey of Cottage Industries in Bengal* (Calcutta, 1924), 30, on Murshidabad; Indian Tariff Board, *Written Evidence Recorded During Enquiry on the Grant of Protection to the Sericultural Industry*, vol. I (Delhi, 1935), 302, on Aurangabad and Paithan; and Raghbir Sahai, *Report on the Survey of the Handloom Weaving and Dyeing Industries in HEH Nizam's Dominion* (Hyderabad, 1933), 96, on Aurangabad (from where *jari* workers migrated to Yeola in the 1920s), and 131, on Paithan.

[30] G. N. Frankau, 'The Gilt Wire and Tinsel Industry at Burhanpur, Central Provinces', *Journal of Indian Industries and Labour*, 1, 1 (1921), 52.

[31] Hadaway, *Monograph on Tinsel and Wire*, 2, 4.

clear. What is clear is that the Madura Sourashtras were actively engaging in imported *jari* trade. A 1920s account suggests that Madura's own surviving *jari* industry consisted of a few Muslim families who used north Indian methods.[32] The thread was inferior enough to have its market limited to embroidery, a class never very popular among the Hindus of the south. When these artisans were seen at all, they were seen working in Madras. The 1901 census also reported a few Muslim families in Tirunelveli and Malabar engaged in lace, in twisted thread, and the cruder process of shine.[33] Subsequently, this class of manufacture was forgotten.

Another example of decline is eastern India. Patna is known to have had a *jari* industry in the nineteenth century feeding a local embroidery tradition. In 1929, there were only eight to ten factories left. They were starved of market, working capital, and credit, and could not compete with the organization and scale of Benares. Several firms in Calcutta made *jari* for the embroiderers of Murshidabad. In the 1920s, they were found to be in decline because of German thread. Around 1900, Calcutta also had a small industry in tinsel-making, which consisted of a few family firms. German manufacturers reportedly visited them in their better days, and had copied the work successfully. In the 1920s, the art of needlework spread in middle-class homes. 'Cultured ladies' of Indian Christian and Brahmo families took it up on a noticeable scale. Some of this occupation became commercialized under the initiative, among others, of a Chinsura (Chuchura) entrepreneur. Much of this new revival, however, involved *chikan*, that is, silk-cotton embroidery. Metal thread was rarely used in such work.[34]

There were two independent reasons for the competitive decline and survival in *jari*, which became entwined in the interwar period. These were internal competition, a factor present in all skilled crafts once they tended to compete in the same market, and external competition, which was specific to a craft like *jari*. These reasons were no longer independent in 1930. By then, the ability to substitute imports by technical adaptations determined the survival of *both* competitions. In this process, Surat and Benares were notably more successful than almost any other older site of *jari* production. The rest of this chapter describes this dynamic.

---

[32] K. R. R. Sastry, *The Madura Saurashtra Community* (Bangalore, 1927).

[33] Census of India, 1901, *Madras*, vol. xv, Part I (Report) (Madras, 1902), 249.

[34] Bengal, *Report on the Survey of Cottage Industries in Bengal*, second edition (Calcutta, 1929), 38.

Import-substitution

French thread became a serious competitor of the Indian industry between approximately 1900 and 1914. There were sporadic attempts at this time to compete with imports. The first attempt was that of the India Gold Thread Mills at Perambur, started as early as 1908 by two enterprising merchants. The company's board consisted of Sourashtra members, who at that time controlled the *jari* trade of south India.[35] The firm set up a lace factory with integrated *jari* production, procured a plant from France, hired a French forewoman and a French lace-maker, who was soon dismissed on being found to be a better theoretician than a practitioner.[36] When interviewed by the Tariff Board twenty years later, the firm's representative made no reference to lace, and considered wire-drawing to have no great advantage over Benares methods. But, on the strength of gilding, the firm maintained a niche, though the quality of the finished thread was still not comparable to the best of imported thread. Alfred Chatterton, in an initiative not very widely known, went to Lyons in 1911 to study the techniques. On hearing he was from India, 'the factories shut their doors firmly on his face'.[37] He did, however, have some important things to say about the quality and construction of the French thread.

The First World War dislocated imports, and provided more serious attempts at import-substitution by emulating Lyons methods in India. The Gauri Gold and Silver Works of Surat, started in 1916 with power-driven draw-benches of British manufacture, was the most notable of these. Similar attempts were reported from Bombay, Kanpur, Coimbatore, and Salem. Some of the new firms were set up to supply silver wire to the jewellery industry. Imported machines were marginally adapted. In one instance, a manufacturer in Benares found a way, 'now a trade secret', to fix two arrangements to the winding process, one of which avoided the touch of grease, oil or dirt on the thread at the final stages, and the other automatically stopped the reel when a wire snapped.[38] The import of *jari* revived quickly at the end of the war. The two years of overvalued exchange in 1921–2 encouraged the import of *jari*, though they also encouraged the import of machinery to manufacture *jari*. At this stage, the Indian Tariff Board intervened.

With the competition in *jari* arising from non-British sources, the Tariff Board faced less of a moral dilemma than it usually did in dealing with the question of protective tariffs in interwar India. The Board's

[35] Sastry, *The Madura Saurashtra Community.*
[36] Hadaway, *Monograph on Tinsel and Wire*, 2.
[37] Mehta, *Gilt Wire and Tinsel*, 26.   [38] *Ibid.*, pp. 16–7.

members sought to answer the same question they did with the other nascent or distressed industries that asked for protection: did it have a natural, long-term competitive advantage to justify the infant industry argument? The answer, as in most other cases, was obscure, and the evidence fragmentary. But, unlike elsewhere, in *jari*, the enquiry was briskly performed, and the action was swift and decisive. An existing revenue tariff of 10 per cent *ad valorem* on fine *jari* and *lametta* was raised in 1921–2 to 20 per cent, to 30 per cent the next year, to 38 per cent in April 1930, and finally to 50 per cent in October the same year. Protection was extended to *jari*-using fabrics four years later. Interestingly, 'imitation' *jari*, in which base metal was used in place of silver, carried lower duties. The import of imitations did increase, but to a limited extent, since imitations were recognized as an inferior substitute.

Imports into Bombay and Madras in value more than halved during the 1920s. The main port of entry was Madras, where imports dwindled further after the 38 per cent duty. Import into the French territories of Pondicherry and Karaikal, however, soared. Thousands of rupees worth of *jari* was carried as small passenger baggage across a porous land frontier, easily bypassing nominally effective check-posts. The approximate value of smuggled thread in 1931 was Rs. 1 million. Till then, the only steps taken to curb illicit trade were an informal agreement between the Indian government and the Lyons manufacturers to sell consignments as far as possible to British India, and a small tax imposed by the Government of Pondicherry. A smaller illicit trade also occurred at the Kathiawar port in Gujarat.

Tariffs and smuggling had rather curious effects on the *jari* trade of south India. In the interwar period, the control of the southern *jari* trade had witnessed a shift. Before the war, the Sourashtras of Madura controlled much of the imported *jari* trade. In 1910, Hadaway found no European interest in the southern *jari* trade. In the 1920s, however, European 'managing agents' such as the Coimbatore-based Peirce Leslie, were dominant in the official import trade. The Sourashtras' local advantage consisted in the fact that they were also in substantial control of silk cloth and yarn trades.[39] But this proved to be insecure in the face of changes in trading systems. In the prewar period, much of the *jari* imports happened by postal consignments. After the First World War, the trade seems to have preferred sole-agency contracts with European firms. The exact antecedents of this shift are not clear, but a surge of speculation during the war could have contributed to it.[40] The smuggling finally finished off what was left of the Indian

[39] Hadaway, *Monograph on Tinsel and Wire*, 3.
[40] Implied in Mehta, *Gilt Wire and Tinsel*, 24.

trade.[41] Interestingly, the Sourashtras' acclaimed mastery in dyeing, and their extensive investment in dye-houses, were almost contemporary achievements. It is not unlikely that capital shifted out of *jari* into these more profitable fields. The smuggling, however, threatened the managing agencies. Their determined lobbying achieved the little checks that came to be imposed on the land frontier.[42] By 1939, both the official and the illicit trades subsided decisively.

The combined pressure of the European firms seeking curbs on illegal trade, and that of the Surat industry led to the final round of duty in October 1930. A later report interpreted that 'the whole purpose' behind the final hike was to enable Surat to capture the south Indian market.[43] The high level, combined with some control on the illicit trade, did seem to bear results, and what was left of cross-border trade was destroyed by the dislocations of the Second World War. By 1950, Surat was indisputably in control of the south Indian trade, vacated first by the Sourashtras, and now by the European trading firms.

With protection, the feeble initiative at import-substitution of the prewar era became more general. Almost all of it took place in Surat, and only to a minor extent in Benares. Indeed, in this process of enhancing competitiveness, the two towns displayed quite different types of response.

Surat, Benares and technical change

Minor adaptations of various kind were taking place in the prewar *jari* industry, presumably in response to internal competition on quality. One important change in wire-drawing technology in the early part of the century involved the drawing plate. Plates of standardized dimensions, with better resistance to wear and tear, began to be imported and fitted onto the old frames where the artisan worked. Steel was replaced by firmer metals (hard metal-coated drawing holes), or by 'gold-plated steel', which is more likely to have been a brass plate.[44] One of the first allied crafts to disappear was that of the *tania*'s, boring holes in the draw plate. The plate earlier used to be of good steel, being cut off from old swords. The process of boring with hammer and punch was not only hard work, but unpaying for the skill involved. It was wasteful, because the *tania* needed to make more holes than were necessary at the

---

[41] Indian Tariff Board, *Evidence Recorded*, 75, E. G. Cornet.

[42] *Ibid.*, 69, W. J. Campbell, Director of Peirce Leslie.

[43] India, *Report of the Indian Tariff Board on the Continuance of Protection to the Silver Thread and Wire Industry* (Bombay, 1948).

[44] See Ray, *A Monograph on Wire and Tinsel*, 2, on processes, and changes in the disc in eastern India; see Gwynne, *Monograph on the Manufacture*, 8, on northern India.

prevailing level of dimensional exactitude. Being also the wire-drawers themselves, an overaggregation of labour resulted. The situation changed quickly with the availability of German and English brass plates from 1900, and, about twenty years later, of ruby- and diamond-coated discs. By the early 1920s, discs were being made in Surat and Ahmedabad.[45] In the prewar period, flattening of wire and spinning saw some changes. By 1923, the artisan *tardabkiya*, as the flattener was called, had disappeared from Benares, and, while the motive power still came from hand, a transition had been made to a system that could be converted into electric power.[46] However ingenious the spinning method seemed to the unfamiliar eye, it was far too labour-intensive. It became rare at the turn of the century in the larger *jari* towns, and was replaced, wherever the workshop owner had the means, by spools and reels.[47]

The imported thread had an uneven impact on technical change. In wire-drawing, in terms of cost and quality of labour, the gap between India and Europe was narrow or non-existent, but only where the process was carried on by highly skilled artisans. Benares enjoyed an advantage over Surat in this respect. So much so that, as late as 1960, primary wire-drawing in the town was done manually.[48] Benares wire-drawing can perhaps be seen as an extension of a whole tradition in decorative silver work for which the city was well known. Apart from skilled labour, Benares' adherence to conventional *jari* was said to derive from its climate, which favoured the use of silver, though the exact benefits of the climate are obscure. Benares was relatively insulated from competition by several circumstances. First, the French thread landed mainly in Madras, and not in Calcutta, such that transport costs escalated by the time it reached Benares. Benares was closer to silk supplies from Kashmir, a material better suited to high-quality twisted thread than the Mysore silk used in Surat. More importantly, Benares brocades provided a large local market for *jari*. The value of output and employment show that Benares brocades were a bigger consumer of *jari* than any other textile town in 1960. Moreover, the scale of weaving expanded greatly in the first half of the twentieth century. Gwynn reported 2,000 weavers in 1910. In 1960, there were 20,000 looms employing 46,000 workers.[49] By then, these looms had diversified, but Benares' image in textiles still derived from brocades. It is this immense

[45] Mehta, *Gilt Wire and Tinsel*, 10–11.
[46] United Provinces, *Industrial Survey of the United Provinces* (Allahabad, 1922–4), Benares District.
[47] Gwynne, *Monograph on the Manufacture*, 8.
[48] India, *Report on the Jari Industry at Important Centres*, All India Handicrafts Board (Delhi, 1961), 2–3.
[49] India, *Report on the Survey of the Brocade Industry at Varanasi*, All India Handicrafts

pull of the local market which insulated Benares *jari* to some extent from competition. While imports did cause a decline, they produced far less alarm than in Surat. An indication is the noticeably poor representation of Benares in the Tariff Board enquiries, almost suggesting mutual disinterest, whereas the Surat lobby visibly dominated the proceedings.

The gap between imported and local *jari* was widest in spinning and gilding. By 1930 Surat and Benares had access to cheap electricity. In both towns, the decade witnessed a more or less complete switchover to electro-plating.[50] Within a decade from 1921, French thread was 'totally ousted' from the Benares market, electric processes of gilding began replacing oil engines that had been installed briefly, and the demand for local thread expanded. A considerable part of Benares' output at this time did not use silk, but English cotton thread, as foundation. From this point on, Surat and Benares diverged. Surat searched and found new markets, and Benares supplied its traditional markets, the local brocade and Punjab embroidery. While hand-processes in wire-drawing and spinning persisted in Benares,[51] in Surat there was mechanization and the growth of larger firms in these processes. Surat increasingly moved out of 'real' or silver *jari* and into 'imitation *jari*', whereas Benares did not, reinforcing a product differentiation that originated from skills in wire-drawing.[52] Imitation thread, in turn, encouraged the mechanization of wire-drawing.[53]

There were two elements in Surat's dynamism: trading acumen and imitation *jari*. Imported thread not only eclipsed many smaller towns once well known for *jari*, and threatened the reputed ones, it also integrated markets for *jari*. It was Surat's merchants who tried to break into this trade, and were eventually successful. Since the hub of the trade was southern India, Surat's proximity to the south may have helped. But there was also a difference in the quality of enterprise and trading institutions. Benares was after all an artisan town, itself consuming a large quantity of the *jari* it made, whereas Surat was developing into a centre of trade. From 1930, Surat's market was increasingly non-

Board (Delhi, 1960). Two-thirds of the *jari* requirements of this industry came from within the town.
[50] United Provinces, *Industrial Survey*, 11, Benares.
[51] Indian Tariff Board, *Evidence Recorded*, 51, The Industrial and Trade Association, Benares.
[52] The additional reason cited for Surat's move to imitation during the war was a short-term one: the restrictions on gold exports necessitated a verification of *jari* exports from Surat on gold content. The costs of this verification were large, since Surat did much of its business by post, whereas only the customs office or shipping agents were authorized to do the check. D. R. Gadgil and R. K. Patil, *Gold and Silver Thread Industry in Surat* (Surat, 1953).
[53] *Ibid.*, p. 7.

local. The need to capture the southern market made the traders highly mobile. Already in the 1940s, shops owned by Surat merchants were being established at Coimbatore, Dindigul, Madura, and elsewhere in the south. After 1947, this tendency strengthened considerably. The tendency had old roots. Surati artisans were known for their hawking. They travelled around in consuming towns nearby selling their ware. Whereas the travelling artisans sold what they made, and returned after their journeys, the merchants following their example arranged to make what they sold. They settled in distant parts, specialized in trade, and specialized by type of thread.[54]

What was imitation thread? The twisted thread, called *kasab* in the case of Surat imitations and *kalabatun* in the north, was a finished product, ready for the loom or the needle, when the silver thread had the required golden shine. In the older processes, where the silver bar was gold-plated, the thread was usually finished at the spinning stage. Alternatively, where the thread was a mixture of silk or cotton and base metals, the shine was added by a crude process of heating-cum-dyeing the metal, a class of work for which Bareilly was once famous. But the resultant thread was recognized as 'imitation', and a poor one. Imitation in this sense served a plebeian demand for embroidered cloth and brocades, a demand that might even have grown.[55] But it was quickly rendered obsolete by a more powerful process of manufacturing imitations, which Surat specialized in.

The most important impact of imports on domestic practices was the increased usage of the mechanized processes of lustring, namely, electro-plating. This not only eliminated the gold-plating of the silver bar, and hence unnecessary costs, it made possible an increased use of base metals as the foundation for the thread, for the lustration process had now separated itself, and had no essential link with the metal. The market still respected the difference between a genuine and imitation thread, such that the two cities with two images could co-exist. But by addressing a potential everyday usage of *jari*, and the middle-class demand, the imitation offered better growth prospects.

In 1910, Nissim compared Surat with the more conservative and smaller *jari* industry at Yeola, and stated that Surat's competitive strength lay in the diversity of the local textiles that used *jari*. This factor made the industry there better equipped, merchants more enterprising, but diluted the adherence to the purity of the metal. By then, the purity of the silver was the sole weapon left to any town where *jari* was in a declining state and costlier than imported *jari*, but still made as part of

[54] *Ibid.*, 1–2.
[55] See, for this inference, Gwynne, *Monograph on the Manufacture*, 3.

the old textile tradition.[56] As time went on, the difference became sharper. The principle of adaptation in Surat came to be: 'adjust[ing] their products to that all controlling factor – the market price'.[57] By cheapening inputs, Surat extended its own market and the total market for *jari*. In the process, local handlooms as a source of demand were eclipsed. In 1960, Surat was more or less completely specialized in imitation thread.

Surat's modernization began at the end of the First World War, when the Government of Bombay sponsored a study team to go to Europe, consisting of B. J. G. Sastri of the Gauri works, and J. K. Chapadia. Their report, published in 1923, had an apparent impact. Surat acquired greater knowledge and skill at electro-plating from this point. Surat's manufacturers guarded the specific recipe for gilding so closely that occasional attempts by Benares to break into imitation did not succeed.[58] In fact, in the early 1920s, some Benares real silver wire was being sent to Surat to be finished into *kalabatun*.[59] Possibly from the 1930s, the switch to imitation began. From the Second World War, the engineering side of the industry began to develop. Nearly all machinery and parts, including ruby dies, were now locally manufactured in Surat. In Benares too, a firm began to manufacture dies, but this branch of the industry was relatively smaller in Benares.

In the early parts of the interwar period, Surat quickly captured the western Indian market. As 'the quality of the indigenous product . . . improved greatly', Surat strengthened its position in the global *jari* market, a role that was probably threatened in the early twentieth century but never quite extinct. In the 1930s, a part of the city's output was carried over the land route to Afghanistan, and, after 1950, towards the Middle East, East Africa, and Malaya. In the late 1930s, as much as one-third of Surat's output was exported.[60] The hardest market to crack, however, was south India. At the end of the 1920s, Surat's thread was by no means generally acceptable to the fine silk weavers of the Tamil Nadu towns. Madura and Kanchipuram refused any but trifling quantities of Surati *jari*, and what they did get of 'country-made goods' was used in the off-season for inferior cloths to be sold locally by itinerant hawkers.[61] Surat's industrialists responded by demanding further protection, and, in the process, sharpened the conflict of interest between the makers and the users of the product, in this case a conflict

[56] Nissim, *Monograph on Wire and Tinsel*, 11.
[57] Gadgil and Patil, *Gold and Silver Thread*, 17.
[58] India, *Report on Jari*, 33.
[59] United Provinces, *Industrial Survey*, 12, Benares.
[60] India, *Report of the Indian Tariff Board on . . . Silver Thread and Wire*, 4–6.
[61] Indian Tariff Board, *Evidence Recorded*, 75, E. G. Cornet, and 125, Karanjia.

also between the north and the south of India. The conflict was eventually settled by protection, and the south's shift to imitation.

The existence of a local brocade industry was probably an advantage and a weakness for Benares, for it contributed to a somewhat static survival of *jari* in Benares. While Benares remained bound to a dominant textile tradition, Surat specialized in inputs. This divergence accounts for subsequent adaptations. The Surat *jari* industry, for example, could adapt its machinery to non-textile uses, since it was capable of handling a variety of metals; whereas Benares *jari* was more dependent on the fortunes of the local brocade weaving. Unlike Surat's local consumers, the lace weavers, Benares' weavers were more adaptable, as they could apply their skills and the broad-width looms to a wider range of uses. Nevertheless, the transition to a more diversified industrial base created more opportunities in Surat, leading to a flow of *jari* workers from Benares to Surat from the early interwar period. The migrants were probably weavers of brocades. As Surat's *jari* merchants extended their operations to all regions of the country, and finally abroad, Benares lost its traditional markets in north India, especially Punjab.

Nevertheless, in the 1940s, both towns benefited from tariffs and subsequent adaptations, each in its own way. The scale of expansion can be seen from Table 4.1 and the figures below. Here are assembled some estimates of varying reliability. But they are revealing nevertheless. In the first decade of the century, Surat employed about 2–8,000 workers in *jari*. In 1931, workers in *jari* and allied processes were estimated to be 19,000. Of them, weavers of *jari* cloth who had migrated from Benares numbered 2,500. Manufacturers of lace numbered 5,000, spinners 3,000, embroiderers 2,000, and gold-plating by older processes employed 3,000. Six larger wire-drawing factories employed 180 persons, and gold-plating by power-driven machinery 1,200. The Surat Electric Supply Company had connected 412 factories to its mains. The value of output, estimated by conversion of silver bars and wires imported into the city, was Rs. 5 million in 1919, at least Rs. 2 million in the early 1920s, and Rs. 11 million in 1931. Growth was present in Benares as well. In 1923, Benares *jari* employed approximately 5,000 persons, and sold Rs. 1 million worth of thread. In 1945, there were about 10,000 persons working in the industry, with an output of Rs. 10 million, predominantly real *jari*.[62] The scale of production in the immediate post-war years was probably unusual in both towns, for employment and output declined thereafter. In 1958, Benares employed 3,000

---

[62] United Provinces, *Industrial Survey*, Benares District, 10; and India, *Report of the Indian Tariff Board . . . on Silver Thread and Wire*.

Table 4.1 *Production and employment in the* jari *industry at Surat*

	1910	1924–5	1930–1	1945
Average annual production (Rs. million)	–	2	11	30 (real)
				7 (others)
				23 (allied products)
Employment	2–8,000	2,000	19,000	20,000 (real)
				10,000 (others)
Factories	–	60	–	1,000 (real)
				500 (others)

Notes: Approximate weighted non-agricultural price indices, with 1924 as base, would be 71 in 1930, and 101 in 1945. The employment figures fluctuate a great deal, not entirely because the estimates are impressionistic, but depending on the inclusion of *jari*-using sectors in the figure. The category 'others' consists mainly of imitation *jari*, and allied products, probably of cloth and lace. In addition to the number of workers indicated, there were, in 1945, about 1,500 part-time women workers in the industry.
Sources: Nissim, *Monograph on Wire and Tinsel*; Indian Tariff Board, *Evidence Recorded*, 167–9, P. B. Advani, Director of Industries, Bombay; India, *Report of the Indian Tariff Board*, 3.

workers in about 250 units, and manufactured Rs. 4.3 million worth of thread, and Surat employed 3,300 workers (an obvious underestimate), turning out Rs. 4 million in output. Lace weaving employed in Surat about 1,000 looms, whereas in Benares the number had shrunk to 200. In the late 1970s, Surat's *jari* and allied crafts employed 6–7,000 persons.[63] By then, the diffusion of electricity had again made the industry somewhat mobile.

Except perhaps for wire-drawing, innovations were incremental in nature, that is, added on to the existing tools and processes. In this sense, innovations maintained a compatibility with the nature of the existing firms, rather than inviting new entry. The point leads us to change and continuity in the nature of the firm.

Contracts

The general tendency of market-integration created opportunities of accumulation in trade in several crafts. In *jari*, we have seen some of the post-1920 changes in the network and control of trade. The prewar phase of the process remains obscure. Silver trade may have been one of the earliest points of accumulation. The silver trade, and especially the

[63] India, *Report on the Working Conditions of Workers in the Jari Industry at Surat (Gujarat)*, Labour Bureau (Chandigarh, 1978), 3.

Figure 4.2 *Jari* weavers in Surat, *c*.1950

melting of silver, was carried on in Lucknow, Burhanpur, Lahore, Delhi, and Benares under strict quality control by the trading community, a practice that created powerful silver-cum-lace dealers' guilds in many *jari* towns. In 1880, Lucknow, the most well-known site of lace production, maintained a common furnace to melt silver. The institution was a response to the need to control silver quality, and continued to exist several decades after 1880.[64] In the interwar period, French thread loosened the bond between the silver trade and the *jari* trade in the north, and destroyed it in the south. The silver merchant thus becomes rarer in connection with *jari* in sources after 1930. At the same time, the detachment enhanced the control of *jari* and cloth traders in the north, and that of import firms in the south.

Textile production was an enduring source of capital into *jari*, as the example of the Sourashtras suggests. In embroidered cloth, where the resident Europeans partly offset the loss of domestic demand, trade seemed to polarize into two networks, one meeting the demand from rich Indians and the Europeans, and the other that of the 'Indian

---

[64] See William Hoey, *A Monograph on Trade and Manufactures in Northern India* (Lucknow, 1880); and Gwynne, *Monograph on the Manufacture*, 7.

Figure 4.3 *Jari* manufacture by mechanized process, *c.*1950. The process shown is yarn winding.

purchasers of humble means'. The former segment innovated on designs, its merchant needed to 'consult his clientele'. All these reasons encouraged trade on larger scale and closer control on *jari* manufacture. The other network was of older vintage, involved smaller-sized traders, and innovated on material rather than designs. This latter type of traders was more open to imitation *jari*.[65] In the 1920s, the sale of *jari*-embroidered cloth was done typically by 'petty dalals who roam about in the Chowk trying to get hold of unwary purchasers'.[66] In north India, the interwar period did not witness a substantial change in this pattern.

In 1900, cloth merchants in north India were generally in command of *jari* manufacture wherever *jari* retained its market among local weaving. The artisans worked neither in a factory, nor in the bosom of their families under conventional putting-out contracts. The merchant hired a combination of teams, gave out the metal, coordinated the processes, and received the *jari*.[67] Sometimes, the coordination job was

[65] Gwynne, *Monograph on the Manufacture*, 4.
[66] United Provinces, *Industrial Survey*, Lucknow District, 25.
[67] Gwynne, *Monograph on the Manufacture*, 6.

done by specialist artisans. They are equivalent to the *karkhanadar*. But this term is rather rare in sources on northern *jari*. Their origin was seemingly in *jari* production rather than in the cloth trade, for there were among them master artisans who employed workers. In Benares, there were many such persons who coordinated production, but were not known as traders. The increasing articulation of an artisan-contractor class in the twentieth century can be inferred from two changes. First, the producers tended to become heterogeneous among themselves, both by a natural process of growth and immigration, and via uneven rates of technological change between processes. The need for coordination, in other words, increased. Secondly, contractual work developed on the input side. Wire-makers were rigidly bound to the thread-makers, though the latter were loosely contract-bound to the thread or cloth merchants. Some of the thread-makers worked on their own account, owing to the increased scale of their production.[68] In other words, the number of intermediaries increased.

Descriptions of Surat in the first half of the twentieth century are dominated by two relatively well-defined classes. The *akhadedars* were artisans usually working with household labour. The other group consisted of the merchants. Haynes describes production relations in Surat broadly in the following terms.[69] The *akhadedar*–merchant contract proceeded towards greater dependence, as the former 'bartered independent positions in the market for greater security'. Imports probably accounted for the increasing uncertainty. These relationships, though economically unequal, were based upon personal contact and acquaintance, and, thus, upon ties of clientage and affection. Similar ties could be seen at work when the *akhadedar* recruited workers from the same caste or from acquaintances. They were also visible in the strongly caste-based diffusion of technical information, and in the system of wage payments which fused wages with informal credit. A sense of ethnic solidarity not only transformed the Golas, formerly engaged in rice-pounding, into skilled manufacturers, but also gave them possession of 'a near-monopoly of the knowledge of the new techniques' in imitation *jari*.[70] Their case conforms to several others, usually from textiles, of caste-based cooperation that contributed to the diffusion of technology.

Both Surat and Benares had, or developed, wage labour and factories. The extent of wage labour and small factories partly depended on the

---

[68] India, *Report on Jari*, 6.
[69] Douglas Haynes, 'The Dynamics of Continuity in Indian Domestic Industry: *Jari* Manufacture in Surat, 1900–47', *Indian Economic and Social History Review*, 23, 2 (1986).
[70] *Ibid.*, 145–8.

stage of manufacture. Wire-drawing tended to be performed with hired labour or non-family apprentices, because the work was too strenuous to be performed by family labour. It also appears that the number of participant firms in Benares was higher than in Surat, for the conversion of the same quantity of metal and fibre into *jari*. This seemingly greater division of labour in Benares was associated with the practice of apprenticeship and scarcity of family units in Benares *jari*. Apprenticeship tended to involve specialization by task, and therefore, the de-integration of tasks.

Factories were started in both towns in the interwar period. They were induced by attempts at import-substitution. Some of these were large and integrated ventures. But most of them were started to perform only the gilding stage. Some of the gilding factories were owned by *jari* merchants. The others were enlarged versions of the artisan-owned workshop. In Surat, the size of unit, and the presence of hired labour, increased in the first stages of wire-drawing after the introduction of power.[71] It seems that most of these firms were enlarged versions of artisan workshops. One effect of selective mechanization, and labour-hiring induced by mechanization, was a sharper distinction between the manual-labour intensive, and machine-operated segments of the industry. In the 1950s, piece-wage contracts, the sign of putting-out, still prevailed in the former, but time wages prevailed in the latter.[72]

In 1945, Surat artisans were differentiated according to the stage of manufacture and the extent of the integration of stages. For an example of integration, some artisans possessed handlooms in their premises.[73] The merchants were differentiated by the extent of investment in owning workshops. For the early twentieth century, Haynes has suggested not only the increasing dependence of the ordinary artisan, but also that technical adaptations needed to be consistent with the stability of the family as a firm. The tools changed but gradually, and the investments were divisible and marginal. Equally gradual were changes in relationships. A report thirty years later suggests a more accelerated pace of change in the postwar years. There was considerable expansion of large-scale workshops. Merchants with industrial premises became more common and divisions within the *akhadedars* became more muted. Merchants usually meant 'merchant-manufacturers', who owned factories and gave out contract to *akhadedars*.[74] In the late 1970s, any

---

[71] *Ibid.*, 143–4.   [72] India, *Report on Jari*, 5.
[73] Gadgil and Patil, *Gold and Silver Thread*, 3.
[74] India, *Report on the Working Condition*, 3.

connection of *jari* artisans with handlooms was unknown. At the same time, artisan workshops in specific processes also expanded. There was investment in fixed capital by merchants, richer artisan families, and even by factory labourers who set up their own workshops. It is not clear where the labourers came from. Since neither migration nor interoccupational shifts are mentioned in these sources, it can be inferred that the workers had the same origin as the majority of the capitalists, namely, those of erstwhile *akhadedar* status.

The tendency for labourers to start workshops in Surat suggests a relative ease of mobility. The possibility meant that, in times of depressed demand, some workers tried to take over marginally viable units, typically leasing them from their owners. Such progressions are rare in other craft towns, and are possible only under much easier market for informal credit. There are indeed signs of the existence of a smooth credit market in this town. For example, time wage payments in Surat involved a credit element. Wages were based on *annual* contracts. The employers agreed to keep a part of the dues to their workers as a deposit, whereas, in times of distress, workers could borrow from the employers almost as an entitlement. The workers drew upon this fund from time to time, and were permitted overdrafts. Leaving the contract was conditional on the prospective employer clearing off the previous account. The system had its hazards, but the hazards arose from the imbalances of demand and supply of skilled labour, not from an inherent tendency to fraud.[75] Here was a credit market at work, but not credit for production, only credit as a means of smoothing consumption flows. This institution will reappear in chapter 7 on carpets, where it was known as *baqi*. A more relevant feature of the Surat informal credit market was the presence of silver dealers as a source of finance. Unsecured trade credit was given routinely, as anywhere else. But probably in Surat alone, unsecured capital loans were given too. For artisans to begin trade or to expand production, therefore, was stated to be 'very easy'. The credit market was competitive, and information on personal solvency easily available, two conditions that facilitated the functioning of the market. Easy finance characterized not only dealings between the silver trader and the artisan aspiring to be a merchant, but also those between the merchant-manufacturer and the labourer who wished to invest in a workshop. 'The more skilled and prudent of the labourers can without much difficulty put themselves up as artisans', for the cost of one or two machines could easily be raised from the market.[76]

---

[75] Gadgil and Patil, *Gold and Silver Thread*, 6.   [76] *Ibid.*

The extension of wage labour led to a general rise in disputes in Surat in the postwar period. During a trade depression of 1951–3, widespread wage cuts generated a demand for the stricter implementation of certain basic clauses of the Factories Act, especially those on fixation of contract wage, regularization of hours, bonuses and weekly holidays. The strains were unfolding for a decade, and were mentioned by the 1945 Tariff Board report. But the outburst took ten more years. The small employers, typically of artisan background, resisted the implementation of labour laws on the ground that *jari* was a 'cottage industry' performed in the residence of the employers, and that the capacity to pay varied greatly between employers. The Tariff Board, on the other hand, observed that some of them did employ 'a large number of hired workers and earn[ed] large profits', and recommended a phased introduction of the Act.[77] An industrial tribunal, probably the first of its kind in a craft in transition, acted decisively in favour of the workers, but could not push the reform.[78]

Conclusion

The fact that *jari* was an input, and not a differentiated finished good like cloth, explains its vulnerability to competition from machinery. European thread destroyed *jari* manufacture in a large number of textile towns roughly between the 1880s and the 1920s. But, towards the end of this period, the two main sites of the industry were stable, able to compete with imports, and at least one possessed a powerful lobby to raise and push through the demand for protection. In the history of import-substitution, we can trace two roads. Surat produced for non-local markets, and developed the capability to produce cheaper raw material of good quality. Benares was primarily an artisan town, which produced mainly for its own weavers, and which remained loyal to real *jari* much longer.

The emergence of factories, merchant-manufacturers, and the extension of wage employment were some of the effects of import-substitution and relocation. A few of the factories were large integrated units set up with European machinery and manpower. But the majority of the factories were small in size, and bunched in certain processes where the skill difference between European and Indian *jari* manufacture was the widest, such as gilding. The factories did not either replace or swamp the family firm working on contract. But they were a twentieth-century

[77] India, *Report of the Indian Tariff Board . . . on Silver Thread and Wire*, 9.
[78] Gadgil and Patil, *Gold and Silver Thread*, 62–5.

development, noticeably widespread, and represented the dominant trend in the industry.

If transitions in handloom cloth and *jari* were both driven by imports, in a number of products a similar change was produced by a different means, namely, the integration of the home market. The next chapter studies one such industry, the manufacture of brassware.

5 Brassware

Metal craftsmen in India can be divided into two broad classes: the iron workers mainly engaged in the manufacture and servicing of tools; and the brass, bronze, and copper workers producing utensils. The second group forms the subject of this chapter. It produced a consumer good like cloth; and, not unlike cloth, the product was highly diversified, ranging from the utilitarian to objects of display. The specific skills involved did not face serious threat from mechanized processes. Also, the product being bulky, transport costs would not have justified imports. The dominant source of change in this craft, therefore, was a commercialization that involved locally produced wares. Pursuing this theme, this chapter describes sharper intra-craft competition, consequent pressures to raise productivity and quality, institutional and technological changes as a result of the latter, and, finally, the part that subtle conflicts between utility and craftsmanship played in these adaptation processes.

The first section deals with general developments of the brassware market. The next two sections outline the constraints that these very developments imposed on the artisans, the second dealing with the utilitarian, and the third with that branch of the industry intensive in craftsmanship. The fourth section describes institutional and technological changes, partly in consequence of these tendencies in demand, and partly in consequence of broader developments in location and input markets.

Consumption

The most important metals used in India for consumption were brass (copper and zinc), bronze (copper and tin), and copper. Older descriptions refer to a greater variety of metals, but these were usually minor variations in the alloy, and were standardized over time. The metals were subjected to two basic processes: forging and casting, the products of which could be quite different. In general, forging on sheet metal

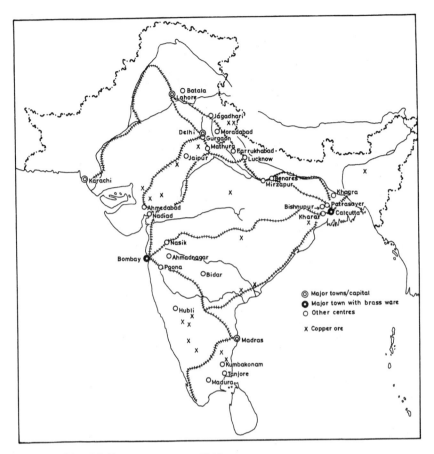

Map 5.1 Brassware centres, *c*.1940

tended to serve the utilitarian end of the market, whereas casting could
not only render a diversified range of goods, but also produce vessels
that could be decorated on the outside. The decorative skills varied, but
can be reduced to two broad types: brightening the surface by polishing
or plating, and designing the exterior. Designs were effected by hand:
engraving on the surface, engraving on a layer of tin fixed to the exterior,
or, more rarely, *repoussé*. Usually, the engravings were coloured by
lacquer, and the specific combinations between the colours of the lines
and that of the surface distinguished towns such as Bidar and Moradabad. Major centres of manufacture possessed both hammerers and
engravers, but a few were especially well known for their decorative
work.

The assortment of metals and design techniques in different manufacturing regions varied due to, among other reasons, the specific preferences of communities. Hindus appeared to prefer alloys. Cast iron was both awkward and impure to eat from, copper too sacred, and bronze, a metal seemingly not so popular in south Asia, was considered inferior. Bronze did circulate, but on a smaller scale than brass, its production was more ruralized, and it is not known to have been used extensively for effecting designs. The Muslims, on the other hand, had a weakness for copper, but only after plating both the interior and the exterior. The layer applied outside rendered itself to ornamentation. Thus, it was in towns with large and prosperous Muslim settlements that the brazier's art tended to unite with that of the engraver.

General utensil manufacture was not constrained to locate near natural raw material sources, for, in large part, the raw material used was scrap, and not ores. Copper deposits in India occur in the southern Andhra coast, Rajputana, Punjab, along the Himalayas, and Chotanagpur. It is an interesting speculation that the further back one goes, and the rarer scrap becomes, the more the industry might be seen to retreat to these areas. Remnants of this layer of manufacture, that evolved from ore smelting and had visible tribalist roots both in technologies and the artifact turned out, are still found in little hamlets scattered over some of these areas.[1]

The dependence on scrap did not make the industry wholly urban, but nor was brassware nearly as diffused or rural as textiles or leather. In general, the industry occurred in small towns and clusters of villages close to major consuming points. A list of such locations appears in the detailed accounts of the crafts prepared in the last quarter of the nineteenth century.[2] An important function in this scheme belonged to the peddlers who trudged the surrounding countryside exchanging, 'like the lamp-seller in Aladdin's story', new vessels for old. The poorer and more rural the region, the wider the distance covered, longer the periods of credit, and the riskier the business. And, where the brazier was himself the hawker, as in certain parts of the Deccan, his travels added to the costs of production. These costs, real or monetary, would have

---

[1] For an example of survival, see India, *Report on Cast Metal Industry in Dariapur*, All India Handicrafts Board (New Delhi, 1964). See also the monograph by Meera Mukherjee, *Metalcraftsmen in India*, Anthropological Survey of India (Calcutta, 1978). The connection of brassware with smelting, which dissolved later on, is indicated in the following: 'in the hilly districts of western Bengal, metal artisans, or at least certain sections of them, seem to have gradually evolved out of the aboriginal . . . iron-smelters.' T. N. Mukharji, *A Monograph on the Brass, Bronze and Copper Manufactures of Bengal* (Calcutta, 1903), 4.

[2] For example, G. C. Birdwood, *The Industrial Arts of India*, Part II (London, 1887); and T. N. Mukharji, *Arts and Manufactures of India* (Calcutta, 1888).

been greater than, say, what the weaver-hawker had to bear, the finished good in brass being much bulkier. It is for these reasons that concentration in towns was a strong tendency in brass.

Only a few of the places appearing in the early craft monographs reappear in the middle of the twentieth century, whereas most of these towns grew considerably in the meantime. One reason for the increased concentration was a change in raw material. Foreign trade did not expose brassware to any significant competition, but it did substitute scrap by imported sheets wherever possible. Evidence of the direct cost saving involved is not available, except perhaps through a minor reference in Hoey's profit calculations for Lucknow artisans.[3] But it is plausible that the gain was large. Brass sheets eliminated the need to melt the scrap in crude furnaces. Copper needing a high temperature to melt, rendered itself to economies of scale which had been absent. Moreover, sheets standardized the composition and quality of the metal, needed for the mass production of utensils.[4]

The other major change in recent times concerns the market for brasswares. Accounts of the industry in the first decade of the century or earlier suggest that brass entered a market which had probably grown since the advent of the railways. In the interwar period, the optimism was replaced by greater caution, but there was no depression in evidence for many decades to come. There were indeed several reasons to believe in expanding demand for brasswares.

First, metals replaced earthenware wherever possible. Durability would have been an attraction for metals, but perhaps not the only one. In fact, the Hindus' dislike for being served on a used vessel in a mixed company had always made the easy replaceability of earthenware attractive as well. What possibly turned the balance was, a relaxation of prejudices apart, cheaper transportation, and the resultant growth in the internal trade and integration of markets. Apart from some indeterminate reduction in costs, trade would have increased the choice for consumers. In this process, metals commanded an advantage over earthenware, being the more transportable of the two.

Indeed, the increased scale and variety of metals at the end of the century was attributed to a general tendency for consumption to

---

[3] William Hoey, *A Monograph on Trade and Manufactures in Northern India* (Lucknow, 1880).

[4] Interestingly, there were episodes in the late nineteenth century, when imported metal had become scarce, of defunct copper coins being unearthed from hoards to be melted. This happened in south India with Negapatnam coins, used in art-metal of Tanjore and Madura. The archaeologist's loss was the art historian's gain. See Edwin Holder, 'Brass and Copper Ware of the Madras Presidency', *Journal of Indian Art (and Industry)*, 6, 46–53 (1896), 83.

diversify. The latter, in turn, was believed to reflect, in cities like Calcutta, an 'increase in wealth and love of luxury'. In rural areas that exported cash crops, it was attributed to a prosperity that induced some classes of farmers to possess more utensils than they did formerly, and make gifts of a larger assortment of such articles in marriages.[5]

Diversified consumption was, at least partly, an effect of imports. The greater variety of consumer goods and especially the lighter durables the Europeans brought to India for their own use, not only altered the tastes of the relatively affluent and urbanite Indians, but also, almost immediately, were copied by the artisans engaged in comparable work. The copies were sometimes of equivalent quality, and almost always much cheaper. Examples of the newly acquired tastes that could be locally met would include certain kinds of footwear and hollow glassware, numerous cast metal goods such as lamps, scissors, or locks, and printed textiles.[6] Imports, in other words, induced import-substitution by artisans, and at times the artisans were successful. This is rather an important process which historians have taken little note of.

That is not all. Half a century of railways, of safer passage through forest roads, and the elimination of road-taxes that, in the times of the Mughals and the Marathas, tended to proliferate around the holy cities, had increased traffic to and from the latter. Many of these were well known for brasswares. 'Every pilgrim who comes to Benares generally purchases at least one brass *lota* . . . as a souvenir of his visit to this sacred city.'[7] This *lota*, in which Ganges water was carried away, is as popular today, and has not been replaced by steel.[8] The same could be said of a part of Nasik's output, of the idols made in Kumbakonam and Swamimalai, and of Mathura's images 'eagerly bought by Hindus as household gods'.

The articles the temple towns specialized in involved specific skills that justified their use as treasured mementos and objects of display or

[5] Central Provinces and Berar, *Report of the Industrial Survey of the Central Provinces and Berar* (Nagpur, 1908–9), 82; and Mukharji, *Monograph*, 12–13, 15. If prosperity increased the use of metals, famines did the reverse. The 1901 census attributed a decline in brass and the increased use of earthenware to the 1896 famine, Census of India, 1901, *Bombay*, vol. IX, Part I, (Report) (Bombay, 1902).

[6] Including 'a general growth in smoking habit' in and around the major cities. However, 'at the end of the decade [1920s] came the boycott of imported cigarettes and the *Beedi* came into its own'. Census of India, 1931, *India*, vol. I, Part I (Report) (Delhi, 1933), 2.

[7] United Provinces, *Industrial Survey of the United Provinces* (Allahabad, 1922–4), Benares district, 23.

[8] When pilgrim inflow into Benares was smaller, in the eighteenth century, the *lota* itself travelled out. Alexander Hamilton wrote: 'Priests fill Brass and Copper Pots, made in the shape of short-necked Bottles, with *Ganges's* Water, which they consecrate and seal up, and send these bottles, which contain about 4 *English* Gallons, all over *India*, to their Benefactors.' *A New Account of the East Indies* (London, 1739), 23.

of religious significance. These skills, consisting in the quality of polishing, casting, and the engraving, lacquer, or damascening on the outside, also occurred in a few other artisan settlements, most notably Moradabad, Jaipur, and Bidar. A general growth in trade brought these objects to the notice of the European residents, initiating an export market that was promising in the interwar period, and pivotal since independence. An article in the first issue of the *Journal of Indian Art* (1886) was probably the earliest to refer to a growing interest among European residents in decorated metals.[9] But, in the 1880s, this consumption was kept in check by the average English officer's 'nomadic habits'. Metals after all were the least portable of objects. As sedentary occupations expanded, the demand would have increased too. Thus, another article published twenty years later wrote about a 'craze among Europeans' for engraved wares. In 1920–3, an American firm began to engrave thermos flask covers in Moradabad. The town 'extended its foreign market considerably as a result of the publicity it was given at the Wembley Exhibition'. By the 1940s, close to 80 per cent of the town's output in value went abroad.[10] The foreign market, and specifically American interest in Jaipur's and Bidar's work, flourished from the Second World War, but a sporadic traffic had begun much earlier. Mathura's images, cherished by Hindus as household gods, were equally cherished by Europeans as paperweights.[11]

Did artisan population and employment reflect this growth of trade? Employment over the long period of nearly a century seemed to remain surprisingly stable. Census 'actual workers' in brass and bronze expanded, from about 125,000 in 1891 to 145,000 in 1901, declined in 1921 to 106,000,[12] was 120,000 in 1931, and thereafter, for three decades, it remained stationary at a little over 100,000. The censuses of 1971 and 1981 club these activities under 'metal products', but the overall employment figure shows no significant change. There can be only two possible explanations of this long stability consistent with our hypothesis that the market for brass did expand. First, productivity

---

[9] J. L. Kipling, 'Brass and Copper Ware of the Punjab and Kashmir', *Journal of Indian Art (and Industry)*, 1, 1 (1886), 6.

[10] The exhibition referred to is probably the British Empire Exhibition, 1924. United Provinces, *Industrial Survey, Moradabad District*, 21; Census of India, 1931, *United Provinces of Agra and Oudh*, vol. XVIII, Part I, (Report) (Allahabad, 1931).

[11] G. D. Ganguli, 'The Art Industries of the United Provinces', *Report of the First Indian Industrial Conference (Benares, 1905)* (Allahabad, 1906), 346. On the beginning of European interest in decorated brass, and the hunt for the *purana chiz* in brass and copper in the Indian bazaars, see the reminiscent piece by J. H. Rivett-Carnac, 'Specimens of Indian Metal-Work', *Journal of Indian Art (and Industry)*, 9, 70 (1902).

[12] Part of the decline can be accounted for by a general decline in employment, probably an after-effect of the influenza epidemic, and by raw material shortages during the war.

improved. And, secondly, the very growth of the market, and the appearance of new markets, created certain problems for the artisans.

In fact, the aggregate employment statistics itself provides an indirect confirmation of the former. Interestingly, an unusually large component of brassware employment (50 per cent) in the 1961 census was 'non-household', that is, wage labour. Already in 1921, the Industrial Census had shown that 13–14 per cent of actual workers were employees in the 300 or so brassware factories, 260 of which did not use mechanical power. This is consistent with a trend towards concentration in a number of other crafts, but the proportions are higher in brass. The proportion of non-household workers in 1961 was above average in all the major states, except Madras. It also appears, but cannot be conclusively tested without adjusting for provincial borders, that, between 1931 and 1961, brassware employment expanded in the major provinces: Maharashtra-Gujarat, Bengal, Uttar Pradesh, and Tamil Nadu, and declined elsewhere. But relative growth was smaller in the east, and employment sharply declined in the Punjab, the eastern districts of which used to be a major brass producer.

At the same time, the very process of growth also carried within itself constraints, by creating need for adaptations which not everyone could meet with success. These challenges differed somewhat depending on whether the product was utilitarian or decorative, but, in both, they showed up through heightened competition within the craft.

Sites of production

If a part of brassware growth came about through the substitution of earthenware, then a levelling-off is expected, brass being more durable. Moreover, the space vacated was potentially available to more recent alternatives like china, aluminium, enamelled iron, and, decades later, steel. None posed an immediate or vital threat to brass, but they did exist, and were being tried out.[13] To a limited extent aluminium replaced copper vessels, as copper prices rose in the prewar decade. Substitutions were also reported in heavy and large vessels by galvanized iron, in fashionable articles by porcelain, and in articles consumed in poorer households by enamelled iron. But aluminium was not as versatile as brass, and the affluent Hindu's inclination for country-made earthenware in certain contexts was exactly matched by a 'great dislike'

---

[13] As early as 1872, B. H. Baden-Powell wrote of Punjab, that 'glass and crockery are coming more and more into use, even among those [Indians] who do not ape foreign manners at all', *Handbook of the Economic Products of the Punjab*, vol. II (Lahore, 1872), 141.

for imported porcelain.[14] Thus, the threat from other metals was real, but substitution happened slowly, and was absent in ornamental work.

The dominant source of change in those twentieth-century crafts that did not compete with foreign goods was 'an industrial contest within'.[15] Brassware was no exception. With easier communication and trade, larger towns able to utilize economies of scale, effect quality control, and establish brand images expanded the reach of their wares. Simultaneously, small colonies of artisans were as a rule vulnerable. This tendency characterized both the utilitarian and the ornamental branches of the work, but the nature of the constraint and the forms of adaptation differed.

In utility wares, the collapse of the small-town manufactures is reflected most clearly in the experience of Bombay and Bengal. There are parallels from other regions as well. In the Bombay–Deccan, the main brassware towns in the 1880s were Nasik, Poona, Ahmadnagar, and Hubli. 'By 1884, the introduction of railways had greatly helped the brass and copper industry . . . as it cheapened the cost of transport' of both inputs from Bombay city, and of finished goods to a wider range of destinations.[16] In relatively plainer work, the benefits of cheaper transportation should vary positively with the weight-to-price ratio. The metals' gains from the railways, therefore, were relatively greater than, say, that of cloth. But as part of the same movement, the next two or three decades witnessed a gradual shift of trade and manufacture first from Ahmadnagar to Hubli, Nasik, and Poona, and then from Nasik to Poona. By 1910, there was also a spatial relocation of trade. Poona supplied all of Deccan's demand. Nasik supplied the local demand from pilgrims, and markets in Hyderabad. Some of the smaller centres appeared to be moving into bronze, whose demand was usually rural. The growth of Poona is reflected in the diversity of the products. In the 1880s, 132 types of utensils and other goods were produced in Poona for uses ranging from storage to rituals, and from jewellery to musical instruments.

About 1900, Bombay was a large town of brass manufacture, with 4,000 workers. Most of the workers were recent immigrants.[17] Braziers

---

[14] For examples of these preferences, see A. C. Chatterjee, *Notes on the Industries of the United Provinces* (Allahabad, 1908), 117; P. G. Shah, 'The Copper and Brass Industries in India', *Report of the Eighth Indian Industrial Conference, Bankipore, 1912* (Amraoti, 1913), 22, 56; and Bengal, *Report on the Survey of Cottage Industries of Bengal*, second edition (Calcutta, 1929), 35.

[15] Census of India, 1901, *Bombay*.

[16] N. M. Joshi, *Urban Handicrafts of Bombay Deccan*, Gokhale Institute of Politics and Economics (Poona, 1936), 56.

[17] Shah, 'The Copper and Brass Industries', 28.

might well have been as mobile as the other skilled artisans, but, brass being a smaller craft than, say, leather or textiles, little is known about these migrations. In the interwar period, cheaper Bombay products destroyed much of Gujarat's brasswares, which relocated into Nadiad and Ahmedabad, both producing ornamental ware.[18] In the more rural industry of the Central Provinces, 'concentration in certain places' was attributed to cheap transport, and to 'decay of the village commercial system and specialization of manufacture'.[19]

The fragility and high costs of the 'village commercial system' were probably the reasons for concentration in Bengal as well. A comparison of two reports twenty years apart (Mukharji's of 1903, and the Industry Department's in 1924) shows the extent. Of the ten brass locations in the Presidency division listed in the former, three reappear, and two are added to these, both in the suburbs of Calcutta. In the Burdwan division, of the thirty-four centres of manufacture, only nine reappear. These include the three major rural clusters that subsequently supplied much of the province's consumption: Khagra in central Bengal, Kharar in Midnapore, and Bishnupur-Patrasayer in Bankura. The other major survival, in the Jalpaiguri division, was the Nawabganj group of villages. But, while many locations disappear, Calcutta's industry, concentrated in Kansaripara in the north of the town, expanded.[20] And a notable metal town, Kanchannagar near Burdwan, gave up brass to specialize in cast-iron tools.

The Bengal trading system was especially reliant on travelling vendors. The *beparies* and the *paikars* represent a proliferation of inter-mediaries rather unique to the region. The risk they bore being high, 'they . . . are compelled to make much profit'.[21] Any option that could substitute these intermediate networks would mean an advantage for the producers and the consumers. Relocation did just that. But there is possibly another reason for the relocation: a partial destruction of the craft. Bengal brassware was generally plainer work, more often forged than cast. Hammered vessels were of a limited range, purely utilitarian, and were vulnerable to the available alternatives since here the quality of the metal mattered relatively more. In other regions, when the simpler kinds of manufacture moved, they moved towards towns with a reputa-tion in technology, which generally implied the presence of a well-developed cast metal industry. Eastern India, with a few exceptions, did

---

[18] *Ibid.*, 53; and A. B. Trivedi, *Post-War Gujarat* (Bombay, 1949), 165.

[19] Central Provinces and Berar, *Report of the Industrial Survey*, 82.

[20] 'Of late years the manufacture of many new articles in brass has commenced in and around Calcutta to meet the new wants created . . . among the people.' Mukharji, *A Monograph*, 12–13.

[21] Bengal, *Report on the Survey*, 83.

not seem to have one. Where it did, the methods used were evidently crude.[22]

In Punjab, 'ever since the Annexation the scattered forges and bhattis of village brass and coppersmiths have been gradually disappearing'.[23] Kipling wrote in the 1880s:

The popular notion is that there are braziers and coppersmiths in every town of any importance, but a slow change is taking place in this respect. Thus in a town where there are . . . representatives of the usual number of other trades, the writer was informed their only thathera had left, and their wares imported from other places . . . On the other hand, the middleman pushes trade to a greater extent.[24]

The industry relocated itself in towns of which three flourished in generalized metalwork later: Jagadhari, Batala, and Gurgaon. The Punjab industry also partially succumbed to better finished United Provinces ware. In United Provinces itself, a comparison of Ganguli's ('Art and Industries') list in 1905 and those prepared in the interwar period would show a disappearance of some of the metalworker colonies, especially in copper and bronze. Simultaneously, the surviving towns seemed to extend the reach of their wares. Farrukhabad captured the market in the hills and the Punjab; Mirzapur sent 'enormous quantities of utensils all the way to Gorakhpur and Basti' in the eastern districts; and Moradabad's market was already reaching beyond India. The town also contracted to engrave and polish wares made in such distant towns as Poona.[25]

Moradabad deserves a more detailed description. Brassware in this town was an old industry, but the pre-seventeenth-century history is undistinguished. Its later growth came through a combination of brass casting initially for firearms, engraving on coins, and an attempt to reproduce a zinc *hukka* made in Bidar. Groups of artisan families, courtiers at Delhi, and their patrons are credited with the development of these skills here. In the eighteenth century, Moradabad traded with, and probably received engraving designs from, Persia, Turkey, and Egypt. However, the most spectacular period of growth began in the late nineteenth century as, within a few decades, two crucial railways intersected here, the East Indian towards Calcutta and Aligarh, and the

---

[22] For example, in our period, moulds were generally of wax in Bengal, but of wood in Moradabad. The use of wooden models in castings implied mass production and a greater division of labour, for a specialized branch of carpenters did this work.

[23] Shah, 'Copper and Brass Industries', 57.

[24] Kipling, 'Brass and Copper Ware of the Punjab and Kashmir', 6.

[25] United Province, *Industrial Survey*, Mirzapur District, 12. Some of this trade still went in carts, the railways being unpopular as they 'ruthlessly knocked about' the vessels. See also *ibid.*, Farrukhabad and Moradabad.

Avadh–Tirhut with an access to the hills. With the railways came not only easier transport, but also godowns and storage space. For a bulk-intensive industry this was important. An essay in the 1885 issue of the *Journal of Indian Art* mentioned that lacquerware in the town saw 'great strides during the last few years', resulting in expansion and diversification into 'an infinite variety of articles both for ornaments and for utility'. This was an effect of a widening long-distance trade. In 1945, railway returns show that Moradabad wares went to 266 towns, no one destination being dominant, spread all over the north from Karachi to Calcutta. In 1924, the town had 7–8,000 full-time brassworkers, in 1945 and 1960 about 10,000, and in the late 1970s, 13,500. From the middle of the century, Moradabad was by far the largest concentration in the country. Productivity, measured by rough weight-to-worker ratios, increased dramatically,[26] the number and average scale of factories increased, ancillaries developed,[27] average earnings in Moradabad were higher than in the other brassware towns, wage spread within the town increased,[28] and the nature of the market and technologies changed. The last development will be seen in more detail below.

There are several reasons why urbanization might have led to the shedding of labour without significant changes in output. First, it would have streamlined the marketing systems by making a large body of peddlers redundant. Secondly, it utilized an already existing more advanced division of labour in the towns. Thirdly, as a consequence of the last, it would have provided the artisans with greater choices on diversification, and, hence, on the manner of raising productivity. And, fourthly, as we shall see below, it concentrated capital and, conse-

[26] For 1924, United Provinces, *Industrial Survey* furnishes the value of output, the number of workers and the cost of brass sheets. For 1945, workers and weight are available from V. P. Chaturvedi, *Moradabad mein Pital ke Bartanon ka Gharelu Udyog wa Vyavasaya* [The Cottage Industry and Trade in Moradabad Brassware] (Allahabad, 1950). This yields a per worker weight of raw metal used that increased about 2.9 times in twenty years. If this appears to be an overestimate, the possible reasons could be the following. Chaturvedi's figures consist of scrap imported into the city, as recorded in the dealer accounts, and of the number of workers. Relative to conventional figures, Chaturvedi scaled up scrap, and scaled down workers. Scrap was only partly imported by the railways, so there was a guess involved. But, even in the most conservative case, there would remain a large increase in per worker output.

[27] In 1924, there were 300 factories of eight to ten workers each. In the late 1970s, there were 2,136 factories, of which 273 were registered under the Factories Act, with about nineteen workers each.

[28] For this comparison, the engravers who were the most skilled workers and usually worked at home or in jointly rented sheds, are treated as the equivalent of the smaller factory owners. Combining various sources, wage comparisons, on average or by kind of artisan, are possible between United Provinces brass towns in 1907 and in the 1920s; between the Deccan and Moradabad in the 1950s; and between Bengal and United Provinces in the first decade of the century.

quently, created a tendency to mechanize processes. This tendency seems to gather force from the end of the interwar period.

Quality of production

Integrated markets and competition within the industry exposed an inherent weakness of craftsmanship. To understand this, we first have to examine more closely the products made in the towns known for their ornamental work.

Between the purely utilitarian domestic utensils, sometimes of graceful and imaginative shapes but rarely decorated or well finished, and the purely 'ornamental' idols or richly worked trays, jugs, flagons, hukkas, candlesticks, spice and cosmetic boxes, and vases catering to the nobility, lay a wide and undefined range of articles combining utility and aesthetics in various degrees. This space was not a characteristic of metals alone, but of numerous Indian crafts. Here existed the potential for entirely new products serving the urbanite, the middle class, the European residents, and exports. Each one was a mass market for skills that could not be reproduced in machinery. Bearing similarity with textiles, in metals too this dynamic space began to accommodate enterprising artisans moving into it from both ends. There was enough room here for a whole range of skills, from the relatively simple to the more complex. At its upper end were arabesque engravings on goods meant for the reasonably wealthy, and at the other was the 'growing popularity of tinned wares among the poor'. Tin-plating copper was quite a concentrated industry, and an early source of Moradabad's fame.

Traces of this movement are clearly seen in nearly every town known for ornamental work. Benares, commonly identified with idols and ritualist paraphernalia, had, in 1912, a considerable trade in paper knives, salvers, and jardinieres 'which look rather unnatural by the strange mixture of eastern art and western patterns'.[29] Jaipur was fortunate in having the only school of art with brassware courses, and a zealously patronizing State, enabling the craftsmen easily to fuse their designs with a range of unconventional goods. The 'utilitarian spirit of the times' showed itself in the increased output of household goods in place of sword-hilts, plates, etc. Engraving skills also extended to architectural uses.[30] Of the numerous temple towns in the south with colonies of brazier producing ornamental work, the most magnificent

---

[29] Shah, 'Copper and Brass Industries', 42.
[30] *The Imperial Gazetteer of India*, The Indian Empire, vol. III (Economic) (Oxford, 1907), 238; and Shah, 'Copper and Brass Industries', 54.

example of which were colossal many-branched lamps, Tanjore and Madura were among the few survivors. Both towns used their engraving skills to produce a kind of silver-inlayed copper which had a growing market.[31] Bidar, known for designs inlaid on a surface polished black, modernized designs, and found cheaper ways of creating the effect on products like cigarette cases, knives, and bowls.[32] Diversifications in Moradabad are more difficult to generalize about, the product composition being more complex here. The range of Moradabad's output in the twentieth century was enormous, and every description of the industry mentions some forms of experiment. These involved processes by which decorations were effected, standardized, made more durable, or, sometimes, consciously degraded to accommodate rising raw material costs. Moradabad, with common ancestry in engraving craftsmanship with Jaipur and Bidar, departed from both styles in the twentieth century, one component of the change being superior lacquering. The other probable component, evident from the average prices of the goods made, was a larger output of cheaper wares.[33]

The 'utilitarian spirit' afflicting ornamental brassware generated a crisis universal in decorative crafts experimenting with new products or new designs. The increased 'pressure of work' on the artisans, the 'lack of true and correct appreciation of Indian artistic ware' from the new consumers, and 'the interference in direct art education of the people' as demand for novelties built up, combined to degrade quality. In 1907, Chatterjee wrote: 'the artistic work of both Benares and Moradabad has considerably deteriorated of late years.' Bad shapes, inartistic designs, crowded work, lack of finish, desire for cheapness were all symptoms of the affliction. 'The brass figures and images are very inferior in conception and execution to the similar wares of Jaipur', and the engraving 'does not compare favourably with the minute finish of the brass engraving of Madura.'[34] Jaipur, in turn, was faulted for 'an abundance of colours in questionable taste'.[35] Following the development of exports, 'mass production methods' were again blamed for a deterioration in

[31] Shah, 'Copper and Brass Industries', 47. For a more recent description of Tanjore products, see Census of India, 1961, *Art Metal Wares of Tanjavur*, vol. IX, Part VII-A, No. iii (Delhi, 1964).

[32] S. S. Mensinkai, *A Survey of Handicrafts in Eight Districts of the Mysore State*, Karnatak University (Dharwar, 1961), 10.

[33] Engraved cutlery is one example: *Imperial Gazetteer*, 238; in hammered ware, there was a constant change of product: Chaturvedi, *The Cottage Industry*, 23; firms switching from tin-plating to nickel or silver were also 'taking up new lines of manufacture': United Provinces, *Report of the Director of Industries* (Allahabad, 1922–3), 19.

[34] Chatterjee, *Notes on the Industries*, 123–4.

[35] *Imperial Gazetteer*, 238.

quality.[36] The same tendency was alleged in Benares.[37] Of central Indian decorated ware, Ganguli wrote: 'the production of grotesque images in brass which the artisans now indulge in cannot be too severely condemned.'[38] During the Second World War, Moradabad attained a certain notoriety for trying to replace tin by lead in processes where such substitutions affected quality.

It is of a certain interest that art brassware received little or no government assistance, which, in textiles or dyeing, had at least a role in creating awareness of the crisis, and, occasionally, in the diffusion of information. The Lucknow School of Arts and Crafts, started in 1911, was the only institution with a course in metalware designs, but, until 1919, it was utilized by the offspring of goldsmiths.[39]

It would perhaps be valid to conjecture that the crisis in quality was partly perceived, and not real, as art brassware of different places came to compete in the same market, and hence were more closely compared. The artisans would have realized that survival in this market depended on emphatic product differentiation, and the creation of brand images. But when frantic experiments were going on everywhere, survival would also require standardization and quality control. This point was highlighted in, for example, L. C. Jain's informative note on Moradabad submitted to the Banking Enquiry Commission of 1929–30, and exemplified in the role of one dealer whose firm initiated and dominated the export trade by dint of reputation for quality.[40]

To the extent there was a real crisis, how did the artisans respond? Since complaints on quality become rarer in post-1950 sources, there must have been attempts at quality enforcement. Further, the craft tended to concentrate in fewer towns, and perhaps in fewer hands. Establishing brand image was easier when one ware was uniquely identifiable with one town, and this fact might well be a reason for the concentration. Some of the numerous instances of trade and production relocating towards the better known towns explicitly involve quality differences in similar work.[41] At the same time, consumers became better informed and more discriminating about what they bought. But,

[36] Census of India, 1931, *United Provinces*, 425.
[37] United Provinces, *Industrial Survey*, Benares District, 24.
[38] G. D. Ganguli cited in Central Provinces, *Industrial Survey*, 85; also, 'with no better guide to regulate their skill other than the fancy of their numerous customers, the brass workers of the present day have adopted models, which in point of elegance and purity of design, can hardly bear comparison with the art product of former years': Ganguli, 'The Art Industries', 347.
[39] *Indian Industrial Commission*, Evidence, vol. I, United Provinces, 194.
[40] Mohammad Yaar Khan: see Chaturvedi, *The Cottage Industry*, 56.
[41] On the decline of the industry in Lucknow with the rise of Moradabad, see A. Bhattacharya, 'A Survey of the Small Urban Industries of Lucknow', in United

it is probable that, in spite of these adaptations, a part of the export market was lost to East Asia.

As part of these adaptations, new institutions developed to enforce quality control. In textiles, the latter took two forms: mass production whether under putting-out or factories, and where possible, revival of caste-associations and other forms of collective. In brassware, an increased scale of production did take place, but the role that product-quality played in it remains inferential.

Producers

The general tendency in north Indian metalwork is described adequately in this citation from Dampier of the 1890s:

in the small towns and villages the industry has barely emerged from the state where the handicraftsman is workman, master, producer, and retailer all in one. In Benares, Aligarh, Moradabad, Agra, and other important cities, differentiation of labour has taken place . . . to such a point that each separate process is allowed to claim the undivided attention of a separate workman.

The increased division of labour usually meant an increase in the average scale of town workshops:

These large factories will employ up to twenty or more men and be owned by some rich capitalist Banya or Kasera, who supplies his employés with loans, etc.[42]

Most north Indian sites of brassware in the early twentieth century were characterized by a three-tier exchange of products and labour, the 'classes' engaged being termed dealers, *karkhanadars*, and workers. Chatterjee's description in 1907 of the usual practice in United Provinces had the dealer obtaining scrap from the peddlers, and the 'headman' of a brass factory turning it into wares for a charge.[43] Between one place and another, the dealer could be more or less specialized, and more or less distinct from the *karkhanadars*. Similarly, systems of work and payment at the shopfloor could differ as well. But, in general, work was bound almost everywhere by a contract between a merchant and a sort of headman of the workers. A *karkhanadar* was not necessarily an actual workshop owner. But he was invariably an artisan

---

Provinces, *United Provinces Provincial Banking Enquiry Committee*, vol. II (Allahabad, 1930), 404–5.

[42] G. R. Dampier, *A Monograph on the Brass and Copper Wares of the North-Western Provinces and Oudh* (Allahabad, 1894), 11. D. C. Johnstone, *Monograph on Brass and Copper Ware in the Punjab, 1886–87* (Lahore, 1888), 7, presents a similar picture of urban division of labour.

[43] Chatterjee, *Notes on Industries*, 118–19.

intermediary. At times, he was an employer of labour, or a workshop owner, or a master (*ustad*) or head of a team, or a combination of these.

The uniformity with which the three-tier exchange and the *karkhana* appear in early descriptions of brasswares derives partly from the greater north Indian *karkhanadari* tradition (see also chapters 2 and 7), and partly from a technological reason. Before the imports of brass sheets, and in cast-metal work even after imports started, the main capital needed in the work was a furnace which required, at a time, three to five workers to operate and fully utilize. The entire requirement of labour could not come from the family, since female labour was not usually employed in metals. A well-developed apprenticeship helped recruit unpaid assistants, sometimes from the extended family. But the craft still required non-family labour, to a much greater extent than, say, textiles.

This component of labour was paid, but interestingly, the further back one goes, there appears a strong element of *sharing* the value added, which characterized even the largest of the brassware towns. Forms of cooperative work in the crafts were frequently based on caste,[44] but material on brass and coppersmith castes in recent times is too scant to investigate this point. The contrast between a craft such as brass, and weaving which tended to utilize domestic labour heavily, is conspicuous, and extends to their long-term dynamics. In our period, both crafts witnessed an extension of the labour market, and increased hiring-in. But, in textiles, the process created 'classes' out of domestic labour. That is, it implied changes in the opportunity cost of domestic labour. In brass, on the other hand, the movement was of a different kind: classes formed out of apprenticeship or team-work. Traces of this movement can be found in major brass towns, as we shall see, mainly in a long-continued intermeshing of both cooperative and hierarchical systems of employment.

A convenient way of describing how market developments altered production and exchange systems would be to see how the roles in which the three actors – dealers, *karkhanadars*, and workers – appear tended to change in relation to the market, and in relation to each other.

The raw material trade concentrated as a result of market expansion and easier communication. In the new role, the 'dealer' was no longer one who merely bought vessels from peddlers to forward them to the artisans, and who retailed the finished goods in turn. The dealer could

---

[44] Thus, 'whenever a cottage industry is in the hands of a particular caste, it easily assimilates itself to the workshop system', United Provinces, *Banking Enquiry Committee*, Report, 252. Caste, though utilizable this way, was neither a necessary nor a sufficient precondition for workshops to develop.

now be an importer. And by switching from scrap to imported sheets the industry required that the merchants 'incur all the risks of the violent fluctuations in prices in the brass and copper markets'.[45] The dealer, further, must be wealthy enough to afford shops, spaces, and godowns in the town. And, since foreign inputs were not just cheaper, they were available from a world market in which price and supply were both uncertain, the dealer occasionally needed to be someone with privileged access to inputs, say, by holding licences during both the world wars. Licences, at the same time, were a barrier to entry for many others.[46] An effect of increasing scale, concentration, and specialization of capital was a sharper distinction between the biggest of the input dealers and those among the finished goods merchants. However, there were many intermediaries below them who seemed to combine both.

Moradabad had, in the 1920s, about a dozen large-scale importers of brasssheets, who supplied not only the local industry, but also brass manufacturers elsewhere. Simultaneously, the trade in scrap vessels concentrated. Moradabad was getting part of its supplies not from peddlers any more, but from scrap dealers in the northern cities.[47] The increased scale of trade can be seen from the emergence of merchants who could adopt modern marketing practices, maintain agents in distant cities, advertise, and try to create brands.[48] Export prospects, in particular, made local merchants more mobile, and allowed them to station agents in the port cities. Joshi, in describing the industry in Deccan, stated that dealer–*karkhanadar* contracts were extended in the interwar period under conditions of raw material scarcity and consequent difficulty of access.[49] In the middle of the 1930s, Poona witnessed the establishment of a merchants' trade guild, which was supposed to arbitrate disputes between local and outside merchants, but 'by levying fees on new entrants . . . it was almost acting like a handicraft guild'.[50]

The increased scale of trade usually went along with an extension of contractual work, between the dealer and the *karkhanadars*. Were these contracts exploitative? Here regional experiences and perceptions differ. In towns such as Moradabad, with a large industry and reputed craftsmanship, the dealers obviously competed for the *karkhanadars*'

[45] Chatterjee, *Notes on Industries*, 121.
[46] See Mensinkai, *A Survey of Handicrafts*, on dealers in the Deccan.
[47] United Provinces, *Industrial Survey*, Moradabad, 20.
[48] United Provinces, *Banking Enquiry Committee*, vol. II, 132. In Moradabad, big dealers allowed their long-time employees to become agents. Some remained paid employees, and some became full-fledged merchants. Chaturvedi, *The Cottage Industry*.
[49] Joshi, *Urban Handicrafts*, 123.
[50] R. D. Choksey, *Economic Life in the Bombay–Deccan (1918–1939)* (Bombay, 1955), 189.

labour. The 'contract' was defined as an undertaking to complete the work, but not necessarily to sell the wares at predetermined prices. There was, moreover, no obligation to continue transacting with specific parties, and the participants were known to change frequently between turnovers.[51] In a similar situation in Bengal, the extension of dealer-producer contracts had quite different implications for the producers. The two major clusters in western Bengal, the Kharar group of villages and the Bankura cluster, were both engaged in relatively simple utility articles. Here, *mahajans* or petty traders themselves owned the brass workshops. All raw material came from, and the entire output was sold in, Calcutta. The *mahajans* were rich, had 'these poor unfortunates absolutely in their clutches', and appropriated the 'lion's share of the profits'. The workers had an almost complete lack of knowledge about markets, a condition which Bengal's rural production and urban marketing secured in a number of crafts. 'They are kept in such ignorance that some of them do not even know the current prices of the goods they make.'[52] In the other major centre in Bengal, Khagra, the workshops were owned by the headmen-cum-intermediary, and the workers themselves seemed somewhat better off. To generalize, the increased scale and concentration of trade could be exploitative or advantageous for the workers depending on, at least, the following features: whether the workers or the foremen owned the necessary fixed capital; and whether market information was easily accessible to all.

We turn now to the *karkhanadars*. The *karkhanadars'* options differed somewhat depending on the nature of the product. Especially in north India, in complex and decorative work, the division of labour was well advanced, production processes were separate, and the *karkhanadar* was usually a subcontractor of the dealer. Moradabad's engravings are an example. In plainer work, on the other hand, the *karkhanadar* could be a direct employer, owning a furnace or a set of forging equipments. A *karkhana*, in other words, was not necessarily a full-fledged factory. The word could variously imply, as in Chaturvedi's usage: (i) a shed containing the most capital-intensive processes (furnace); (ii) a shed containing the most labour-intensive processes (moulding); (iii) a shed the owner of which is also a merchant of inputs or of product; and (iv) a unit subcontracting work contracted by merchants.

There are several references earlier (pre-1930s) to *karkhanadars* who

---

[51] In 1907, 'there is . . . a great deal of competition among the dealers and profits are cut very fine': Chatterjee, *Notes on Industries*, 125. On flexible contracts, see Baljit Singh, *The Economics of Small-Scale Industries. A Case Study of Small-Scale Industrial Establishments of Moradabad* (Bombay, 1961), 20.

[52] Bengal, *Report on the Survey*, 31–3, 56.

were not rigidly contract-bound, who had shops and could thus retail the wares they made. There is also mention of merchants who owned and supervised workshops.[53] If these ambiguous entities were products of a change, then these changes continued, such that, of a certain class of people, the two terms tended to be used interchangeably even in the later sources.[54] In general, however, the instances of *karkhanadars* trading independently or contracting with smaller *karkhanadars*, and thus gradually specializing as dealers, were more common than that of the dealer moving into production. The examples of the former come from Moradabad art brassware where brand images were often associated with producers rather than traders. Here, mobility was freer, *karkhanadars* could rise from the ranks,[55] and there was always a certain number of artisans who 'dislike being employed . . . and endeavour to set up a business of their own'. This was reported in 1908. Forty years later, once again, 'the *karkhanadar* has greatly improved his position and has begun to buy raw material from wholesalers and making utensils outside dealer-contracts, directly engaging craftsmen on their own, and occasionally selling to outside merchants directly'.[56] That is, in skill-intensive work, the tendency of *karkhanadars* beginning to trade was noticeably strong. In an atmosphere of degraded quality, this option would be even easier for the more skilled *karkhanadars* to undertake.

The other movement the *karkhanadars* frequently undertook consisted in employing more labour, different kinds of labour, and enlarging the workshed. This course was open to those who actually owned a shed. A common precondition for this, present since the interwar period and strengthened later, was for the *karkhanadar* to be a skilled craftsman, the skill being such as could not be mechanized. Polishing, and plating of vessels with a layer of tin, are two such processes, both originally major considerations in Moradabad's fame. Immediately after the First World War, several new concerns were reported to be experimenting with power-driven technologies in polishing. The manual lathes once used were replaced by power-operated ones in one firm.

---

[53] On *karkhanadars* trading (Mirzapur), see Chatterjee, *Notes on Industries*, 121; on factories belonging to 'men of substance' who were not themselves workmen, see Chatterjee, *Notes on Industries*, 120, on Moradabad engraving, and 122, on Benares. In the early 1930s, *karkhanas* in Poona were owned by 'rich capitalists', who owned shops in the city. Some of these worked on contract, and some were independent. Joshi, *Urban Handicrafts*, 124.

[54] In the 1960s, a section of Moradabad dealers were called *karkhanadars*: see India, *Report on the Survey of the Brassware Industry at Moradabad*, All India Handicrafts Board, New Delhi, 1964.

[55] United Provinces, *Banking Enquiry Committee*, vol. II, 131.

[56] Chatterjee, *Notes on Industries*, 120; Chaturvedi, *The Cottage Industry*, 27; and Singh, *Economics of Small-Scale*, 21.

And tinning by hand was replaced by electro-plating in nickel and silver in another.[57] Interestingly, both firms faced 'much opposition' from manufacturers, since their action implied not just substitution of 'labour', but of a whole distinct kind of artisans called *kalaigars*. The lesson of this conflict, it was stated, was that greater integration between processes was desirable so that the mechanizing firm could make finished goods on its own without having to depend on others. Thirty years later, electro-plating was common in the town, having dramatically increased during the war. Significantly, manual processes had suffered a certain de-skilling owing to a shortage of tin during the war. Power lathes were more common, though here the manual process of polishing, an extremely tiring one, had retained its image of qualitative superiority.[58] It must be remembered, moreover, that substitution in each case needed long experiments to make the technologies suit rigidly specified product quality, and hence were abandoned many times before being finally adopted.[59] Power-operated forges and the use of dies and presses had meanwhile also gradually progressed. The earliest venture here too dated far back.[60] Of less visibility, but present nonetheless, were gradual shifts from hand- to wheel-operated bellows, and from clay to graphite in moulding despite an old reputation for Moradabad clay.

There were even indications in the 1950s of engraving work coming to the *karkhanas*. A new division of labour, between the master who drew the design, and the workers who executed it, was now in place.[61] This is indeed significant, for engraving was the least concentrated of the activities for a long time, being dependent on individual competence. But then the tendency of craftsmanship to become divorced from its execution was not unique to brass, but present in several other design-intensive crafts about the same time.

All this would perhaps suggest that the size of the workshop tended to increase. Indeed, of brass it was stated that 'the superiority and the economy of the small-scale sector does not lie in its smallest . . . size of establishment'.[62] Economies of scale did exist, but, significantly, they also reversed beyond a point. The most dynamic units in Moradabad town were those in between the smallest (three to five workers) and the large factories. Such units faced a higher mortality, but they were also

---

[57] United Provinces, *Industrial Survey*, Moradabad, 22.

[58] Chaturvedi, *The Cottage Industry*, 25; and India, *Report on the Survey*, 6–8.

[59] For example, where the vessel was lacquered, the lathe needed to move slowly and controllably, and the assistant turning the lathe had to have knowledge of the master-craftsman's techniques.

[60] 'A leading brass dealer of Moradabad informed me that he was making arrangements to set up a die-press in that town.' Chatterjee, *Notes on Industries*, 125.

[61] Singh, *Economics of Small-Scale*, 54.   [62] *Ibid.*

more adaptable to sudden changes in demand than the larger factories. This flexibility in starting up and winding up work as the market dictated implied a certain persistent surplus capacity, the possible sources of which were underpaid and underemployed apprentices, and the poorer or the less talented artisans.[63]

There was another kind of mechanization proceeding along with the increased scale and the upgradation of the *karkhana*: this was import-substitution in raw materials, where *karkhanadar* enterprise was probably rarer. Both the wars, and especially the second, had shown the vulnerability of the industry to fluctuations in the input market, and encouraged import-substitution. This involved setting up rolling mills that turned billets from scraps, and then made rounds, sheets, and plates out of these. The origin of enterprise here is not clear. The scale of investments needed would suggest large dealers to be the source of capital. This movement was aided by another long-term development: the concentration in the scrap market. Moradabad and Jagadhari in Punjab are mentioned in connection with interwar diversification into billets.[64] Interestingly, in this case, the equipment mechanized, the furnace or the forge, could with some adjustments adapt to other metals. That, in turn, created the possibility of switching from brass to iron, and from utensils to instruments, tools or components. That several Jagadhari firms did diversify in this way in the 1950s is clear. Of these, one grew into a major rolling mill of northern India. Press-shops in Poona used aluminium and steel as well as brass in the 1940s. Those in Bombay and Calcutta had long been engaged in partially meeting the needs of the cotton and jute mills. The Bombay firms moved flexibly between metals during the Second World War.[65]

Finally, what sort of new options did the workers confront? In skill-intensive crafts, the 'go-ahead worker' starting up as a *karkhanadar* was not unknown. But this was probably not very common either, and rarely encountered in beaten articles. Joshi, on the other hand, found workshop owners in the Deccan becoming 'completely dependent'. They worked in the fewer and bigger factories on monthly wages.[66] Setting aside such dramatic turns of fortune, the important change was perhaps a more

---

[63] Interpreting data supplied in *ibid.*

[64] Chaturvedi, *The Cottage Industry*; and United Province, *Industrial Survey*, Moradabad.

[65] On Punjab, see *Haryana District Gazetteer*, Ambala District (Chandigarh, 1984), 129; Punjab, *Report on Industrial Survey of Punjab* (Chandigarh, 1960), 86–7; on Bombay, see Shah, 'Copper and Brass Industries', 53; Bombay, *Report of the Bombay Economic and Industrial Survey Committee, 1938–1940* (Bombay, 1940), 74; on Calcutta, see Mukharji, *Monograph*, 12–13; and on Poona, see *Gazetteer of the Bombay State*, Poona District (Bombay, 1954), 270–2.

[66] Joshi, *Urban Handicrafts*, 124.

subtle one: the transformation of 'craftsmen', the *karkhanadar*'s collaborators, and experts in specific processes, into the latter's 'employees'.

There was indeed a period, the length and boundaries of which varied between major brass towns, when worker–*karkhanadar* contracts in many branches of the industry retained elements of cooperation, in decision-making as well as in modes of payment. Consider Chatterjee's description of the usual shopfloor contract in the United Provinces towns: the skilled workers (furnace-man, turner), the semi-skilled (mould-maker, mould-finisher, filer, assistant turner), and the apprentices received *fixed proportions* of the net income.[67] One of the skilled workers was the owner of the shop. In Moradabad of the 1940s, groups of workers 'employed' by *karkhanadars* had the freedom to negotiate sales on behalf of their employers.[68] Fixed proportion wages also appear in the Deccan in the middle of the 1930s. The workers here offered their labour as a gang, and divided the wages in an agreed ratio. The headman, usually the chief beater, was not the *karkhanadar*, however.[69] Likewise, in the rural cluster of Nawabganj in central Bengal, 'a band of hammerers (6 men) works alternatively in 4 shops'. The area was close to a concentration of mango orchards, and the workers were part-time mango-harvesters and sellers. The factories in consequence went through periodic shortages, met with a system of labour exchange whereby surplus labour in one shop could be temporarily 'borrowed' by another.[70]

The inevitable traits of labour markets of this kind were, first, piece-rates, and, secondly, artisans identifying themselves with the process, not the workplace. A third feature was that the *karkhanadar* (or the *kothiwala*, literally the 'shed-owner') 'serves the useful function of a coordinating agent'[71] between the merchant, the engravers, the moulders, the joiners, and so on. Why were such quasi-collaborations commonly encountered in brass? The nature of the final output in brass being simpler in comparison with textiles, it is conceivable that skills were more well defined in this craft. Long apprenticeships, on the other hand, ensured full information about individual abilities. But these may not be sufficient to explain the systems of income-sharing. Possibly, all these forms were variations on the apprenticeship system, which appears as a culturally rooted institution in urban north India (see also chapter 2).

It must be pointed out, however, that the freedom implied in being able to identify oneself with processes rather than employers was

[67] Chatterjee, *Notes on Industries*, 119.   [68] Chaturvedi, *The Cottage Industry*, 27.
[69] Joshi, *Urban Handicrafts*, 125.   [70] Bengal, *Report on the Survey*, 81–2.
[71] Bhattacharya, 'A Survey', 402.

restricted by the artisans' inability to stock up and withhold work in the case of disputes, and the inconvenience of sale by 'the tedious and tardy method of hawking'.[72] The merchant was crucial for the artisan's survival in brasswares, more than in cloth where the output was both lighter to carry, and took up less space. There was, thus, a constantly present tendency to tie the labourers to the work or the workshop via contracts that could not be easily broken by the workers, if the merchants or manufacturers needed such ties.

Usually, explicit attempts at tying labour involved some form of personal credit. In Moradabad in the interwar period, a system of consumption loans (*baqi*), extended by *karkhanadars* to workers, was common. It prevailed in many United Provinces craft towns and was a useful system for the workers (see also chapter 7). *Baqi* could be bypassed, if the *karkhanadar* persuaded the prospective dealer to take over the burden, which in times of shortage the latter gladly did. *Baqi* was also not hereditary. The money was 'unwisely spent' on drinks, gambling, betting on partridges and quail, 'for they regard it as an unearned income'. The small *karkhanadars*, being equally profligate, were no better examples.[73] The system, however, was made illegal in the 1930s, and gradually faded. The more stable system of tied labour was probably apprenticeship. In nearly all *karkhanas*, the younger male members of the *karkhanadar*'s family, relatives, and workers' children necessarily went through a long stretch of training, sometimes for several years.

In the middle of the 1930s, the Deccan towns were in a transition, seen from the establishment of the first workers' unions, and the first chambers of commerce.[74] Several towns where the industry was in crisis, Lucknow for example, experienced the first strikes and wage disputes in the early 1930s. Such times displayed the relative strengths and the sources of bargaining power. The Lucknow artisans, for example, commanded skill but without Moradabad's brand image, so that, if pushed, the traders could after all replace local with imported wares.[75] In Moradabad the transition was a more tranquil one. About 1950, chambers of commerce and unions were established to settle wage disputes and regulate entry.[76] Over the next thirty or so years, payments gradually changed over completely to time rates, and from daily to monthly rates, a large body of the workforce became 'permanent', and workers' role in negotiating sales faded away. The most significant of

---

[72] *Ibid.*, 404.   [73] United Provinces, *Banking Enquiry Committee*, vol. II, 23.
[74] Choksey, *The Economic Life*, 189.   [75] Bhattacharya, 'A Survey', 404.
[76] Census of India, 1961, *Brass and Copperware Industry in Uttar Pradesh*, vol. XV, Part VII-A, No. 4 (Delhi, 1964).

these trends was, perhaps, government intervention in the labour market. The Factories Act transformed artisans into employees by defining *karkhanas* as factories. The wages now included allowances, thanks to statutory minimum wages, and leave and welfare benefits had been extended. In the 1980s in Moradabad, a large number of *karkhanas* were still not subject to the Act. Between them and those that were, the difference was that of minimum wage implementation, whereas the maximum wages offered, being efficiency-guided, varied relatively little.[77] It is tempting to speculate that enforcement of minimum wages perhaps induced the factories to diversify into more skill-intensive products. The hypothesis receives some support from a 1960s report on the Deccan towns.[78]

This outline will remain incomplete without reference to caste, or the social identities that influenced economic mobility deeply in the contemporary crafts, manifestly in textiles and leather. We saw that, among the handloom weavers, who were divided in a complex and elaborate hierarchy, social status often indicated entrepreneurial prospects. For status tended to be associated with the product woven, with ability and willingness to acquire technical and general learning, and with business organizations. In the case of tanners, degraded status in the village was clearly a major factor in the urbanization of the industry, the emigration of labour, and the creation of labour markets out of a customary transaction (chapter 6). What does brassware tell us about the specific interactions between caste and mobility? Answering this question in any detail must await further research, for the material available on brassware castes is extremely inadequate. However, a few tentative conclusions can be drawn based on what exists, and by way of comparison with other crafts.

The number and population of brassware castes were smaller than in textiles, and socially brassworkers were not underprivileged in the way leather artisans were. In north India and the Deccan, the three main castes were the Kasera or Kasar or Kansari, the Thathera or Thathiar, and the Tamera or Tambat. More rarely, one also comes across the occupational terms, Chhatera, the engraver, or Bhartya, the foundry owner. But these were not caste denominators. The three caste groups

---

[77] India, *Report on the Working and Living Conditions of Workers in the Metalware Industry at Moradabad*, Ministry of Labour and Rehabilitation (New Delhi, 1982), tables. The study contains fascinating information on the levels of living of Moradabad brassworkers. By income, wealth, and welfare indices, they were placed somewhere in the middle classes of the town. It would seem, however, that over the preceding decades, the workers' distance from the workplace had increased, reflecting general urban growth.

[78] Mensinkai, *A Survey of Handicrafts*, 89.

were unevenly distributed, with Kasera concentration increasing towards the east, Thatheras towards the north, and Tambats in central India. The Thatheras included a large number of Muslims. Etymologically, the first could be identified with brass or bronze, the third with copper, and, from the way the name sounds, the Thatheras were likely to have been wielders of the hammer. The Tameras, indeed, were a small and probably depleting group in the early twentieth century, reflecting the fate of pure copper work. The other two were said to be as freely taking up other occupations as outsiders were entering brass, but the census statistics on caste–work correspondence, the usual means to infer such changes, are not detailed enough to confirm this. The metal-wise and process-wise specializations, if any, between them had also long since disappeared.

The comparative homogeneity of the work, and of the workers, may account for the following two features of the industry. First, it may explain why, unlike in cloth, social inequalities did not show up in striking ways in brass. And, secondly and relatedly, the distance between the merchants and the artisans was much less apparent than in crafts like textiles or leather. The two 'classes' in brassware were usually from the same caste, or, at least, class did not indicate systematic social origin. If this impression holds, it would define brass as an industry with prospects of economic mobility relatively unhampered by social hierarchy.

Recognizing that merchants and workers were not socially divided makes it easier to tackle the rather confusing attempts at defining caste occupations in the twentieth-century sources. According to N. M. Joshi, Poona Kasars were master-hammerers in the 1880s, the Nasik ones were rich dealers. L. C. Jain's evidence before the United Provinces Banking Enquiry suggests that the Moradabad merchants were Hindu banias (Kaseras?), whereas the workers were Muslims (many north Indian Thatheras were Muslims). Chaturvedi's Moradabad survey twenty years later, however, shows that merchants too were predominantly Muslims. P. G. Shah's informative article at the Bankipore industrial conference of 1912 identified Kasars as the 'capitalist class', and Thatheras as the 'workmen class'. In Bengal, Kansari is a corruption of Kansabanik, 'banik' standing for merchant. G. R. Dampier in 1894, D. C. Johnstone in 1888, J. L. Kipling in 1884, and Baden-Powell in 1872, all describe the north Indian Thathiyar as 'polisher', 'beater', or 'the hammer-anvil man', whereas Kaseras are traders.[79] If these usages seem temptingly suggestive of a pattern, Denzil Ibbetson frus-

---

[79] Though several of them did acknowledge that 'the [caste] names are often applied to both' classes.

trates it by confidently asserting that 'the Thathera is the man who sells, as the Kasera is the man who makes vessels'. William Crooke has a similar assessment. And Enthoven's caste anthology of 1922 describes an origin myth of the Gujarat Kaseras, unambiguously defining them as hammerers.

One way to resolve this apparent paradox would be to suggest the following. In their origins, the Kaseras might have been the cast-metal workers and Thatheras the hammerers. But also, in origin, when neither product was extensively traded, economic distinctions between cast-metal and hammer-anvil workers might have been relatively indistinct. However, with the emergence of cast-metal as the traded good, the distinction between the two technologies, and between capitalists and artisans, would become sharper. There were capitalists and artisans in both technologies, but it is inevitable that capital was more visible in cast-metal work, or among Kaseras. It is probable that the man who became a merchant was usually engaged in cast-metal work. That is, he was one who possessed enough resources to maintain a furnace, crucibles, and adequate space, was able to turn out articles that could add value by polishing, plating or engraving, had enough influence or contacts to coordinate such work, and had the space to store the finished goods. It is also plausible that the hammerer, whose job was basically physical-labour intensive, was usually the person without capital.

Interestingly, the 1961 census monograph on Benares brassware mentions that a part of the factory workforce was constituted of outsiders.[80] The connection between new entrants and non-caste entrants among *karkhana* workers has important examples from textiles, and suggests how occupations open up in an old industry. In fact, in textiles, it also shows why relations of production differ between one kind of factory and another. In brass, unfortunately, we have only one example.

Conclusion

On the effect of commercialization, the experience of brassware has both typical and unexpected elements. The growth in market size and market destinations enabled trade increasingly to specialize. However, the outcome of the process on market structure could be variable. Trade could either concentrate, or become more competitive, or encourage the entry of many intermediaries. It also appears that the markets differed in degree of transparency, that is, in the degree of the ease of access to information for the artisans. Perhaps, the most dynamic craft towns like

[80] Census of India, 1961, *Brass and Copperware Industry in Uttar Pradesh*, 17.

Moradabad are examples of increasing competitiveness, transparency, and scale, all together and in an interdependent way. Markets also induced mass production, utilizing manual skills and the existing division of labour since no mechanized alternative was yet available. The main actors in this story were the *karkhanadars*, who developed new products and better designs, and probably the raw material merchants, who helped substitute imported materials. A class formation did result out of this process.

The final output of brassware was relatively insulated from foreign trade, except in the case of Moradabad. In a number of other crafts, export played a more explicit and a more powerful role. The next two chapters deal with two examples of this role, beginning with leather, a relatively unskilled work, and following up with carpets, a skilled craft.

6   Leather

Most kinds of craft in mid-nineteenth-century India can be classified into two types: commodities, and non-marketed services.[1] Whether a craft functioned as a service or as a commodity depended on the product, and on the producer's caste. Leather and agricultural implements were industries for which a clientele outside the village, or a market inside it, seems to have been rare. On the other hand, in textiles, it was caste that usually distinguished the sellers of a commodity from the providers of a service. The coarse weaving practised by the 'menial' castes of central India had the character of a service, one of several that these castes were supposed to perform for the village. They were not 'weavers' as caste, and the fact that they rarely specialized as weavers on leaving the village, suggests that there were implicit barriers to their specializing. In contrast, weavers by caste freely sold cloth, whether at the village bazaar or to the merchant engaged in long-distance trade, and, when migrating, tended to settle, and were settled by local rulers, as weavers.[2]

Both sorts of craft were transformed in the colonial period, though historians have been mainly concerned with textiles, an industry already commercialized. On textiles, recent scholarship has argued that the expansion in trade and infrastructure in the second half of the nineteenth century did not quite destroy Indian weaving, but induced institutional and technological changes by integrating markets, making

---

[1] By 'service' here is meant serving a patron or benefactor, and not the activities that constitute the tertiary sector. 'Service' is opposed to 'commodities', which refers to any product of labour that is sold. The distinction is generally useful in classifying craftsmen's labour, but can become blurred under certain conditions. For example, when a service commercializes, or when a commodity is produced under exploitative contracts.

[2] Artisan castes in this sense were typically those identifiable with the manufacture and trade of specific products. Over sufficiently long periods of time, these identities, and the correspondence between caste and occupation, could evolve. The identities assumed here, therefore, are legitimate only in the context of the late-nineteenth-century conditions. See also the discussion on weaver castes in chapter 3.

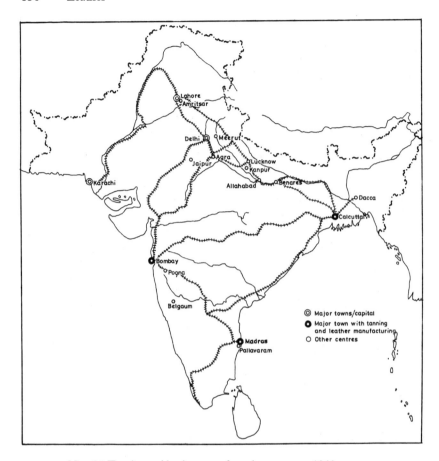

Map 6.1 Tanning and leather manufacturing centres, *c.*1940

labour mobile, and hastening urbanization. This line of reasoning obviously lends itself to generalizations. Trade, markets, and railways might well have transformed a whole range of industries in the same way as they did weaving, including and especially the more or less custom-bound services, thus forcing rural society to adapt.

Leather was probably the most important of the quasi-services that commercialized during the colonial period. The following description in Watt's *Dictionary of Economic Products* can be taken to be fairly representative of the industry as it existed before the 1860s in most parts of India:

Each village has its own workers in leather, who are also, to a large extent, their own tanners; and it is part of their recognized duties to keep their patrons in boots, and to cure and make up the hides required for the leathern buckets made for irrigation.[3]

Domestic trade was not absent, for there was an urban and an army demand for leather, but this was relatively small. The situation was vastly different in the last decade of the century. By then, India was one of the world's largest exporters of tanned hides, and an importer of boots and shoes from Europe. The scale of export trade, at Rs. 60 million in 1890 was many times that of domestic rural–urban trade, estimated at Rs. 8 million by a source cited in Watt.[4] The change was an outcome of expansion in the leather industry, and improvements in tanning technology, in the West. It is tempting to say that leather was an example of India turning into a raw material supplier and finished goods importer in the world market. But that would be a trivial conclusion, besides being a half-truth.

First, the process was not complete, and imports replaced domestic leather goods only to a very limited extent. Secondly, the real impact of trade was felt, not in the extent of specialization, but in the way technology and organization in both tanning and leatherworking changed at the imperative of a much enlarged market. And, thirdly, for some of the most numerous and exploited castes, the process involved a social transition as the market opened up avenues of mobility which the society previously denied them.

The present chapter will sketch this transition in broad outline. The period begins about the 1870s, when exports increased rapidly, and ends before the Second World War. The chapter is divided in six sections. The first describes the producers and the technology prior to the expansion in the export trade. The next three show how exports affected tanning. The specific themes are the rise of new sites of production and migration into these; the rise of the factory and new capitalists; and technological change. The fifth section outlines changes in leather manufactures in response to increased competition and shortages of raw material. The last section discusses the nature of capital in tanning.

---

[3] George Watt, *A Dictionary of the Economic Products of India*, vol. IV (London and Calcutta, 1890), 613.
[4] An estimate based on data in *Review of the Inland Trade of India*, 1888–9, in Watt, *Dictionary*.

Tanning as it was

As far as we can tell, tanning in the early nineteenth century was almost wholly a rural industry. Although large tanner colonies were known to have been settled on land grants in or near some north Indian cities at least as late as the eighteenth century, these were exceptional.[5] By and large, tanning was rural because it needed to be so. Consumption of beef being restricted, so was the slaughtering of cattle for consumption. The government-owned urban slaughterhouse was a later institution, so the raw hide came exclusively from 'fallen', that is, naturally dead, cattle, or *murdari* as opposed to *halali* in north Indian trade parlance. Such cattle were, of course, all rural. The 'green' hide, or the hide in its raw state, if not cured within a few hours of death becomes irretrievable as leather. The risk is so great that even in the age of the railways, the green hide was never transported. This necessitated the tanner, who was usually the curer, to stay in close proximity to the cattle population.[6] The tanning substances, moreover, grew in the wild, were collected by the craftsmen, and were rarely traded. The bark of the ubiquitous babul (*Acacia arabica*), the nuts of myrobalan (*Terminalia chebula*), and the south's avaram bark (*Cassia auriculata*, also well-known as *tarwad* in western India, and as 'tanner's *cassia*' inside tanneries) were the best known tannin, whereas curing was usually done with saline earth.[7] The raw material frequently drew tanning into the neighbourhood of forests, which in turn led to the somewhat more delicate industry in skins of wild animals. Thus, the northern borders of Rajputana and the foothills of the Kumaon and Garhwal Himalayas became famous for Sambar

---

[5] The origin of a colony in Lucknow is related in H. G. Walton, *A Monograph on Tanning and Working in Leather in the United Provinces of Agra and Oudh* (Allahabad, 1903), 25–6. Lucknow appears in nineteenth-century sources as a town which had inherited a diversified leather and hide production and trade, but which did not participate in the great expansion of the tanning trade from the 1870s onwards. Until the rise of Kanpur, Lucknow might have been north India's most important 'hide emporium': William Hoey, *A Monograph on Trade and Manufactures in Northern India* (Lucknow, 1880), 27.

[6] This also explains the stubborn persistence of crude curing methods even as tanning came to the towns.

[7] The tannin just mentioned were the 'big three', whose usage continues to date. Other popular tannin included several varieties of *Acacia*, particularly cutch and wattle barks. A detailed description of the processes and materials can be found in M. V. Edwards, R. L. Badhwar, and A. C. Dey, *The Vegetable Tanning Materials of India and Burma*, Indian Forest Records (New Series), Chemistry and Minor Forest Products, I, 2 (Delhi, 1952). However, by the time this informative report was published, some indigenous processes had become extinct. For two earlier and much briefer reviews, see W. A. Fraymouth, 'Note on the Progress of Researches to Apply the Natural Tanstuffs of Northern India to the Production of War Leathers', and J. A. Pilgrim, 'The Future of Tannin Extract in India', both in Indian Munitions Board, *Industrial Handbook* (Calcutta, 1919). The authors were leather technologists in government employment.

skins. Gorakhpur town had a reputation for embroidery of skins of black-bucks from the Nepal forests. Nilgai skin was used for charpai covers in the north, and for the larger of the portable water-bags (*mot* or *charsa*) in western India.[8] These activities further strengthened the contact between tanners and the forest. In the largely forested regions like the Central Provinces:

> the tanning Chamars are frequently to be found in a separate little hamlet, the huts of which form a ring, in the middle of which are set the pits, wells and large earthen vessels, belonging to the trade. These settlements are generally in the neighbourhood of *malguzari* jungles, whence the supply of tanning material can be drawn.[9]

The 'respectable distance from the villages of the caste people'[10] was universal, and necessitated by the Hindus' aversion to the craft because of its association with flesh, while the Muslims found the Chamars' habit of keeping 'that foul beast, the pig' equally offensive.[11] Within the colony, work was usually cooperative and the pits were jointly used. Similar descriptions of the tanners' colony suggest that, while the craft needed space, it had perpetually limited access to it.[12]

The rural location of tanning was reinforced by caste. The Chamars of the northern plains from Bengal to Punjab, the Mahars (Dheds) of central India and Gujarat, the Dhors of Bombay–Deccan, the Madigas of the Telugu countryside, and the Chakkiliyans of the Tamil country, were all castes that performed a variety of services in the village. Coarse weaving was one of these; agricultural labour in the busy seasons was another; scavenging and associated leather processes was a third. The Chamar was known to thatch roofs and occasionally carry palanquins. The Chamarin was a midwife. The tanning castes were also found to be the village musicians, performing at festivals.[13] Denzil Ibbetson

---

[8] A. C. Chatterjee, *Notes on the Industries of the United Provinces* (Allahabad, 1908), 99; United Provinces, *Industrial Survey of the United Provinces* (Allahabad, 1922–4), Almora District; and J. R. Martin, *Monograph on Tanning and Working in Leather in the Bombay Presidency* (Bombay, 1903), 21.

[9] Central Provinces and Berar, *Report of the Industrial Survey of the Central Provinces and Berar* (Nagpur, 1908–9).

[10] A. C. Chatterton, *A Monograph on Tanning and Working on Leather in the Madras Presidency* (Madras, 1904), 10.

[11] W. Crooke, *The Natives of Northern India* (London, 1907), 122.

[12] 'Village chamars have to depend upon zamindars to have a suitable place for their tanning ... For a small man in the villages it is not easy ... and the tanner will have to pay ... heavy penalty.' This statement appears in Chowdhry Mukhtar Singh, *Cottage and Small-Scale Industries* (Allahabad, 1947), 156. The author, however, did not substantiate it.

[13] The Madigas were known to play the drum: see Chatterton, *Monograph on Tanning*, 10. The north Indian Chamar was a drum-player too: see William Crooke, *The Tribes and Castes of the North-Western Provinces*, vol. II (Calcutta, 1896), 196. The Pardeshi-Mang Chamar of Nasik were also called *vajantris*, or instrument-players: *Bombay District*

hypothesized that the integration of the vagrant and the tribal into settled rural life involved an evolution wherein scavenging, tanning, and weaving were adjacently placed occupations. In 1916, he could observe various stages of this process completed in the Gangetic plains.[14] Coarse weaving and tanning did not require great skills, and hence a specialist artisan caste. They were also ideal as off-season employment for agricultural labour. The Mahar was additionally the village watchman and the general purpose labourer, commandeered 'whenever a pair of shoulders are required to bear some burden, it may be the revenue records from field to field or a petty official's kit'.[15] Payment took the form of customary entitlements like rights to reusable wastes, crop-share, and sometimes piece-rates, the mix being variable between regions and classes, and over time.[16] As if to justify their function in rural society,

---

Gazetteers, Nasik District (Bombay, 1884), 257. The Ahmadnagar Mochi played the pipe and the drum: *Bombay District Gazetteer*, Ahmadnagar District (Bombay, 1884), 122. The Mahar was a hereditary drummer, and the first Bhiwandi riot in 1837 was sparked off by Mahars refusing to perform at a festival connected with Muharram: *Bombay District Gazetteer*, Thane District (Bombay, 1884), 514. There are many other instances of the link between tanning and music, of which perhaps the most extraordinary is the following. Descriptions of the central Bengal's silk industry *c.* 1900 mention the prodigiously talented Dubraj. He was a Chamar in origin, began his life as a drummer, turned into a composer of verse though he was not literate, became the leader of a 'gang of *impromptu* singers (*Kabis*)', and, later in life, apprenticed himself to a Muslim weaver of Baluchar. At his death, Dubraj was the most famous master-weaver in figured patterns. See N. G. Mukherji, *A Monograph on the Silk Fabrics of Bengal* (Calcutta, 1903), 42. Technologically, the association is obvious: the making of drums, and several other instruments, involved tanning skins or working with guts. It is, therefore, possible that tanners tended to make instruments, and then became musicians themselves. It is also possible that tanners by caste were recruited from musicians, indicating the probable tribalist roots of tanners in some areas. There is involved here a problem in the evolution of products and occupations: which leather article came first, the water-bag used by the peasants for irrigation, or the prehistoric drum?

[14] Thus, 'the Khatik who is a scavenger in the east turns into a tanner in the west; we see the Koli Chamar abandon leather-making and take to weaving, and turn into a Chamar-Julaha or Bunia; we see that in some districts most of the Mochis are weavers rather than leather-makers.' Denzil Ibbetson, *Panjab Castes* (Lahore, 1916), 267. Consistent with this hypothesis, the vagrant Paraiyans of Madras were increasingly turning towards leather over the period of the 1911–31 censuses.

[15] M. L. Darling, *Wisdom and Waste in the Punjab Village* (Bombay, 1934), 265.

[16] On customary services in Punjab, or *sep*, see Harish C. Sharma, *Artisans of the Punjab* (Delhi, 1996), chapter 2. Among sources on leather, A. J. Grant, *Monograph on the Leather Industry of the Punjab, 1891–92* (Lahore, 1893), 3–5, describes various kinds of *sep*. Grant mentions the existence of a 'fixed share or fixed amount of the produce'. Occasional references in the caste anthologies also suggest that the various ways the leather castes were paid back by their patrons included crop-share and/or rights to rent-free land. In some areas this seems to have evolved into a tenancy of an undefined sort, though usually the tanners were field labourers. See, for example, H. V. Nanjundayya and L. K. Ananthakrishna Iyer, *The Mysore Tribes and Castes* (Mysore, 1931), vol. IV, 'Madiga'.

the tanners also invariably carried a degraded image. There is, in fact, a surprising constancy in this image across distant regions in India.[17]

When a cow died in a central Indian village, the owner tied a rope to it, dragged it as far to the edge of the village as he could, and informed the Mahar. The latter then dragged it out of the village and flayed it. He could 'keep the hide free in return for services performed for the village community'.[18] The hide was then cured and either tanned by the scavengers themselves, or sold to tanners. The latter, in turn, either were themselves duty-bound to supply their 'patrons' with a fixed number of shoes, ox-goads and irrigation implements, or sold the leather to the leatherworkers, who were thus duty-bound. The intervention of a market, or the extent of division of labour, seems to have depended on the region, and, relatedly, on the tanning processes followed in different parts. In the villages of the northern plains, the three actors quite often collapsed into one caste, the Chamar.[19] The Madigas and the Chakkiliyans of the south too were frequently leatherworkers as well.[20] In Gujarat, flayers and tanners merged, but leather artisans, Mochis, were distinct. In the Deccan, flayers were the Mahars, tanning was done by the Dhors, and leather was the Chamars' responsibility.[21] This increased division of labour might account for the great reputation of Dhor bag-tannage in Kolhapur-Satara-Poona area, the origin of the Kolhapuri sandal. Wherever a division of labour was elementary or absent, the tanner was engaged in making the simplest kind of articles with an essentially local demand, chiefly the water-bag and crude footwear. On the other hand, the separation between tanners and leatherworkers was decisive whenever the article involved some sort of skill and/or had an urban clientele. In fact, in that case, subdivision appeared among the leather workers themselves.

It was this last stage in the leather chain, the manufacture of finished goods, that was considerably more commercialized and dispersed. The

[17] They were 'wily, filthy, and of low morals', as numerous north Indian proverbs about the Chamar expressed. Proverbial, too, was the landed and other upper castes' weakness for the Chamarin, or her southern counterpart. Two representative compilation of proverbs and lore are Herbert Risley, *The People of India* (Calcutta, 1908); and Edgar Thurston, *Tribes and Castes of Southern India* (Madras, 1909), 'Chakkiliyan'.

[18] Central Provinces and Berar, *Industrial Survey*, 58.

[19] For customary exchanges in Punjab, see Darling, *Wisdom and Waste*, 265; and in United Provinces, see Chatterjee, *Notes on the Industries*, 99. In the 1870s, the leather-artisan Mochi, existed as a separate caste only in the towns of northern India, whereas the three occupations, flayer, tanner, and leather artisan, tended to converge in the villages. See M. A. Sherring, *Hindu Tribes and Castes*, vol. II (Calcutta, 1879), 'Chamar', 'Mochi'. Walton, *Monograph on Tanning*, 26, confirms: 'Chamars on their promotion. . . . call themselves Mochis.'.

[20] Chatterton, *Monograph on Tanning*, 10–11.

[21] A. Guthrie, *Report on Leather Industries of the Bombay Presidency* (Bombay, 1910).

leather craftsman, the Mochi, was also socially better off, probably because he did not have to touch flesh. The product that seems to have been the most thoroughly integrated into urban trade was a covered footwear with or without decoration, the indigenous shoe appearing universally as one made of reddish leather with a curled front, thin sole, and covering the feet to a little above the toes. This ubiquitous article was nowhere a mass consumable or working-class attire, but was worn by the relatively wealthy, the city-dweller, or that class subject to 'the unwritten ordinance' which required the removal of shoes as a courtesy to the superior.[22] In rare instances, this curled shoe was made in craft towns, came into contact with forms of local embroidery, with artisans engaged in gold-thread manufacture, and was transformed into a richly designed object. Lucknow had developed this craft of gilded and embroidered shoes to excellence; other examples of a fusion between footwear and *jari* come from Jaipur, Delhi, Raichur, and Chanda.[23] Further, many northern towns housed garrisons which needed the leather craftsmen for saddlery and harnesses. The cities also used leather jars to carry *ghi* and oil, and to store scents. These bags were, in the 1880s, 'familiar to every one who has once passed through an Indian bazaar'.[24] The cities, and mobile populations like the armies or administrators, needed water-carriers, or *mashaks*, which were made by a small occupational group, the Bhishtis.

Some of these products were surely traded, and yet references to leather goods entering long distance or urban trade remain rather rare. The final output of the leather artisan was usually rural. Tanned hides and skins are not objects commonly encountered in internal trade prior to the railways: there may well have been an aversion to carrying such goods over long distances. In Gujarat, an ancient sea trade in both unwrought and worked leather survived till the early colonial period. The best known description of this trade belongs to Marco Polo who had noticed, among other objects, 'unicorn' hides in the merchandise.

[22] T. N. Mukharji, *Art-Manufactures of India* (Calcutta, 1888), 302. Mukharji, the author of this eminent book and a major figure in Bengali literature, was a curator of the Indian Museum at Calcutta.

[23] *Ibid.*, 301–2. Delhi was a major exporter of embroidered shoes in the 1880s: J. L. Kipling, 'The Industries of the Punjab', *Journal of Indian Art (and Industry)*, 2 (1887–8), 29. Possibly the last time a large sample of living traditions in embroidered, engraved, and embossed leather articles were collected together was on the occasion of the Indian Art Exhibition at Delhi, 1903(?). See George Watt and Percy Brown, *Indian Arts and Crafts*, Official Catalogue of the Indian Art Exhibition (Delhi, 1904), 199–205.

[24] See Hoey, *Monograph on Trade*, 138, on the *kuppesaz*, the maker and seller of *kuppas*, leather jars in Lucknow. In Punjab, the craft involved a group of artisans who once functioned almost like a caste, but appear to have become extinct through the interwar censuses: see Ibbetson, *Panjab Castes*, 301–2.

The tanning processes were exceedingly simple, if back-breaking. The simplicity explains the ease with which tanning could be combined with other labour. Flaying was usually done with a short and sharp knife called a *rampi*. This implement, considered much too sharp by observers of the practice,[25] acquired notoriety in the nineteenth century as increasing 'butcher's cuts' impaired the worth of the exportable hide. The shape of the knife had changed somewhat earlier in Europe. The next process was 'curing' the raw hide of bacteria that could destroy it. Curing was done by either sun-drying, or salting the hide. In the first case, the hide was merely left in the sun flesh side up for several weeks till it was completely drained of moisture and bacteria. The process yielded a crumpled and hard substance, so hard that the subsequent soaking and softening became difficult and hazardous.[26] A better method was air-drying where the hide was stretched on a frame and kept under shade. But the method most preferred by tanners was salt-cure where salt solutions were repeatedly painted on the flesh side of the hide. The process became known as 'pickling' in salt. But, as neither edible salt nor frames nor artificial shade was easily accessible to the average village curer, the larger part of Indian hides was *sukties* or sun-dried. It is reported in at least one source that, during 1880–1914, the usual method of curing in India tended to shift from wet-salted to dry.[27] This remains rather an isolated statement, but, if true, the tendency can be explained in terms of a preference in the export market for raw hides with the minimum of processing, and, possibly, a desire to avoid false weights added via wet-salting, 'a native science'.

Tanning began with a preliminary soaking, first in water to de-salt the skin, then in lime solutions to remove hair, a stage avoided with skins of wild animals, and finally in tannin solutions, under close and extremely long contact with the bark of the required tree. The skin was placed between barks, and soaked in bark solutions, 'good, strong liquor' as they were called in the European tanneries, with the solution periodically changed and made stronger. This process could either happen in a pit, or the skin was sewn up in a bag containing the solution that was repeatedly changed. Finally, the leather was finished, that is, smoothed and scoured (a process known as 'currying'), oiled, and sometimes dyed. The longer the soaking the better for the hide, but in villages the processes could, in fact, be much simpler: the skin was merely wrapped in bark and soaked in water, and almost never finished. On average, the

---

[25] For a reference, see Bombay, *Report of the Bombay Leather Survey* (Bombay, 1960), 21.

[26] India, *The Hides Cess Enquiry Committee*, vol. II (Delhi, 1929), M. B. Hudlikar, Harcourt Butler Technological Institute, Cawnpore (Kanpur), 54–5.

[27] Imperial Institute Committee for India, *Reports on Hides and Skins* (London, 1920), 90.

tanning process took about thirty to fifty days to complete, though the time depended on the material used, the state of the cured hide, and on whether the process involved bag- or bark-tanning, the former being somewhat quicker. By the end of the nineteenth century, chrome-tanning had been invented in the US, cutting down the time to as little as a day. In India, Alfred Chatterton, Director of Industries in the Madras Government, introduced it in demonstrations.[28] But it was not until the First World War that chrome-tanning became popular, and even then it was practised only in factories in a few towns. It needed large investments, imported tannin, and the leather cost more (it was also more durable). But, even if not popular locally, the global stride of chrome-tanning did affect the demand for Indian hides in the world market, as we shall see.

A slow transition in the old state of affairs began in the 1830s with the first exports of Indian hides to Europe. That India had a surplus to sell to the world was well known. In a short and informative monograph about Bengal written in 1804, the civil servant Colebrooke argued the possibility of England replacing her supplies of hides from Brazil by those available in Bengal.[29] But it was not until the 1870s that trade surged. In fact, several circumstances combined in one decade to create this boom that did not seem to wane till long afterwards. The growth owed much to the repeal of a 3 per cent export duty on hides in 1875. Public auctions in hides began in London about this time. The trade in hides was 'immensely stimulated' during and after the devastating southern famines of 1876–8 and 1896–8.[30] Cattle mortality was so high in some months of the famine that hides sold almost for free. William Digby, author of probably the best first-hand account of 1876, 'the greatest disaster ... which had visited India during the century', described what he saw on a winter morning in 1876 in Sholapur:

I spent some time in Tuesday's cattle market. There were perhaps 1,500 or 2,000 head. But people scarcely care even to drive them a few hundred yards into the market. There are no buyers but butchers, who buy them for two or three annas, solely for their skin ... 700 were forcibly driven into the Sholapur mill compound, and there deserted ... The Hindus were forgetting their prejudices, and the butchers were busy slaughtering the beasts that were literally brought to them for nothing.[31]

[28] On this initiative, see Padmini Swaminathan, 'State Intervention in Industrialisation: A Case Study of the Madras Presidency', *Indian Economic and Social History Review*, 29, 4 (1992).

[29] H. T. Colebrooke, *Remarks on the Husbandry and Internal Commerce of Bengal* (Calcutta, 1804), 115.

[30] See Martin, *Monograph on Tanning*, 4 on famine mortality forcing exports. Generally, on the significance of the 1870s, see also Chatterton, *Monograph on Tanning*, 4.

[31] William Digby, *The Famine Campaign in Southern India*, vol. I (London, 1878), 265–8.

Table 6.1 *Export of hides and skins by sea, 1890–1939*

	Cured		Tanned		Unwrought leather		Hides in export value (percent-age)	Unit value index[a]	Terms of trade[b]
	thousand tonnes	Rs. million[c]	thousand tonnes	Rs. million[c]	thousand tonnes	Rs. million[c]			
1890–4	43.9	83.5	_[d]	_[d]	–	–	5.3	100	1.0
1895–9	62.3	91.0	_[d]	_[d]	–	–	6.6	77	0.7
1900–4	58.2	71.0	15.2	32.0	–	–	5.4	74	0.7
1905–9	67.2	92.1	16.2	48.4	–	–	8.4	88	0.6
1910–14	74.5	99.5	16.3	44.3	–	–	6.6	83	0.6
1915–19	55.8	130.0	24.4	87.1	–	–	8.9	142	0.8
1920–4	44.4	61.2	13.8	51.3	–	–	4.6	101	0.5
1925–9	57.0	81.5	20.9	81.6	–	–	5.0	110	0.5
1930–4	11.4	11.7	3.4	10.6	0.3	1.2	1.4	81	0.7
1935–9	13.1	13.4	4.5	11.5	1.3	5.2	1.7	84	0.8

Notes: [a] Unit value index is average for all products. [b] Terms of trade is unit value index as a ratio of weighted agricultural prices. [c] Figures are available in pound sterling. They have been converted into rupees at the current exchange rates. Exchange rates were Rs. 15 to £1 in 1890–1917, Rs. 13.3 to £1 in 1926–39, and floating in between. [d] Included under 'Cured'.
Source: India, *Review of Seaborne Trade of British India* (Calcutta, various years).

The decade witnessed substantial progress in the trunk railways connecting Madras, Bombay, and Calcutta with the major hides- and skins-producing regions. Germany's advance in mineral dyeing, a contemporary development, made her the only country able to manufacture coloured leather. The conclusion of the Franco-Prussian war and the resumption of peace saw Germany re-enter the world market. In the last quarter of the century, Germany and Austria were the main buyers of Indian raw hides, a trade organized by a group of 'German or quasi-German' firms, based in Calcutta and forming a strong cartel. In America at the same time, chrome tanning created a demand for raw or semi-tanned skins for which India was the ideal source.

India possessed the largest cattle population in the world, and, despite the near-absence of meat consumption and hence of slaughtering, India had one of the world's largest supplies of hides and skins due to high natural mortality. From 1890 onwards, leather constituted 5–9 per cent of total private merchandise exports. The composition was changing gradually from cured to tanned, and, later, to processed leather (Table 6.1). That is, it was changing towards higher value-added goods. The importance of the trade dropped sharply and temporarily after the Great Depression. But, by then, the industry had revolutionized. The export market for Indian hides had forced traders to regulate supply and quality.

New sites and migration

Two changes, both locational, are immediately discernible. First, the direction of internal trade changed. The major source of raw hides was the region formed of Punjab, United Provinces and Central Provinces, and western Bihar. If earlier tanning was mainly local, now undressed hides (cattle) began to move out of this region towards Calcutta and Bombay, and undressed skins (goat and sheep) from the north as well as the south towards Madras. Secondly, as a natural development, tanneries were set up at the ports and major points of hide trade. The opening of the trunk railways was a clear inducement for this movement. Railway stations at source had special godowns for hides. The agents of merchants in the port cities operated at these points, Bombay's merchants, for example, had agents stationed as far as Peshawar, Rawal Pindi, Aligarh, and Agra. Madras subagents had a major station in Daund, 600 miles northeast of Madras, at one end of the great savannas of the southern peninsula. The gradual decline in the proportion of cured hides, that is, sun-dried in the village, in total exports (see Table 6.1) is a rough indicator of the urbanization of the industry. The impact of the railways in facilitating trade was relatively much stronger in leather than, say, in textiles, for the country tanner had little access to traditional modes of transportation.[32]

But a wide transport network in itself was not sufficient to access sources of hides. Nor can an expanding trade rely on famine mortality or on the natural death of animals. The market would eventually need to exercise control on mortality, which is possible only through slaughter-houses. Supervision of slaughtering was also needed to control quality, since most defects in Indian hides arose from bad flaying. Municipal slaughter-houses were set up from about the end of the century, and were busy by the 1920s.[33] Slaughtered cattle supplied better hides than fallen cattle not only due to better flaying, but also to the quality of the

---

[32] Even as late as the 1950s, the village tanner encountered great resistance to carriage of his wares by bullock-carts, and had to pay higher charges, 'whatever demanded by the vehicle owner': Central Leather Research Institute, *Symposium on Tanning as a Small Scale and Cottage Industry* (Madras, 1959), 28, in W. N. Pandav's article on Bombay State.

[33] The first slaughterhouse in Calcutta's Tangra area, which later became the main tanning centre of the city, was established in 1869. But this is probably a very early example of the municipal slaughterhouse. P. Thankappan Nair, 'Civic and Public Services in Old Calcutta' in S. Chaudhuri (ed.), *Calcutta. The Living City*, vol. I (Calcutta, 1990), 232.

animal itself. The hides of fallen cattle were a gift of nature, and came from starved and diseased animals. The slaughterhouse, on the other hand, was a business from the start. Further, the prospects of hide exports improved along with the prospects of meat exports.[34] In the early twentieth century an export trade to Burma developed in dried oxen and buffalo meat, and major slaughtering centres in the United Provinces specialized in this trade.[35] Roughly about one-quarter of the estimated 20 million hides produced annually in the early 1920s came from the slaughterhouse.[36] This was a direct inducement for tanneries to develop in the towns. Centralized slaughter created a network of merchants to collect dry cattle from the villages. It allowed the urban tanneries to avoid middlemen and contract directly with the butchers. It also allowed them to avoid, though partially, the badly cured hides from the villages, and to modernize processes.[37]

For the remaining supplies that still came from 'deads', a major redefinition of caste roles was under way with the creation of a market. First of all, flaying was more rarely the right or duty attaching to castes. In some cases the caste involved refused to accept the duty;[38] in other cases their patrons refused to part with a product that had now acquired a price. And, at the spiritual level, 'revulsion to consume the carcasses of dead animals is gaining ground' among the scavengers, as a signal to society at large.[39] The customary exchange was breaking down every-where. In one exceptional instance, it broke down because the landlords tried to enclose common lands where the Chamars were settled.[40] More frequently, custom broke down because the hide had now acquired a price. In central India, 'owners of cattle are less disposed to ... [the] custom [of gifting away carcasses]'. Briggs observed in the north that 'the increased value of leather has led the landlord to question the chamars' traditional right to raw skin'. Thurston noticed the tendency of the *ryots* 'to dispense with the services of family Madigas, and resort to the open market'; or, if the hide was transferred to the Madigas, to

[34] Reversing Walton's conclusion at the turn of the century, tanning in India 'suffers ... from having a very poor meat market': *Monograph on Tanning*, 5.

[35] India, *Hides Cess Enquiry*, evidence of Forrester Walker, Government Harness and Saddlery Factory, Kanpur, 20–1.

[36] *Ibid.*, evidence of P. J. Kerr, Veterinary Adviser to the Government of Bengal.

[37] *Ibid.*, evidence of Mehtab Singh, Industrial Surveyor, Delhi, 484; and of bark tanners of Pallavaram, 300.

[38] In parts of Bombay, the Mahars refused to flay animals, 'due to new awakening', Bombay, *Report of Bombay Leather Survey*, 11.

[39] So, interestingly, was the refusal to play the drum on traditional occasions: Chatterton, *Monograph on Tanning*, 10–11.

[40] R. L. Anand and Ram Lal, *Tanning Industry in the Punjab*, Board of Economic Inquiry, Publication No. 61 (Lahore, 1931), 35.

demand payment. The Madigas themselves began to 'poach on each other's monopoly of certain houses'. In Bombay, the traders tried to enforce a market by insisting that the tanners enter into a bond promising none would acquire hides except from the traders.[41] The extent of the change can be gauged from a comparison of two situations. In 1804, there was so much fallen hide available to the artisan that 'the currrier often neglects to take the hides'.[42] By the 1920s, a tannery owner in Bombay professed ignorance about 'any custom by which the hide of the dead animals belong to the *chamars* or sweepers'.[43] And, in the south, the 'qualified kind of serfdom ... has all but died out' by the early 1930s.[44]

There was a curious sidelight to this development. It seems that the north Indian tanner's repertoire included the art of poisoning diseased cattle. By the turn of the century, as hides were no longer plentiful in the village and customs no longer respected, rumours of its unauthorized usage were rampant.[45] It is not clear how much of this allegation was real, and how much fabricated, perhaps to create a hostility that reinforced the collapse of tradition. In any case, it became an inseparable part of the image of the Chamar. 'A humorous allusion to this practice ... may be traced to the proverb which represents the Chamar as enquiring after the health of the village headman's buffalo.'[46]

It is perhaps this detachment of tanning from the rural economy that shows up in a long decline in the number and proportion of traditional leather castes engaged in the craft. In northern India, according to the

[41] These examples are from India, *Hides Cess Enquiry*, evidence of A. A. Pillai, Director of Industries, Madras, 332; Thurston, *Tribes and Castes*, 'Madiga; Central Provinces and Berar, *Industrial Survey*, 58; Chatterton, *Monograph on Tanning*, 10–11, reference to the Madigas; G. W. Briggs, *The Chamars* (Calcutta, 1920), 58; and *Indian Industrial Commission*, Evidence, vol. IV (Calcutta, 1918), evidence of R. B. Ewbank, Registrar of Cooperative Societies, 546.

[42] Colebrooke, *Remarks on the Husbandry*, 115.

[43] India, *Hides Cess Enquiry*, evidence of Pratap Pandit, Director of Western India Tannery, Bombay, 388.

[44] Nanjundayya and Ananthakrishna Iyer, *The Mysore Tribes and Castes*, vol. IV, 'Madiga'.

[45] Cattle poisoning is a constant element in nearly every portrait of the rural tanner between the 1880s and the 1920s. The possibility of selling hides at the urban market was stated, or implied, to be the motivation to clandestine poisoning. One of the earliest references is, possibly, Hoey, *Monograph on Trade and Manufacture*, 91. See also Central Provinces and Berar, *Industrial Survey*, 58; E. A. H. Blunt, *The Caste System of Northern India* (Lucknow, 1931), 119; Briggs, *The Chamars*, 235; Risley, *People of India*, 133; and Watt, *Dictionary*, 248. A little packet of arsenic 'craftily wrapped in a leaf or a petal of the mohua-flower' was dropped where the cattle were grazing: Risley. In some of these sources, Risley and Watt for example, 'cattle poisoning' is mentioned as a profession in itself. If indeed there were specialist poisoners, nothing very much seems to be known about them. The usual allegations of unlawful use referred to the tanners who as a rule practised it on the side.

[46] Risley, *People of India*, 133.

census, 'actual workers' employed in leather did not decline over 1901–31, though employment may have been stagnant. But participation in tanning by castes identified with leather definitely reduced (see Table 6.2). Further, in contrast with the percentages of traditional leather castes engaged in leather in northern India, the proportions were on average low in the south throughout the census period. This could be due to the entry on a fairly large scale of labouring castes into leather in the south.

Responding to the creation of a market for his services, the village servant was evidently specializing. All over the country, some were giving up leather to become agricultural labourers or to enter 'cleaner' occupations, whereas others were becoming specialist tanners. Often, the attempts to exit leather and to improve social status were reinforced by conversion.[47] Three sorts of avenue seemed to be open to those specializing in leather: to become subcontractors of hide merchants; to become workers in tanneries; and to become traders themselves.

The Chamar who lost hereditary access to fallen cattle was often replaced by the 'contractor', the itinerant agent of the export merchant, or of tanneries, or, in the case of live animals, of the slaughterhouse. The Chamar, however, was frequently a subagent, and privileged to be so, being the only one available to flay and cure the hide locally. For the same reason, the landlord to whom the cattle belonged could ask for a price, but could not displace the Chamar from the trade, since the agent had an advance contract with the Chamar.[48] In the 1890s, Grant found in Punjab that specialist artisans who contracted with the merchants 'on cash principles of ordinary business' were 'absorbing

[47] On options being limited, in the towns of Rajasthan, if Chamars or Mochis tried to become entrepreneurs, or to enter services like running eatery or hotels, 'Savarna Hindus' stoutly resisted them: T. S. Katiyar, *Social Life in Rajasthan* (Allahabad, 1964), 24, 77. For instances of exit from tanning and entry into agriculture or other occupations, see the following: on western India, *Indian Industrial Commission, Evidence*, vol. IV, evidence of Ewbank, Bombay, 546; on Mysore, Nanjundayya and Ananthakrishna Iyer, *The Mysore Tribes and Castes*, vol. IV, 'Madiga'; and in Punjab, the same process was observed later by Tom Kessinger, *Vilayatpur, 1848–1968: Social and Economic Change in a North Indian Village* (Berkeley, 1974), 160–1. In cases, conversion to Sikhism encouraged exit from leather: Darling, *Wisdom and Waste*, 265. In Punjab, the Muslim Chamars did not depend on agriculture at all, whereas a large number of the Ramdasi, Hindus, and Sikhs worked as farmers and labourers: Punjab, *Report of the Punjab Provincial Banking Enquiry Committee, 1929–30* (Lahore, 1930), 302–4. Grant reported in 1891 that some Punjab Hindu Chamars had converted into Islam and called themselves Mochis, that is, they diversified at the same time: *Monograph on the Leather Industry*, 7. The Madigas' refusal to perform village services followed conversion to Christianity: Chatterton, *Monograph on Tanning*, 10.

[48] India, *Hides Cess Enquiry*, evidence of P. B. Advani, Director of Industries, Bombay, 401.

Table 6.2 *Employment in leather, 1901–1931*[a]

	Number of male workers (000s)			
	1901	1911	1921	1931[b]
'Actual workers' in leather:				
Madras	170	160	128	113
Bengal	71	45	53	32
United Provinces	–	120	130	–
Punjab	215	240	–	211
Actual workers in leather from leather castes:				
Madras	58	–	58	–
Bengal	71	–	53	33
United Provinces	–	1-8	119	–
Punjab	–	226	215	178
Proportion of actual workers following traditional occupation (%):				
Madras: Madiga	26	24	18	–
Madras: Chakkiliyan	18	–	13	–
Bengal: Chamar and Mochi	25	32	27	26
United Provinces: Chamar	6	5	–	5
Punjab: Chamar	–	36	35	26
Punjab: Mochi	–	66	73	72

Notes: [a] In the censuses, 'tanning' is defined as a separate order under the general class 'exploitation of materials', but leather products are variously classified by usage. The most important usage is footwear, classified under 'articles of clothing'. We have considered only this item, which implies exclusion of minor products like leather containers, etc. [b] 1931 data refer to 'earner with principal occupation as leather'.
Source: Census of India, 1901, 1911, 1931, *India*, vol. I, Part II (Tables) (Calcutta and Delhi, 1902, 1912, 1933), and Part II (Tables) of corresponding volumes on the major provinces.

and swamping' those still in customary services.[49] A Punjab report of 1930 found that most rural tanners still in the trade had become permanent clients of contractors. The few who could contract directly with the tanneries noticeably prospered. But the majority was without the means to 'hold up their goods for any length of time', and had to rely on intermediaries.[50]

Many others turned to the city, to work in the newly established large tanneries. These could find only Chamars willing to work in the tanning processes, a situation that has changed very slowly to the present day. The movement was something like an exodus: 'In some parts of the country as many as 25 per cent of [the male rural Chamars] are away

[49] Grant, *Monograph on Leather*, 3.
[50] Punjab, *Provincial Banking Enquiry Committee*, 304.

from home half the year.'[51] They were not all working in the tanneries, though tanning remained the occupation where they were most naturally acceptable. The western Indian Mahars moved to 'the cotton mills, gin factories, and railways'. Some of the vacuum, in Khandesh for example, seems to have been filled with migrant Chamars. Their sect names – Dakshini, Pardeshi, Bengali, Hindustani, Marvadi, or Madrasi – indicated diverse origin.[52] The Malas and Madigas of southern Andhra went to the gins and presses.[53] Chhattisgarh Chamars were found in the Assam tea gardens, in the railway workshops of Kharagpur and Chakradharpur, as porters in the railway stations all over the east, and of course, as labourers in Calcutta.[54] Chamars and Mochis formed the largest relatively homogeneous component of labour in the mines and factories in Bengal.[55] Even as early as the 1870s, the central Indian Chamar was known to be very mobile, leaving the village at 'a very slight cause', but usually they tended to return.[56] The first half of the twentieth century, in contrast, witnessed many more permanent migrations. A reference in a 1939 report on central India suggests that, with these migrations and with the redirection of the hide trade from the interior, there occurred a 'de-industrialization' of large areas formerly known for tanning.[57]

The two great famines, 1876 and 1896, especially the former, exposed how severely restricted the entitlements of the lowly within the village could be. Unvaryingly, the most vulnerable groups during the famines, the aimless 'wanderers' who died on the roads, who did not believe the relief camps were meant for them, 'accustomed as they are to

---

[51] Briggs, *The Chamars*, 58.

[52] Maharashtra, *Maharashtra State Gazetteers*, Nasik District (Bombay, 1975), 256–7.

[53] Y. R. Gaitonde, *Report on Village Tanning Industry in the Bombay Presidency* (Bombay, 1930), 25; Madras, *Report of the Madras Famine Code Revision Committee*, vol. II, *Appendices* (Madras, 1940), evidence of C. H. Ranga Rao (Supervisor of Industries, Bellary), 231.

[54] R. V. Russell and Hira Lal, *The Tribes and Castes of the Central Provinces and Berar* (Nagpur, 1916), 'Chamar'. The great melting pots, the plantations and the public works, thus performed the humane role of facilitating a disintegration of caste as a barrier to entry. This process, and the migrant labourer, form the backdrop to Jim Corbett's unforgettable tribute to Chamari, an employee at the Mokama station in the first decade of the century, *My India* (Delhi, 1991).

[55] Ranajit Das Gupta, 'Factory Labour in Eastern India: Sources of Supply, 1855–1946. Some Preliminary Findings', *Indian Economic and Social History Review*, 13, 3 (1976), 319; and C. P. Simmons, 'Recruiting and Organizing an Industrial Labour Force in Colonial India: The Case of the Coal Mining Industry, c. 1880–1939', *Indian Economic and Social History Review*, 13, 4 (1976).

[56] Sherring, *Hindu Tribes and Castes*, vol. II, 111.

[57] Central Provinces and Berar, *Report of the Industrial Survey Committee* (Nagpur, 1939), vol. I, Part II, 124.

be treated like unclean beasts by their countrymen',[58] consisted mainly of the services castes. They were returned in official reports variously as unskilled weavers, 'chucklers', or 'rude artisans'. In the longer run, because food prices were rising somewhat faster than prices of leather exported during 1890–1925 (see Table 6.1), an increasing preference for wage work was likely.[59] The cities offered a cash economy. There were implicit earning differentials between the city and the countryside. The village services carried payments, but usually in kind, and the upper castes often reneged on these.[60] Even when the Chamar's work in the village was already commercialized:

wages [in the tanneries] are so high that it pays the hand-to-mouth Chamar or Chikwa [Muslim goat-butchers] to retire from his own business and enter the service of one of the large tanneries. In Cawnpore small independent tanners are extremely rare. The same is the case elsewhere.[61]

The tendency of cattle owners selling hides or animals directly to the slaughterhouse or its contractors gave the rural tanner, those who could not enter trade, no option but to leave the village.[62]

Further, many important uses of leather within the village were in decline, again loosening the tanners' ties with the village. The water-bag for irrigation was going out of use wherever newer and more centralized systems of water distribution became available. This was mentioned as one of the chief reasons for the decline of rural tanning in Gujarat, Khandesh and Marathwada.[63] The peasant, moreover, clearly preferred chrome-tanned leather in irrigation where he had the option, for the country-made *mot* was notorious for its short life and frequent repairs, 'leaving the *ryot* at the mercy of the chuckler'.[64] Numerous forms of household leather containers were being replaced by metalware. The village drums were yielding to the music of the cities as their makers

[58] Digby, *Famine Campaign*, vol. I, 115; the quote talks about the Madigas. 'Such workmen as ... the chuckler ... are the first to suffer and the last to recover': vol. II, 350.

[59] 'High prices of grain' was mentioned as a reason for the decline of customary services in Punjab: Grant, *Monograph on Leather*, 4, 14, Gujranwala and Jhelum districts especially.

[60] The village tanners in Berar were paid in kind for the leather goods made, or were not paid at all: see H. R. Pitke, 'Hides and Skins Industry in Berar', in *Proceedings of the Ninth Indian Industrial Conference at Karachi, 1913* (Amraoti, 1914). In the late 1920s, some Punjab landlords brought a case against the Chamars' refusal to perform *begar*. The ground was a dispute on customary dues. The landlords lost the case. Anand and Lal, *Tanning Industry in the Punjab*, 35.

[61] Walton, *Monograph on Tanning*, 27.

[62] Russell and Hira Lal, *The Tribes and Castes*, 'Chamar'.

[63] Bombay, *Report of Bombay Leather Survey*, 28. See also Grant, *Monograph on Leather*, 5, on the decline of agricultural usage in Punjab.

[64] Chatterton, *Monograph on Tanning*, 42.

themselves migrated. At the same time, the rural tanners were never adept at the infinitely more delicate processing of guts or skins demanded by the instruments played at the courts or the temples.[65]

Along with all this, there was present a desire to leave the customary roles which constrained attempts to specialize. Thus, with the Chhattis-garh tanners who, by 1915, had dispersed all over eastern India, the most likely reason for 'their taste for emigration [was] the resentment felt at their despised position in Chhattisgarh'.[66] Even as times were changing outside, in the village the Chamar remained 'at the beck and call of the others no matter what their own interests may be'.[67] The landlord, the petty officers, and the upper castes all freely laid claim on their time. A revealing example of this was that of a government servant, a Chamar, who was forced by the *zamindar*'s henchmen onto the field when on vacation in his village. Thus, when asked his caste by the census investigator the Punjab Chamar answered 'coolie', he was not only hiding a stigma, but also being truthful.[68] It is easy to see why a Registrar of Cooperative Societies, when asked about the prospects of collectivizing the rural Chamar, honestly rejected the idea: 'I would rather that the local tanners go to the tanneries at once.'[69] In this one instance, the craftsmen, on joining the proletariat, had nothing to lose but centuries of petrified institutionalized degradation.[70]

Both the urban and the rural Chamars included examples of own-account traders. Thus, with Kanpur beginning to emerge as north India's entrepot in hides:

The extension of the leather trade ... made it a great Chamar centre. Many of them have become wealthy and aim at a standard of social respectability much higher than their rural brethren, and some have begun to seclude their women which every native does as soon as he commences to rise in the world.[71]

Outside, but around the town, 'generally hides of dead cattle are collected in villages by *chamars* and sold in village weekly bazars'.[72] In the smaller towns of Bombay, around 1910, 'there is a peculiar sort of

[65] A brief indirect reference to this differential in skills involved in musical instruments, and its urbanizing effect, appears in Bombay, *Report of Bombay Leather Survey*, 73.

[66] Russell and Hira Lal, *The Tribes and Castes*, 'Chamar'.

[67] Briggs, *The Chamars*, 56.

[68] Ibbetson, *Panjab Castes*, 297.

[69] *Indian Industrial Commission*, Evidence, vol. IV, evidence of Ewbank, 557.

[70] The move to the cities and the cash economy formed the bases for movements for social and political power. For example, see Eleanor Zelliot, 'Mahars and the Non-Brahmin Movement in Maharashtra', *Indian Economic and Social History Review*, 7, 3 (1970).

[71] Crooke, *The Tribes and Castes*, vol. II, 191.

[72] The various instances of Chamar enterprise in the north are from *Hides Cess Enquiry*, evidence of W. C. de Noronha, tanner at Kanpur, 81–2; Briggs, *The Chamars*, 57; and Punjab, *Report of the Industrial Survey of Punjab* (Chandigarh, 1960).

"contract" work to be found', wherein one Chamar supplied the physical capital (hides, bark, lime, and vats) to another, and received the tanned hide 'at a price previously arranged'.[73] Already, in the 1880s, the Chamars owned tanneries in Lucknow, and, judging by the size of the units (multiple pits), were believed to have possessed substantial capital.[74] In the 1890s, the Madigas of the Mysore towns were reported to 'have risen to considerable influence ... on account of the rise in the value of skins.'[75] In the 1910s, cattle dealers in Raipur town in Chhattisgarh were usually Chamars.[76] A survey in the 1950s showed that some tanneries in the Punjab towns involved Chamar capital, and in the cities of the Deccan, Dhors owned tanyards.[77]

The Chamar entrepreneur, thus, was not at all rare. Yet, many instances from the transition in tanning also reveal the constraints the entrepreneurs, especially the rural tanner, had to overcome. In the cities where the caste tanner owned yards, rarely was he known to move into chrome-tanning, which needed greater investment, information, and market access. In the largest tanneries of the country, therefore, Chamar involvement was unknown except as labourers. The mobility of the Chamar was restricted by exclusion from existing business institutions. The Hindu moneylender would scarcely advance credit for tanning.[78] 'In Chhattisgarh, the village tanners are below the status in which more than the most trifling credit is available.'[79] In industrial towns, the availability of credit was a less serious problem than its cost. A tanner in Hoshangabad town could get Rs. 300, no small sum, thanks to 'the lender's knowledge of the extent of his transactions'. In Saugar, a banker regularly lent to the Chamars. But, 'owing to the ill odour in which such a trade is held by respectable Hindus, the dealers are not content with the smaller profits of an anna or two in the rupee'.[80] It would seem that the general aversion to financing tanning and the poor creditworthiness of Chamars placed a few moneylenders in a monopolistic position.

---

[73] Guthrie, *Report on Leather Industries*, 19.

[74] Hoey, *Monograph on Trade and Manufacture*, 92.

[75] Mysore census, 1891, cited in Jogendranath Bhattacharya, *Hindu Castes and Sects* (Calcutta, 1896), 214.

[76] Russell and Hira Lal, *The Tribes and Castes*, 'Chamar'.

[77] D. R. Gadgil, *Sholapur City: Socio-economic Studies* (Bombay, 1965), 140–2. See also N. V. Sovani, *Social Survey of Kolhapur City*, vol. II (Bombay, 1951), 106–12, on both tanning and leather manufactures. Both studies form part of the series of surveys of urban economy conducted under D. R. Gadgil's initiative and leadership by the faculty of the Gokhale Institute of Politics and Economics, Pune.

[78] P. V. Mehd, 'Tanning Industry, its Development in India' in *Proceedings of the Ninth Indian Industrial Conference at Karachi, 1913* (Amraoti, 1914).

[79] Central Provinces and Berar, *Industrial Survey*, 71.

[80] *Ibid.*, 71.

Moreover, unlike textiles, in leather the finished goods would rarely be acceptable collateral, or a valid form of repayment.

And yet, the export trade opened an immense mercantile opportunity. There emerged many tiers of mercantile enterprise of which the most prominent were the export traders located in the port cities, and 'the class of middlemen' who 'gradually [came] into prominence' as intermediaries between the rural suppliers of cattle and hides and the urban slaughterhouse or the export trader.[81] In regions with a plentiful supply of hides, tanning represented an attractive investment for just anyone who had some capital. Neither the ordinary artisan nor members of the Hindu trading castes could seize these opportunities. The former was constrained by hierarchy; the latter was repelled by raw hides. These avenues, therefore, attracted mainly non-Hindu and non-artisan capital, as we shall see.

Factories in cities

Since more or less the only capital needed in vegetable tanning was sufficient space, the urbanization of tanning went along with large-scale production. The scale of the average workshop was always larger in the city than in the village, and wage labour was usual in the cities. But both scale, and the extent of wage labour, expanded enormously during the First World War. The small-scale units could not meet the great increase in demand.[82] The composition of export changed from cured to tanned hides, as England's own tanyards were fully occupied. The import of leather spare parts used by Indian mills stopped. And, finally, there was a greater need to control the quality of tanning. The result was a mushrooming of larger factories in the cities, the biggest of which employed several hundred workers each. Wartime ventures normally suffered from high mortality, but they did transform the industry. The magnitude of the change is captured in the approximate percentages worked out by a 1952 report on hides marketing. Village tanners were estimated to process 43 per cent of the hides, whereas the factories processed 50 per cent (30 per cent for export, 20 per cent for domestic leather producers). The remainder consisted of 'raw', that is, semi-cured, hides for export and hides entering other uses.[83] By the 1950s,

[81] Citation from Grant, *Monograph on Leather*, 14.
[82] Many of the early units in the city were no more than small curing yards under either family firm or team-work systems: see United Provinces, *Industrial Survey*, Cawnpore District. In the first three years of the war, exports in volume almost doubled, and in value increased two-and-a-half times.
[83] India, *Report on the Marketing of Hides in India*, Ministry of Food and Agriculture (Delhi, 1952), 56–7.

the town merchant having his own curing yard in the village was also quite common.

A 1940 report on Punjab described a hierarchy of tanning units in the province. The description seems generalizable. At the smallest scale was the 'village tannery'. This was still mainly an artisan-owned unit, working with family and community labour, using local fallen cattle, but heavily indebted and therefore contract-bound to the hide merchant from the small town. In the middle was the 'town tannery', factories with five to ten hired workers each. The owners were well-off, and had the freedom to choose buyers and suppliers. They took part in both contractual and spot-markets. A fair number of them were of artisan background, but the majority was Khoja or Muslim hide traders. At the top of the scale were the 'big factories' employing 100 or more workers each.[84] There was some European capital in these ventures, though the main source was the larger of the Khoja merchant firms. The first type could be found scattered in rural north India. The second occurred in small towns, but those with a slaughterhouse and a large spot-market (*mandi*) in hides. The third was a feature of major ports and industrial towns.

These towns had specific advantages: raw material availability in Kanpur and Madras; and the ports in Calcutta and Bombay. Kanpur, since its occupation in 1801, housed a cantonment. The local Chamars at that time supplied the troops with the necessary articles, gradually adapting quality by observing the British products.[85] When the mutiny demonstrated the need to have army supply bases close to areas of potential trouble, Kanpur was chosen as the site for a government harness and saddlery factory in 1867. The idea was implemented by a young artillery officer, J. Stewart. The first workers were English soldiers with experience in tanyards. The first hides came from 'commissariat cattle', cattle serving the English officers' need for meat. In 1880, a north Indian managing agency started Cooper Allen, shortly to become the source for the entire Indian army's boots, shoes and saddlery.[86] The

---

[84] K. Quddus Pal, 'The Punjab Tanning Industry', unpublished report prepared for the Punjab Government (Lahore, 1940), 70–2.

[85] In one contemporary source, the leather craftsmen were said to be better off than before by having involved themselves more closely with leather goods manufacture. The statement did not refer to any specific context, but the author was really familiar with the United Provinces: Reverend William Tennant, *Indian Recreations; Consisting Chiefly of Strictures on the Domestic and Rural Economy of the Mahommedans and Hindoos* (Edinburgh, 1803), vol. I, 303–4.

[86] 'The largest individual concern in the world which deals in leather from the raw state to the manufactured article': India, *Hides Cess Enquiry*, evidence of the company, 6. On the origin of these two factories, see Walton, *Monograph on Tanning*, 2–3.

town was close to Agra, Aligarh, Delhi, and Meerut, each of which had a meat trade, and therefore local slaughtering. Aligarh was known for the best buffalo in India. The railways integrated Kanpur with Bihar, Punjab, and Central Provinces, the triangular tract that yielded India's best cattle hides, from 'Darbhanga' to 'Multani'. Forests were within easy reach.[87]

Similarly, Pallavaram, a suburb of Madras, and Ambur about 110 miles west, witnessed a spectacular growth of factories shortly before and during the First World War. The region enjoyed proximity to one of the best vegetable tannins in India, the avaram bark. Large army tanneries existed in the early nineteenth century in Bangalore, in Madras, and about thirty miles west of Mysore town, in Hunsur, where an army cattle farm generated one of the earliest tanneries and a carpet and blanket manufactory. But tanning did not attract private enterprise on a large scale until the legendary efforts of a French Eurasian of Pondicherry, Charles de Susa, who discovered the best way of utilizing the avaram bark. Of the major vegetable tannins in India, avaram had the highest tannin percentage, but it was not always used to its full potential. Until the middle of the nineteenth century, avaram bark tanning tended to produce skins that, on exposure to air, suffered a 'fawn red discolourisation which was previously one of the distinguishing features of country-tanned leathers'.[88] De Susa could avoid this effect by treating the leather in a myrobalan bath, subsequent to tanning. From the time his factory at Pondicherry was at work, in the 1840s, there began a tanning industry near Madras. Avaram was generally acknowledged to be superior to the north Indian tannin, but its best use was in skins and not in hides. The Madras industry, therefore, specialized in skins. An added factor in this choice might have been the relative advantages of regions in livestock. The south's lay in goats and sheep, animals more adaptable to drier and drought-prone regions, rather than cattle which thrive on rich grasslands. As in the north, the railways connected Madras town with a wide area stretching from the Tamil countryside to the southern Andhra, and from the Deccan to Orissa, supplying skins. To these natural advantages were added the growth of Madras as a city, and, thus, as a destination of migrant labour. The main body of manual workers, it would seem, was drawn from the agrarian labour castes, chiefly the Paraiyans. The white-

---

[87] A rough impression of the immense pull of Kanpur, and the centralization of the hide trade, over the vast northern plains can be had from the information on the leather industry available in the district reports of United Provinces, *Industrial Survey*.

[88] Chatterton, *Monograph on Tanning*, 2.

Figure 6.1 Tanning house, Cawnpore Tannery, c.1915. Hides are being carried into the pits in the background. The tannery was established in 1896 by the Armenian, A. H. Creet. At the time of the photograph, it was owned by two Muslim hide merchants based in Delhi and Kanpur.

collar jobs, on the other hand, were sometimes performed by people who owned land. In such cases, the interactions between the 'tannery men' and the 'factory men' reproduced, in a much milder way, the hierarchy in the villages that both had left behind.[89]

The advantages enjoyed by Calcutta and Bombay did not consist in proximity to sources of raw material, but in the facility of trade. First of all, they were the premier ports, major points from where hides were sent out, and, therefore, with a plentiful supply of hides. The ports, and especially Calcutta and Bombay, were served by different railways, and, thus, offered manufacturers and traders competitive freight rates and simpler procedures of quotation. These advantages were unavailable to a town in the interior.[90] As ports and as towns they attracted foreign trading firms. Thus, the growth in the hide trade in prewar Calcutta is associated with German enterprise in the city. The Germans

[89] *Indian Industrial Commission*, Evidence, vol. III, evidence of G. A. Chambers of the Chrome Tanning Co., Pallavaram, 323.

[90] This point is empirically demonstrated by R. D. Tiwari, 'Leather Industry: Its Transport Problem', *Journal of the University of Bombay*, 6, 4 (1938).

Figure 6.2 Skin-drying and scaling yard, Muhammad Sharif A. Rahman's export firm, Amritsar, c.1915. The owner was said to be the largest hide exporter in Amritsar. The first yard was established in 1897, the premises were recently rebuilt. 'The imposing premises known as "Sharif Manzil" have been constructed on modern architectural and scientific principles ... provision [being] made for the safe storage of goods' protecting them from the rains.

in 1913 took as much as 60 per cent of the export of cured hides from that port. When the German traders withdrew all of a sudden, the Indo-British managing agencies moved in, not only as traders, but also as manufacturers.[91] In 1914, the city had only six tanneries in the suburbs.

[91] Trade history subsequent to the withdrawal of German enterprise in Calcutta is briefly as follows. England not only became the major destination for Indian hides during the war, in fact India was the major supplier of hides to the British army. Nearly two-thirds of leather uppers for army boots came from East India *kips*. The British trade realized the worth of Indian supplies, and got the Imperial Institute to write a plea for a discriminatory export duty on Indian *kips* under the Imperial Preference. The Institute obliged. 'imperial interests demand that the trade ... should be ... securely in the hands of British firms': Imperial Institute, *Reports on Hides and Skins*, 5. In 1919, a duty of 15 per cent was imposed, with a 10 per cent rebate for export within the empire. The duty does not seem to have destroyed German trade, which did revive, but possibly pushed it towards the better grades of hides: India, *Minutes of Evidence Recorded by the*

Figure 6.3 Selecting hides, Fatehmahomed Dostmahomed's export firm, Amritsar, *c*.1915. The firm was founded in 1860. It purchased hides from northern India, arsenicated them, and exported them. Their godowns and baling presses were spread out from Lahore to Karachi, to Calcutta.

None had any machinery to speak of, the Chamar foremen providing all the expert knowledge, with a combined output not exceeding 100 hides a day. In 1921, there were 240 small and 12 large tanneries, tanning about 1,500 hides and skins a day. In 1929, the city had 300 tanneries, tanning annually 1.9 million hides and skins, and 1.4 million lizard skins.[92] One major byproduct of this boom was the start of commercial chrome tanning. Although many of the wartime concerns failed, the method survived. Towns like Calcutta were also major destinations of migrant labour. The labour force in tanning was entirely made up of migrant Chamars from north India and the coastal south. They adapted

Indian Fiscal Commission (Calcutta, 1923), 351. Also, the trader composition almost certainly diversified in the interwar period, with more British and American participation, and the rise of Indian firms who had started as subcontractors of the Germans. This last tendency will be discussed further below. On the shift from German to English dominance in the trade via Calcutta, see B. R. Rau, *The Economics of the Leather Industry* (Calcutta, 1925), 38–41.

[92] The monitor lizard, once ubiquitous in eastern Bengal, did not survive this assault for long. It is now one of the 'highly endangered' species of wildlife in India.

very quickly to new processes. Although they visited their villages at harvest time, they were beginning to settle down in the city in the 1920s.

Already in 1900, Bombay's 'neighbouring village Dharavi ... is entirely given up to the tanning industry'. The tanneries were owned by the Bohra and Memon merchants, groups controlling Bombay's hide trade, though, interestingly, one tannery belonged to a Mochi. Shortly after the war, the city had thirty tanneries, which number did not seem to increase in the next ten years. One large chrome-tanning unit had started meanwhile. The workforce in Dharavi consisted of Tamil-speaking caste tanners who were reputed to furnish better labour than the local tanners.[93] This efficiency of the Tamil labourers seemingly derived from knowledge of avaram. In Poona and Belgaum, the local tanners tried hard to get the recipe from them, but 'the Madras tanners will not teach them'. This control was a source of some instability. The tanners were routinely accused of 'running away' after they took advances. Such hazards must have eventually declined with the spread of chrome tanning.[94]

Finally, the city and the factory had several decisive advantages over rural tanners on economy in resource use. An important advantage of the big cities was water. Tanning on a large scale was intensive in water, but did not have easy access to water that was common property to the village. It needed a system of centralized supply such as a modern city could offer. Back at the village, not only fallen hides, but access to other commons had also been curtailed. Forest products were now collected on bulk contracts between the government and contractors, and the latter refused to sell them in small lots.[95] Salt had become expensive because of the salt tax. The Salt Act did allow tax-free salt for industrial uses, but only if the user was rich enough to own a *pucca* godown, and to pay quite substantial inspection charges.[96]

The number of large tanneries in India rose from thirteen in 1901 to sixty-six in 1939, and labourers working in them doubled. 1919 was an exceptionally good year. But thereafter the factory sector shrunk somewhat, partly due to the bankruptcy of some wartime concerns, and partly due to enforcement of the Factories Act in 1934. Of the 1921

[93] Among the sources on the two cities, see especially India, *Hides Cess Enquiry*, evidence of B. M. Das, superintendent of Bengal Tanning Institute, 113–16, and evidence of Advani, 401; *Indian Industrial Commission*, Evidence, vol. II, evidence of B. M. Das, 82; and Martin, *Monograph on Tanning*, 2, 30.
[94] Gaitonde, *Report on the Village Tanning*, 48–9, 53, 57, 62 on Dharavi, Kurla, and Madras labour.
[95] *Ibid.*, p. 25.
[96] About Rs. 100 in 1939. 'These regulations are evidently made by persons who have not the slightest knowledge of village conditions ... one hundred rupees is a fortune' to the villager. Central Provinces and Berar, *Report of Industrial Survey Committee*, 24.

census on employment in leather, factories employed 5 per cent in United Provinces, and 4 per cent of tanning workers in Madras. But these figures are an underestimate because the 'factories' here refer only to concerns officially registered as such. A provincial survey of unregistered factories was carried out during the Royal Commission on Labour in 1931.[97] The survey showed that, in Madras, 776 tanneries employed close to 10,000 workers, more than double the 4,000 employed in larger tanneries. According to the 1931 census, the small and large factories engaged about a quarter of the workers in tanning in this province. The survey seems to be less complete for the other provinces. The Bombay and the Bengal ones contain some descriptions of the new organizations. While tanning was usually a male occupation,[98] in some factories in Bombay, women and children were employed sorting wool. These surveys also suggest a survival and relocation of small-scale tanning in the city. In the 1920s in Calcutta, collectives of three or four Chamars hiring a shed, a few workers, and some children above ten were observed.[99] However, such units were not known to perform high-quality tanning.

Already by the turn of the century, a sufficient number of tanners had evolved out of the unfreedom of the peasant economy into a wage labourer, but it was a labour market with fluid and unstable contracts. Walton in 1903 reported a rise in wages in Kanpur:

The presence of many other large employers in Cawnpore makes the cooly an important man, and in a way he is master of the situation. Competition among employers has raised the wages of the ordinary cooly by about Rs. 4 a month. The unskilled labourers can easily command a wage of Rs. 5 to Rs. 8, and the skilled Rs. 10 to Rs. 30. Either of them can live comfortably on Rs. 5 a month.[100]

Labour scarcity also increased the turnover of labour. And it threatened, as Walton noted disapprovingly, the hierarchy within the factory. But these must have been transitional problems, for such complaints were

[97] *Royal Commission on Labour in India*, vol. XI (Supplementary) (London, 1931). Although the survey was claimed to be a census, for many provinces it does not appear to be so.
[98] Employment of women in tanning appears extremely rare. But there do exist some exceptions, from rural tanning as well as factories. Chatterton observed women currying the tanned hide in the south: *Report of the Madras Exhibition*, 1855, cited in Chatterton, *Monograph on Tanning*, 2. A fuller description of women's work can be found in a study on Punjab. In Punjab factories, women ground *sajji*, or saline earth, and babul bark. Inside the homes of the skilled leather artisans, women embroidered shoes, or spun wool. In rural pit tannery, women were mainly engaged in fetching water. Anand and Lal, *Tanning Industry in the Punjab*, 26.
[99] *Royal Commission on Labour*, 38, 62.
[100] Walton, *Monograph on Tanning*, 28.

never raised in the sources on the interwar period, even as the average size of the factory, and the number of factories, expanded greatly.

Technical change

The tendency of the craft to concentrate in larger units in the cities was strengthened by the need to intervene in technology. Exports highlighted the fact that the rural Chamar 'at present ... turns a decent hide into an abominable leather'.[101] In fact, the hide was so poor as to make Indian exports driven by the residual foreign demand, and thus highly unstable: 'If China's or other markets [Java, for example] are low, Indian stuffs do not find sale anywhere.'[102] The relatively poor quality was partly due to the size and health of the animal: the Chinese produced a much heavier hide than the Indian. But there was also bad and careless processing. Curing under the Indian sun so hardened and contracted the fibres of the skin that great efforts were needed to loosen the pores again for the skin to absorb tan. Excessive use of lime damaged the fibres. Systematic and clever adulteration so as to increase the weight of the cured hide sometimes damaged the hide (when too much lime was added), or, at the very least, defrauded the trader (when chalk or plaster was added on the flesh side). Weak finishing produced unattractive leather. Bad flaying left either too much flesh, or too many cuts. The indelible brands on cattle destined for consumption by the troops, marks left by the yoke, and in regions like Bombay where the driving stick had a nail fixed at its end, by the 'merciless' application of the goad, disfigured the leather.[103]

The universal response was to take as many processes as possible away from the rural Chamar to the tannery, leaving to him the barest curing essential. Sources around 1900 described country finishing processes, including dyeing. But by the time of the Hides Cess Enquiry in 1929, descriptions of technology make no reference to finishing. The proportion of cured hides in total exports was falling in the long run in favour of tanned and dressed hides. Cured hides were merely the *sukties* collected from the villages and exported; tanned hides came from the

---

[101] Central Provinces and Berar, *Industrial Survey*, 66.

[102] India, *Hides Cess Enquiry*, evidence of Mohamad Latif, exporter of Kanpur, 37. The witness, however, had an interest in exaggerating instability and thus opposing an export cess.

[103] Branding was an extensive and notorious practice. Other than on 'commissariat' cattle, branding was resorted to in certain sicknesses of the cattle, as a mark of ownership, and with a motive similar to poisoning, to impair the value of the hide and thus preempt claimants. See, on the latter, *Indian Industrial Commission*, Evidence, vol. III, evidence of G. A. Chambers, 321.

urban tanneries. Direct contracting between the slaughterhouse and the tannery eliminated not only the rural Chamar, but also one stage in curing. A second response was to switch from sun-dried to wet-salted curing, less accessible to the average rural tanner. A third form of adaptation involved close supervision by large export firms whose 'mufassil agencies' worked much harder to establish direct contact and dialogue with the village tanner.[104] A fourth response was the Madras 'half-tan'. The half-tan was in fact a nearly finished leather, but carrying a tan easily removable so that the leather could be retanned. Retanning possibilities made the product flexible as an intermediate, suitable for a variety of uses, and increased its export demand. The half-tan industry was in a class of its own. It had a distinct market. Its producers had different interests from those of the north Indian tanning lobby.[105] And its larger extent and more successful career induced not only greater advances in sorting and standardization of material, but also greater local supply of hides and skins.[106] In 1945, Madras had 12 per cent of India's cattle, but 25 per cent of *kips* production (see Table 6.3). Not only the slaughtering rate, but also the proportion of fallen cattle, were higher than average. There being no reason to believe that animals had higher mortality in Madras, reporting and collection must have been better.

But, despite urbanization, the old problems found only limited solutions, for the smaller tanneries in the cities carried on some of the bad practices. B. M. Das, Superintendent of the Calcutta Research Tannery, described a typical small tannery in Calcutta:

A thatched or tiled hut, with a dozen pit and tubs equipped with a couple of unhairing and fleshing palm-tree beams . . . The owners, mostly Muhammadans, do not trouble much about the technical side of the tannery and leave the manufacture entirely in the hands of mistries (chamar foremen). The mistry is usually illiterate and all the wealth of his technical knowledge consists in what has been handed down to him by his fore-fathers. Though he sometimes makes good leathers, his methods are at least half a century behind the times.[107]

The First World War, when demand for good-quality hides increased, exposed the weaknesses of this form of enterprise and encouraged larger and more modern firms to enter the industry.

---

[104] For two examples tying up German firms at Calcutta with their north Bihar suppliers, see J. G. Cumming, *Review of the Industrial Position and Prospects in Bengal in 1908*, Part II of Special Report (Calcutta, 1908), 19.

[105] The Madras half-tanners favoured an export duty on hides, debated and introduced in 1929, whereas the Bombay and Karachi lobbies opposed it.

[106] India, *Hides Cess Enquiry*, Report, 29.

[107] B. M. Das, 'Researches in Tanning and the Calcutta Research Tannery', *Journal of Indian Industries and Labour*, 1, 1 (1921), 35.

Table 6.3 *Production of kips*[a] *in India, 1945*[b]

	Cattle population (million)	Fallen hides in population (percentage)	Slaughtered hides in population (percentage)	Total *kips* produced (million)
Bombay	10.3	8.5	1.6	1.0
Madras	16.6	16.9	4.1	3.5
United Provinces	21.7	4.7	0.6	1.1
West Bengal	8.5	9.4	4.7	1.2
India	140.0	8.8	1.4	14.2

Notes: [a] Lightweight cattle hide. [b] A comparable output figure for the middle of the 1920s comes from A. C. Inskip of Messrs Cooper Allen in his evidence before the Hides Cess Enquiry: 1929. Estimated cattle population: 180 million; assumed mortality: 10 per cent (a generally accepted figure); and estimated hide output: 18 million hides. This is for undivided India, whereas the table refers to the present boundary of India. In 1927, exports at 8.7 million hides constituted 47 per cent of production.
Source: India, *Report on the Marketing of Hides in India*, Ministry of Food and Agriculture (Delhi, 1950).

Meanwhile, new problems arose. A report on Punjab in 1940 listed as many as twenty-two defects of Indian hides, of which eleven occurred in the relatively new sites, the slaughterhouse and the factory floor.[108] The most distressing was the butcher's cuts at the public slaughterhouses. Bad flaying meant that the flayers cut the inner tissues of hides making the piece useless for the tanner. These cuts randomly crisscrossed on the inside of the finished leather.[109] A universal reason for the increase in flaying defects was the partial withdrawal of hereditary tanning castes from the process. Simultaneously, new people entered the craft. In the north, the peak season for slaughtering was the winter, from October to March. Fodder was plentiful in the post-monsoon months, yielding good hides. November to May was the busy season for the collection of forest produce. The hazards of sun-drying hides were smaller. And this was the season meat was dried for export to Burma. Slaughtering and flaying were done in the night until dawn, because the day was spent in sorting and purchases of animals. The building being small, much of the peak season operations took place in the open. The master-butcher had a 'following of young lads of the caste who are being initiated into the art of flaying'.[110] Already distressed by poor light and the chill, the inexper-

[108] Quddus Pal, 'The Punjab Tanning Industry', 29–31.
[109] Cooper Allen, who presumably had better access to good quality hides than the smaller producers, stated: '75 per cent of the hides passing through our hands are damaged by bad flaying': India, *Hides Cess Enquiry*, evidence of Cooper Allen, 7.
[110] *Ibid.*, evidence of A. E. Corbett, exporter of Kanpur, 29.

ienced boys worked as fast as they could to turn a miserable piece-rate of three to five annas per animal into a respectable time wage. Added to these problems were the minor local variations in manners of flaying, which made standardization difficult.[111] Bad flaying, moreover, carried no punishment as the hides were sold on live animals.[112]

During the war, a great deal of persuasion was tried, jointly by the Munitions Board and the Directors of Industries, with some effect. But, after the war, these efforts stopped, 'with the result that things have more or less reverted to their original state in many places'.[113] More noteworthy attempts are associated with larger individual concerns in Peshawar, Calcutta, and Aligarh. Incentives were offered sometimes by the buyer of the hide, and sometimes by the employer of flayers. In Calcutta, the scale of the factory expanded and more Indo-British capital entered production. In the early years of the war, excess demand led to the sale of under-tanned leather. But the recession after the war forced a welcome adaptation in quality. While many small firms failed, 'the standard has now been raised and a very large amount of capital has been brought into the business by the large firms'.[114] Although new problems were created by mass production, it was recognized that the solution had to be found in the framework of mass production. Going back to the rural supplier would not work: 'In the villages buyers would not pay bonus for good flaying', for monitoring quality over a widely dispersed body of producers was impossible.[115]

Despite improvements, Indian hides retained the image of poor quality. This combined with the world depression to cause exports to remain low and stagnant throughout the 1930s. Surprisingly, however, there was no report of a crisis in tanning, 'for the local market has not let [the tanners] down'.[116] Even before the First World War, Chamars in the cotton tracts made unconventional products. These were leather for a variety of mechanical usage, such as covering for gin rollers, for the top rollers of draw frames, sheep skins used in grain mills for polishing grains, etc.[117] This small trade grew during the war. Imports having

---

[111] Guthrie, *Report on Leather Industries*, 3, refers to the hazardous and 'peculiar method of cutting' at the Bandra slaughterhouse.

[112] In Calcutta, butchers' cuts owed to the practice of extracting as much meat as the flayer could: India, *Hides Cess Enquiry*, evidence of B. M. Das, 96.

[113] On the injunctions, see Indian Munitions Board, *Industrial Handbook*, 163–4; Gaitonde, *Report on Village Tanning*, 3; and *Indian Industrial Commission*, Evidence, vol. I, evidence of A. Carnegie, manufacturer, Cawnpore, 121.

[114] Indian Munitions Board, *Industrial Handbook*, 20. The large firms included the Sassoons, Graham and Co., the well-known agency Bird and Co., Grace Bros., etc.

[115] India, *Hides Cess Enquiry*, evidence of Latif, 36–9.

[116] *Ibid.*, evidence of Pandit, 387.

[117] Guthrie, *Report on Leather Industries*, 1.

stopped, many essential industrial implements like belting and roller skins for the textile mills were in short supply. To supply this market, some tanneries in Calcutta and Bombay started leather manufacture.[118] The fact that chrome-tanned leather was especially suited to these new uses was a reason for the expansion in chrome tanning in Calcutta. Import-substitution apart, a more important inducement for the strengthening of domestic demand for hides arose from a change in the craft the Mochi performed.

Effects on leather manufactures

Long-distance trade in raw material had complex effects on the artisan engaged in leather articles. It did help the manufacturer, especially the urban artisan, by improving the quality of hides, and thereby enabling diversification. But it also constrained the rural leatherworker and those engaged in traditional articles. On the demand side, trade altered tastes. On the supply side, trade created a shortage of hides.

A great many old uses for leather were in decline. The oil and perfume containers, the water-bag, saddlery, and embroidered shoes were essential ingredients of urban life in the early nineteenth century, but quickly faded away in the interwar period. Glass and ceramics replaced leather in some of its uses. Piped water did away with the *Bhishtis*. Civil demand for saddlery decreased with the extension of motor transport in the cities. In the case of shoes, the integration of internal commerce at first helped the leather manufacturer. '[I]t is probable', wrote J. L. Kipling, the Principal of the Mayo School of Art at Lahore, 'that the trade [in embroidered shoes of Delhi] has greatly increased [since 1864], for the railway has opened new markets, and shapes unknown in the Punjab are now made, e.g. the Maratha shoes.'[119] But long-distance trade in leather goods was rather exceptional. It was also wholly urban. And, in this sphere, the demand for better finished wares, such as the new imported articles, was on the rise.

About 1900, 'prosperous natives' of Bombay had more or less given up the locally made shoes, and adopted those of western fashion. In

---

[118] 'The mills have themselves discovered that country leather will serve many purposes for which formerly imported leather was used': Indian Munitions Board, *Industrial Handbook*, 19, 42, 167–8. For a brief description of the early history of a firm manufacturing (substituting imports in the process) pickers, a leather shock-absorber in the picking motion of a loom, see I. M. Mansuri, 'Picker Industry in India', in Central Leather Research Institute, *Symposium on Tanning*; another source on the western Indian picker industry is Bombay, *Report of Bombay Leather Survey*, Appendix F, 153–5.

[119] J. L. Kipling, 'The Industries of the Punjab', *Journal of Indian Art (and Industry)*, 2 (1887–8), 29.

1910, in Bombay city, 'some considerable time spent in observing the footwear of those who wore any at all revealed that nearly one-third used European shoes.'[120] In Bengal at the same time, foreign shoes were sold in all bazaars and fairs, whereas 'fifty years back they were to be found only in the largest towns'. In the Central Provinces, foreign shoes had replaced local footwear in the towns and among 'the richer classes of villagers'. Interestingly, foreign shoes were uniformly more expensive, or without any noticeable price advantage. The reason for their popularity lay partly in the quality of the leather, and partly in their better shape and greater range of sizes. The country craftsman was notorious for his disregard for anatomy, forcing his clientele to be as a rule 'content with anything that approximately fits them'.[121] More subtly but universally, foreign shoes served as status symbol: 'the loud creaking ... is a great attraction, as it advertises to all and sundry on the owner's possession of up-to-date footwear.'[122] By the 1920s, the typical country shoe, reddish with a curled front, was beginning to become obscure, and, with it, a whole catalogue of products was on the way to a quiet exit. The *shiroli*, or Poona Brahman shoes, the *marhatti* or the two-toed Ahmednagar shoes, the standard slippers or *chapli* of the entire north and northwest and the *hafti* of the west, the Parsis' Surati *jora*, the Goa *sapat*, the Konkani Muslims' *zenani juta*, the Memons' half-shoes, the *bandhai*, *astaria*, and *alga* of central India, the *salimshahi*, *punjabi*, *golpanja*, and *zerpai* of the north, each serving a specific caste and regional clientele, were no longer products worth remarking in connection with the cobbler's art.[123]

What is remarkable is the ease with which the cobbler seemed to reorient his skills. Long before the mutiny, leather artisans supplied European residents with the style of shoes they wanted.[124] In the 1870s, the Mochis used imported leather in the northern towns to manufacture shoes and saddlery.[125] References to imported inputs become scarce

[120] Guthrie, *Report on Leather Industries*, 3.

[121] Chatterton, *Monograph on Tanning*, 37.

[122] On change of tastes in western India, see Martin, *Monograph on Tanning*, 9; on change of tastes in Bengal, see Rowland N. L. Chandra, *Tanning and Working in Leather in the Province of Bengal* (Calcutta, 1903), 3; the quotation is from Central Provinces and Berar, *Industrial Survey*, 59.

[123] For a description of indigenous north Indian footwear, and of the *jutafarosh* who made and retailed them, see Hoey, *Monograph on Trade and Manufactures*, 124–6; and B. H. Baden-Powell, *Handbook of the Economic Products of the Punjab*, vol. II (Lahore, 1872), 129–36. One instance of survival is the *kolhapuri*. It proved adaptable to the times, apparently due to the superior bag-tanning process for the sole practised by the Dhors in Kolhapur, Satara, and Poona, and to that balanced mix of utility and lightness of design which ensured a future for many other artisan goods.

[124] Tennant, *Indian Recreations*, vol. I, 304.

[125] Baden-Powell, *Handbook of Economic Products*, 125.

later on, but the skills remained. The Mochi could 'copy faithfully any pattern or shape of imported boots, shoes, and other articles'.[126] In 1908, Chatterjee noted in the north a great demand for country-made 'European' shoes better known as the *bút*, 'the supply [of which] is not equal to the demand'. In the towns, those making ornamental shoes began to make boots and shoes of standard shapes, harnesses, bags, and portmanteaux.[127] This was surely 'a profitable trade', as any contemporary account of the Mochis as a caste suggest.[128] Ewbank observed in 1918 that 'the boot-making classes seem to be doing very well'.[129] Indeed, many of them in Gorakhpur, Kanpur, Lucknow, and Calcutta were engaged by army contractors to supply large consignments of *munda* shoes during the war.[130] The 1921 census attributed a rise in the proportion of Mochis following their traditional occupation to these prospects of diversification.

The First World War, and the trade dislocation immediately after the end of the war, was again a decisive event. In 1920–1, a large part of the capacity in tanning that had been created during the war was threatened by unemployment. Input prices were consequently low. At the same time, with the exchange rate having appreciated due to inflation in silver, many new firms decided to import machinery and tools needed for boot and shoe manufacture.[131] Manufacturers had to rely on the home market, for, while the global trade in leather grew, many countries had erected stiff protection for their own leather industries. If the 1870s started the hide trade and the war started larger factory enterprise, the early 1920s were the time of transition from intermediate to finished goods manufacture.

If tanning became urbanized, leather tended to as well. As the village tanner disappeared, so did the connection between tanning and leather-making in the villages. Good hides were found in the cities more cheaply than in the village. To this was added a long inflation in hide prices. By the first decade of the present century, the Kanpur tanneries had 'no leather to spare for the bazar', causing a 'great contraction in the supply of hides and skins for the local industry'.[132] In most places near a big hide market for exports, the Mochis had to be satisfied with 'triple

[126] Gaitonde, *Report on Village Tanning*, 26.
[127] Chatterjee, *Notes on Industries*, 105.
[128] Blunt, *The Caste System*, 237.
[129] *Indian Industrial Commission*, Evidence, vol. IV, evidence of Ewbank, 546.
[130] Indian Munitions Board, *Industrial Handbook*, 21, 42.
[131] See, on the postwar period, H. Ledgard, 'The Hide, Skin and Leather Trades and Boot and Shoe Manufacturing in India', *Journal of Indian Industries and Labour*, 1, 2 (1922).
[132] Chatterjee, *Notes on Industries*, 99–101.

rejections'.[133] In Bombay, similarly, the leather artisans found themselves eliminated from their customary access to hides once the tannery
agents began contracting directly with the Mahars.[134]

Mochis, therefore, moved into the cities. Some worked with families,
but many were labourers in small factories. In 1903, Martin saw
settlements of recently migrated Mochis around Bombay town. They
settled in Dharavi in workshops employing four to six workers on piece-
rates. Whether due to collective work, or to better quality leather, or the
proximity to a market that better reflected tastes, they produced 'a larger
variety of products and a better class of workmanship'. They came from
as far as Bengal; the Bengalis in particular supplied the 'cleverest
workmen'. In 1908, Chatterjee found leather footwear to be a prominent industry in Meerut, Agra, Lucknow, Kanpur, Allahabad, and
Benares. The industry was owned by Mochis who had immigrated
recently. In 1916, Ibbetson stated that 'in the east of the Punjab the
name [Mochi] usually applied only to the more skilled workmen of the
towns'. Chatterjee also came across 'a growing class of Musalmans as
well as Hindus in the province who would be willing to embark on the
enterprise'. Twenty years later, Agra was probably India's largest centre
of leather manufacture. In 1923–4, this industry employed, in Agra
town alone, 25,000 persons: 'small capitalists belonging to the middle
classes take to it more kindly than to leather-making.' In Allahabad in
1930, shoe-making took place in Mochi-owned *karkhanas*. These employed Mochi workers. A few used power-driven machinery and made
innovative styles, to popularize which 'the municipal leather school is
doing a lot'.[135] In 1924, a cottage industry survey found Mochis tending
to settle in the suburbs of Calcutta, Dacca, and the smaller towns. Many
were migrants from the 'up-country', and workers in small factories. As
in tanning, the actual artisans often belonged to the traditional castes.
Possibly only in Calcutta on a large enough scale, the Chinese immigrants had supplied the local demand for European-style footwear from
the late nineteenth century. But, by the end of the 1920s, the axis of
shoe manufacture and trade moved from the Chinese-held central

[133] *Indian Fiscal Commission*, evidence of L. C. Mousell of Calcutta Hides and Skins
Exporters' Association, 350.
[134] Guthrie, *Report on Leather Industries*, 19.
[135] Shanti Prasad Shukla, 'A Survey of Small Urban Industries of Allahabad City', in
United Provinces, *United Provinces Provincial Banking Enquiry Committee*, Evidence,
vol. II (Allahabad, 1930), 420. See also, on Bombay, Martin, *Monograph on Tanning*,
2, 9, 26; on Punjab, Ibbetson, *Panjab Castes*, 300; on United Provinces, Chatterjee,
Notes on Industries, 98, 105; on Agra especially, United Provinces, *Report of the
Industries Reorganisation Committee* (Allahabad, 1934), 21; on Bengal, Chandra,
Tanning and Working in Leather, 2; and, on Bombay generally, see Gaitonde, *Report on
Village Tanning*, 26.

Figure 6.4 Mochi workshop. central India, *c*.1900

Calcutta market, towards the northern suburbs. Here, Punjabi Muslims owned workshops, and north Indian Mochis worked in them. They not only displaced imported shoes completely, but were also known to be so skilful that 'their services are requisitioned even by the reputed European firms'.[136] Thus began a network of subcontracting relationships to which the city's privileged situation in leather trade owed a great deal. In Madras, similarly, the small and scattered collectives of Mochis usually consisted of immigrants from Bombay. Significantly, and bearing a parallel with tanning, the immigrant Mochis asserted a higher social standing than they would command in the lands they came from.[137]

[136] Bengal, *Report on the Survey of Cottage Industries in Bengal*, second edition (Calcutta, 1929), 40.
[137] The Mochis of Madras wove the thread, 'pretensions' that would not be 'admitted on the Bombay side': Chatterton, *Monograph on Tanning*, 13. This reference touches on a fairly universal tendency in artisan history. It would appear that the local societies tended to be more ambiguous about the relative status of the highly skilled commodity-producing craftsmen than they were with the position of the priestly, propertied, or the labouring groups. Artisans, in other words, could realistically try to alter their station by settling in newer territories where their skill was highly valued, but their background was unknown. Hence, we find an almost universal tendency for skilled craftsmen to migrate, or, more precisely, to consider themselves aliens wherever they lived and worked. Usually, this image was associated with social practices and claims invariably disputed by some of the local elite.

The combination of factories, Mochi craftsmen, and middle-class capital is the story of many smaller towns as well in different parts of India. It was not rare for the workshop to belong to the Mochi himself. In Punjab, Badenoch found Mochi enterprise in Karnal supplying government stores, and noted with satisfaction that 'the mochi is quick to learn'.[138] In western India, Sholapur and Satara had a previous history in bag-tanning. As they became points of hide trade, leather workshops sprang up. In Poona and Ahmadnagar, many leather foot-wear *karkhanas* were reported in the middle of the 1930s. They were owned by 'rich Chamhar and Bohara merchants'. Each employed about five to ten 'Pardeshi' (literally 'foreign', sometimes a sectname of the leather artisans) cobblers, used machinery and 'possess[ed] a very high skill in their profession'. Immigrant cobblers could be seen settled in colonies at the outskirts of several towns.

The organization of this industry was less like that of tanning, and resembled that in any skilled craft, 'with its eternal triangle formed by the *karkhanadar*, the independent worker and the dependent worker'.[139] An 'independent' worker was one who sold in a spot-market, and had to absorb the price fluctuations that could prove unbearable. A dependent worker was on a putting-out contract. Dependence was safer and often the only option available to an immigrant artisan. The *karkhana* was a particular form of putting-out, and the preferred option for a trader or substantial artisan trying to establish a brand image for his goods.

Capitalists

Both in tanning and in leather, participation of Hindu castes or artisans in large-scale production was rare. At the same time, entrepreneurship was more diverse here than in any other manufactures. Presumably, the Hindu trading castes' avoidance of the craft had also reduced guild-like barriers to entry for others.

The tanning trade and industry were dominated by Muslims, Europeans, Parsis, Eurasians, and the Chinese. Of them, the Muslim merchant had the closest access to the village. The Muslim rural hide trader was, in different regions, called the Sheikh, Khoja, Quassai (butchers), or the Kachchi. The tanning/scavenging castes were the main collectors of hides, but as agents of the rural trader. In the 1920s,

---

[138] A. C. Badenoch, *Punjab Industries, 1911–12* (Lahore, 1917), 22; and Bombay, *Report of the Bombay Economic and Industrial Survey Committee, 1938–1940* (Bombay, 1940), 68.

[139] Y. S. Pandit, *Economic Conditions in Maharashtra and Karnatak* (Poona, 1936), 125–7.

the Punjab Khojas were described as having 'spr[ung] up recently'.[140] In fact, their rise to prominence began almost four decades ago. In the 1890s, the Khoja was 'to the Mochi what the Bania is to the agriculturist',[141] that is, they were mainly financiers and traders. In the 1930s, they were not only the most important figure in hide trade, but also present as slaughterers and factors. They had the means to stock up hides, which they sold either to the Mochi, or at the local *mandi*. They lent money to their suppliers, the rural artisans, which debts made the contracts almost permanent ones. Sometimes they lent money to and bought hides from somewhat larger tanneries. From unpaid debts in this sphere, many Khoja traders turned factors.[142]

In Madras, the early enterprise in tanning was entirely in the hands of the Eurasians, though 'their lack of energy, improvidence and inferior business capacity enabled Muhammadans and native tanners to cut them out'.[143] The most important factories of the prewar decade were owned by Muslim entrepreneurs. The entrepreneurs did not accumulate money in leather alone, but often entered leather via, or combined it with, major tradables like seeds (H. M. Gibson), timber (Osman Hassan), wool (Hyath Batcha), bark (Bangi Hyath Badsha Saib), and piece-goods (Hyath Batcha). Most of these firms were on the verge of entry in the 1880s or the 1890s. The oldest surviving Madras firms at middle of the century, such as the Parpia family concerns, were set up by merchants who migrated from Kuchch in the 1860s. These firms' interests in raw products necessitated dispersed operations, and, even in 1914, when many were rooted in Madras, their business vitally relied on yards located in towns close to the sources of skin supply, in Bellary, Bombay–Deccan, Rajahmundry, and Eluru. A minority of the Madras firms was European. A young man in his twenties, G. A. Chambers was an assistant in one of the Madras tanneries, when in 1903 he began trading on his own account. Shortly after, he rented a tannery at Pallavaram to start chrome tanning. The largest Madras firm, the Chrome Leather Company, evolved from this venture, its growth owing to a partnership with the great Madras house and coachmakers, Simpsons, who needed chrome leather for upholstery. As in Bombay, the firm also supplied cotton mill spare parts.[144]

In Kanpur, on the other hand, European and Eurasian capital was

---

[140] Punjab, *Provincial Banking Enquiry*, 302–3.
[141] Grant, *Monograph on Leather*, 6.
[142] Quddus Pal, 'The Punjab Tanning Industry', 173–6.
[143] Chatterton, *Monograph on Tanning*, 2.
[144] Based on Somerset Playne, *Southern India: Its History, People, Commerce, and Industrial Resources* (London, 1914–15), 145–6, 213, 688, 701–3; and *Indian Leather Trades and Industries Year-book*, Madras, 1967.

strongly involved.[145] But these ventures could not do without the cooperation of Muslim traders. Thus, there was always an avenue of mobility open to the Muslim hide trader. Some of the most successful Muslim tanners in Kanpur, the firms of H. M. Halim, of Abdul Gafoor, and of M. A. Wasay and H. Nabi Baksh, accumulated capital through the agency of the European tanneries, or as agents of the many German trading firms prominent in the trade through Calcutta. The partial eclipse of the German cartel during the First World War was the chance they needed to consolidate in trade and procurement, and enter manufacture.[146] In Bombay in the late nineteenth century, the Bohras and Memons, the Muslim trading castes, owned tanneries.

In Calcutta, the earliest tannery, possibly the first modern tannery in India, was a European venture started in 1795. This was John Teil's Watgunge yard, which held exclusive army contracts until the establishment of the Kanpur factories in the 1860s, and was a great help in the Anglo-Burmese wars.[147] In prewar Bengal, the largest and the best known tannery was a Bengali *swadeshi* venture, but the war boom was led largely by Chinese tanners.

By contrast with tanning, firms manufacturing leather had the considerable presence of the artisan capitalists, the Mochis. As trade in European-style footwear increased, the Mochi owners of small firms were not displaced but absorbed in subcontracting relationships with large trading firms who arose by and large from a tannery and hide trade

[145] We have already referred to the two integrated government factories at Kanpur. One of the best known and early private tanneries in the city was set up by A. H. Creet, an Armenian born in Persia. Creet migrated to India in 1874, and was first a jeweller in Lucknow, then a dealer in leather *c.* 1880–1, and finally proprietor of the Cawnpore Tannery in 1896. A decade later, the factory was sold to a partnership between one William Stork, Hafiz Abdul Kazi, and Hafiz Mohammad Halim, the last probably the leading hide merchant of Delhi and Kanpur. During the war, the firm did very well, simultaneously executing orders for meat to the troops and hides to the Ordnance Department. These and similar information on firms in Kanpur are taken from Somerset Playne, *The Bombay Presidency, the United Provinces, the Punjab, etc.: Their History, People, Commerce and Natural Resources* (London, 1917–20).

[146] Abdul Gafoor of Allahabad, who established himself in the Kanpur hide trade in the early 1880s, was a procurer for the German firm, Schroeder Smidt. The association continued off and on till 1914 when the war drove out the German firm, and Gafoor, with his sons, set up a tannery. Wasay and Nabi Buksh were hide merchants of Kanpur, and agents of Wuttow Guttman, and later of Cohen and Fuchs. By 1914–16, these collaborations were in trouble. In 1916, they finally broke down and Wasay and Nabi Buksh amalgamated with another trading firm, Mohammad Ismail, to set up the UP Tanneries on Jajmau Road, the tanning hub in the city. Creet's firm, known as Stork, Halim & Co. from 1904, was finally in the possession of Halim in 1907. For the source, see the previous note.

[147] Somerset Playne, *Bengal and Assam Behar and Orissa: Their History, People, Commerce, and Industrial Resources* (London, 1917), 195–6.

background. Even where the buyer was a European multinational like Bata, the subcontracting with the Mochi continued to be of fundamental importance in the manufacture of high-quality leather goods.

By the end of our period, both tanning and leather factories involved fairly significant Hindu capital. This seemed to have entered via several routes, such as money accumulated in the export trade, white-collar employees of large tanneries and leather factories, or leather goods trade. There was at least one notable instance in Madras of a Chettiar moving from banking to leather via the export trade.[148]

Conclusion

The integration of colonial India into a world market created an export boom for Indian hides and skins that began in the 1870s and continued for nearly half a century. Earlier, the craft was performed largely as a service wherein the rural labourer customarily received hides free and supplied finished goods to peasant employers. The export trade created a large demand for hides outside the village, and, in the process, created a market for the craftsman's labour, enabling him to leave the customary labour services. These developments encouraged urbanization of the industry, large-scale migration, and the start of factories in the cities. Yet another effect of export trade was felt in technology, as quality control became imperative. The adaptation once again favoured mass production.

In leather goods, on the other hand, imports were at first a threat to domestic production. Imports also altered tastes and standardized products sold in the home market. Because the competition between the imported and the artisanal footwear was less on cost and more on quality, imports could be substituted. But such an adaptation again pulled the country craftsman closer to the trading points, and turned him into an employer of labour, or a labourer himself. Together, both tanning and leather goods illustrate a particular type of commercialization, one which involved the artisans, was induced by foreign trade, created labour markets where none existed, enabled the accumulation of skills and capital, and, in the process, led to the deepening of a comparative advantage.

Tanning was a relatively unskilled craft, performed earlier under simple and primitive conditions such that changes in industrial organization were especially dramatic in this industry. By contrast, in the skilled crafts, which experienced a similar surge in export and shared with

---

[148] *Indian Leather Trades and Industries Year-book.*

leather the broad direction of the change, the reorganization was both slower and more complex. Craftsmanship played an explicit role in shaping their transition. The most important example of an exportable skilled craft is woollen carpets, and it is to this that we turn in the next chapter.

7 Carpets

The art of pile carpets is an old one in Central and West Asia. From the early sixteenth century, with European trade in the Indian ocean and the Levant, and accelerating with subsequent European penetration into South and West Asia, carpets became an important item of trade, and evolved into a popular consumer good in Europe. The transition is significant for many reasons. In interior decoration, the nineteenth century in Europe was positively 'the age of the *tapissier*'.[1] For few other decorated objects individualized living rooms as effectively as carpets did. Carpets were the orientalist symbol *par excellence*.[2] And the process had profound implications for the makers and sellers of carpets in the regions from where they continued to be exported to Europe, and, gradually, to America.

It is this last effect of a drift in consumption that this chapter addresses, with India as an example. Not as large or as differentiated as the Persian and Turkish carpets, the Indian tradition is one of the most visible examples of the integration of artisans into a world market. For India was better accessible to the West than interior Asia. The weavers' experience, in trying to cope with the new consumption, involved an almost cultural encounter that had much in common with what was going on in other decorative crafts. Before the advent of exports, carpets were made mainly in a context of patronage, for specific uses and/or users. Patronage, by definition, is an exchange between an implicit guarantee of quality and a notional security of tenure. Both attributes weaken in a market. The anonymity of consumers tends to relax standards, and competition can become ruinous. These problems, and attempts to address them, shaped the industry from the middle of the nineteenth century. The chapter proceeds in two stages: an account of the product and its consumption; and the conditions of production.

[1] Michelle Perot (ed.), *A History of Private Life*, vol. IV (Cambridge, MA, 1990), 369.
[2] '[E]xpressed the natural East, free and fettered, fed and starved, irresponsible and meditative': A. U. Dilley, *Oriental Carpets and Rugs* (New York and London, 1931), 270.

Consumption

Floor coverings used in India were of three sorts: cotton woven or pile carpets, called *durries*, woollen pile carpets, and reed or grass mats. This chapter deals only with the second. Reed was a local tradition. It was the medium used in damp and warm climates such as that of Bengal or Kerala, which had neither good sheep nor pastures, no indigenous carpet traditions to speak of, and which were not dry enough to preserve woollens at an affordable cost. In northern India, cotton and woollen carpets co-existed. Despite occasional reports of weavers switching between the two,[3] they were distinct fields. Cotton carpets involved a different technique: the 'pileless' weft operations also involved in the Persian *kilims*, tapestries, and some carpets and rugs of Baluchistan and Sind. There were indeed masterpieces in *durrie*,[4] but usually the designs were of the simplest sort, and the product a cheap and undistinguished one. Consistent with simplicity, the mundane uses, and the fact that the pile made little effect with cotton fibres, cotton evolved independently of woollens, though they did meet at times, probably most often in the prisons where both were woven. Cotton carpets had a diffused market, but woollen carpets had an exclusive one. In raw material, woollen carpets were more closely allied to the livestock economy than to agriculture. The history of woollen textiles reflected the changing conditions under which the shepherds, the rearers, and the breeders performed their trade.

There are references to carpets in pre-Mughal India, but it is not clear if these were of cotton or of woollen pile. There are three well-known instances of absorption of this greater Asian art by Indians. The first is the initiative of the emperor Akbar who settled Persian craftsmen in royal factories at Lahore and Agra.[5] Apparently Akbar wanted them to weave both cotton and woollen, but the former was at best experimental. The period was contemporaneous with the two Safavid rulers most closely identified with carpets. On stylistic and etymological grounds, and on the strength of trade relations, the early Indian masterpieces are placed within the carpet traditions of Herat and Meshed (Mashhad) in eastern Persia, and not the more central traditions of the west and north. An older source, however, is the Kashmiri king Zainul Abedin

---

[3] Census of India, 1961, *Woollen Carpet and Blanket Industry in Uttar Pradesh*, vol. XV, Part VII-A, No. 1 (Delhi, 1964), 20, on Shahjahanpur; and V. R. Chitra and V. Tekumalla, *Cottage Industries of India (Guide Book and Symposium)* (Madras, 1948), 202–3 on Warangal.

[4] See David Black and Clive Loveless (eds.), *The Unappreciated Dhurrie* (London, 1982).

[5] Abù'l-Fazl Allámí, *The Ain-i Akbari*, vol. I, trans. H. Blochmann, third edition (New Delhi, 1977), 57.

who had observed the art in Samarkand in his early youth while a hostage of Timur. The third and the most obscure source involves Masulipatnam, the maritime city on the southeastern coast, whose weavers did not seem to migrate from Akbar's factories. They were either settled by the West Asian merchants of the town, or descended from Persian artisans invited to settle in Golconda.

A specific Indian idiom began to express itself in the first century or so of the industry. The invariable flowers of Herat turned more naturalistic in India, a tendency 'found in the rugs of India but consistently in no other rugs of Persia'. In course of time, typically Indian flowers and animals made their appearance in place of Persian.[6] In antique Indian carpets, this feature justified the later classificatory term 'Indo-Isfahani' – though the reference to Isfahan is probably misleading – applied to the entire stretch from Lahore to Masulipatnam. There was also an important organizational difference between the industries in Central Asia or eastern Persia and that in India. Carpet was partly a nomadic craft in West and Central Asia, jointly occurring with shepherds, the distaff they carried for spinning, and domestic labour. India did not display any of these features. The craft was necessarily sedentary, almost always in factories, and with a few exceptions urban. It needed long-distance trade in wool. The artisans belonged in elaborate contractual systems. Women were secluded in the cities and their place in the workshop taken by young boys. These distinctions narrowed later as the nomads settled, and were always narrow in urban weaving. However, even in settled conditions, carpets remained mainly a household industry in West Asia, but rarely so in India.

Nearly three centuries of Indian carpets remain obscure, punctuated by a few noteworthy specimens. These suggest that officers of the East India Company commissioned some carpets in Lahore, the earliest of which, the Girdlers, was made before 1634.[7] However, from the middle of the eighteenth century, Indian carpets become rare, which has been attributed, probably correctly, to a decline in supply. Some of the factories patronized by the aristocracy, including one in Delhi, were destroyed by Nadir Shah's men in 1731. The same raid also decimated the craft in Herat. Remarkably, however, the craft seemed to spread from the imperial cities to newer locations. One authority on carpets mistakenly attributed the resilience to rural communes and the caste

[6] Dilley, *Oriental Rugs*, 94–5; and S. M. Shah, *Hand-Knotted Carpet Industry of Pakistan* (Peshawar, 1980).
[7] On this carpet, and how it travelled from India to the Victoria and Albert Museum, see William Griggs, *Relics of the Honourable East India Company* (London, 1909), 72–3.

system.[8] The reason for the dispersion is probably political decentralization, which allowed it to flourish in Hyderabad and Kashmir, took it to Arcot, Mysore, Benares, and Bihar, and a few other places where it did not dig deep roots. The potentates followed the example of Akbar, or, in the case of Hyder Ali, were inspired by the Mongol Hulagu, Suleyman the Magnificent, and Nadir Shah. All of them had taken carpet weavers back to their domains. The local chiefs were the main customers of the local industries, though increasingly sharing them with the French, English, and possibly Portuguese residents.[9] There are two rather striking features about this expansion. First, the occurrence of carpets in regions which neither had the best wool, nor the climate suited for the extensive use of wool. And, secondly, while the Indo-Isfahani style became extinct or weaker, there seems to have evolved styles that did break free of Persian influence. Nearly all historical specimens known as Indian carpets are products of this dispersed eighteenth-century craftsmanship.[10]

One factor in the long continuance of carpets in India was surely the cost and easy availability of wool. The region produced a lot of wool, and traded all of it, but did not consume much. One noticeable distinction of an Indian from a nineteenth-century European carpet was the abundance of wool in the former. The English carpets were in reality woven of cotton and hemp, with a light covering of wool that wore away rather quickly. 'In an Indian carpet, the whole fabric sinks under the foot.'[11] Even compared to Persian, the Agra carpets were distinctly heavier. Sheep adapt very well to arid conditions, unlike cattle which need grassland, and many parts of south and north India had indigenous sheep which did not yield the finest wool, but yielded a lot of it. An elite clientele, and long-distance trade in textiles were important determinants of location. But a local production of wool, or wool trade, was usually a necessary condition for manufacturing to develop. The main impetus to rural carpet weaving in the famous band around the 40 degrees north latitude had been precisely the occurrence of some of the

---

[8] J. K. Mumford, *Oriental Rugs* (New York, 1900), 253.

[9] Francis Buchanan, *An Account of the Districts of Bihar and Patna in 1811–1812*, vol. II (Patna, 1934, reprinted Delhi, 1986), 657. The Portuguese association with carpets is based on several intriguing pieces of data, the possible existence of a western coastal carpet which disappeared early, and a trade name 'Portuguese' for a very old Kerman carpet. There are several instances of local weavers tracing their ancestry to the imperial cities, or to Persia itself. Buchanan mentions one such, the weavers of Daudnagar in Gaya district.

[10] One early compilation, with monograph by F. H. Andrews, can be found in *Journal of Indian Art (and Industry)*, 9, 89–94 (1906).

[11] George Watt, *A Dictionary of the Economic Products of India*, vol. II (Calcutta, 1889), 179.

best wool of Asia. Within India, the occurrence of wool may explain a
north–south polarization of the industry, that is, it may explain why the
eastern and the western regions never developed strong carpet weaving.
The relative importance of the factors, however, varied. Wool trade was
probably more critical in Kashmir and Punjab, where carpets were one
branch of a diversified *woollen* industry, than in Masulipatnam, where it
was part of a diversified *textile* tradition.

When the British rediscovered carpets in India, shortly after the 1851
Great Exhibition of the empire,[12] it was manufactured in the following
major locations: a cluster of villages in eastern United Provinces, Agra,
Amritsar, Kashmir, Masulipatnam, and a few towns of Hyderabad.
Smaller centres included several towns in the United Provinces, chiefly
Jewar, Shahjahanpur, Jhansi, and Amroha, Jabbalpur in central India,
Walajahpet and Bangalore in the south, Patna, and a group of villages in
the Gaya district in eastern India. This work will exclude the carpets
woven in the extreme western or northern fringes of British India:
villages in Sind, parts of Gujarat, and areas bordering Baluchistan or
Afghanistan, where carpet formed part of semi-nomadic craft traditions.

By the third quarter of the nineteenth century, Indian carpets were
reincarnated as exports to Britain, almost wherever they survived. For
Britain, it made sense to explore the imperial domain. In Turkey and
western Persia, whose goods left the shores of Asia from Istanbul,
Smyrna (Izmir) or Trebizond (Trabzon), the British shared the trade
with the Germans and the Americans, not to mention Armenians,
Greeks and Persians entrenched in local supplies. More than that, and
though the British did have easy access to some Persian goods that
moved towards Karachi or Bombay ports, interior Persia was by and
large so difficult to access that, even much later, no foreign trader could
be sure just where specific fabrics came from. As for the weavers, the
exports saved them from a painful and protracted extinction. Few of the
local nobility had the means to indulge. The new classes of chiefs and
zamindars displayed a preference for imported symbols of status, the
'gaudy products of second-rate English and continental power-looms',
just as in West Asia, 'the floors of the best houses in many towns . . . are
covered with nightmares of Western color and device'.[13]

The isolated powerlooms of Europe were a remote threat to the Asian
carpets. First, a variety of factors, including the small cost of wool and
labour made Asian carpets unassailably cheap. Secondly, and probably
more importantly, carpets needed to be differentiated. Household

[12] *The Imperial Gazetteer of India*, The Indian Empire, vol. III (Economic) (Oxford, 1907), 214.
[13] Mumford, *Oriental Rugs*, 45.

production, a vast accumulated folklore of designs, and a diversity of styles defying the best attempts at classification of Asian carpets into neat orders, ensured differentiation. Machines could not manage the broad widths that manual methods could implement. Until the 1870s, Asian carpets were closely associated with knowledge of dyeing wool in vegetable and animal substances, and colour was a crucial element of craftsmanship. India too enjoyed these advantages. But if they were safe from technology, a crisis arose in quality.

The sense of wonder with which the modern West greeted Asian carpets – in the 1851 London Great Exhibition or the 1893 Chicago World Fair – gave way soon to a sense of loss, an impression that capitalism corroded craftsmanship. The crisis was partly endogenous. Carpets and rugs used to be made in a context where their use values by far dominated exchange values: women wove their dowry; and rich patrons had them made for palaces and mosques. Few carpets actively entered long-distance trade relative to the scale on which they were made. With European trade, carpets acquired an exchange value, but it inevitably created in its wake scope for opportunism. The consumers were sufficiently anonymous and distant, information on tastes costly to obtain, and the contexts of its new use unknown. All this encouraged relaxation of standards, and with impunity, since the producers were too dispersed for incentive–punishment systems to be enforced. In the first fifty years of the trade, Persian carpets needed to be tested for dead wool, fleeting dyes, short pile, and antique dealers had to be increasingly wary of the new masters of fake antiques, abuses unthinkable in dowry, prayer, or court carpets.[14]

In India, the problem of bad work derived, in common with her competitors, partly from dyeing and unknown tastes. But there were at least two specific sources of decay: intervention in designs; and competition from the jails. It is hard to find material on the first thirty years (from 1851) of English trade in carpets. But, as the problems lingered on at least until the eve of the First World War, several early-twentieth-century sources commented on the crisis extensively. It is thus possible to reconstruct the crisis that overwhelmed and swallowed up the Indo-Isfahani and indigenous styles. So thoroughly, in fact, that none of the early-twentieth-century treatises could find any remaining trace of that style in its pure form.

The problem of dyeing extended to all textiles, but was more crucial to carpets. For carpet was more of a durable item than cotton, more

---

[14] See Mumford, *Oriental Rugs*; W. A. Hawley, *Oriental Rugs* (London, 1913); A. F. Kendrick and C. E. C. Tattersoll, *Hand-Woven Carpets: Oriental and European* (London, 1922), vol. I (Text); and Dilley, *Oriental Rugs*.

even than silk. Further, carpet embodied complex colour schemes, and the fading of any one of the shades that constituted the seheme could destroy the whole effect. On the evidence of antique carpets and rugs, vegetable dyes were believed, on the whole, to 'age gracefully'. The mineral dyes aniline, popularized in the 1870s, had not been in the trade long enough to reveal whether they faded or ripened with time. But the substitution of local material for the easier and cheaper mineral dyes did happen, and happened on a rather weak foundation of skill. Anilines induced a gradual decay of knowledge in indigenous dyeing.[15] Careless handling of the new dyes, that required adherence to recipes, tended to make colours fugitive. And they created whole new shades which encouraged departures from older designs. The prospect caused such an impassioned reaction from craft observers that, quite unlike cotton, in carpets anilines spread slowly, haltingly, and with many reversals. The governments at Kashmir and Persia even banned its entry, a legislation that was at least informally considered in India.[16]

Physically, India was more amenable to communication between the traders and the producers. Stylistically, India was eclectic in the best of times, and had little of the grandeur that 'Turkish' (a generic name in the US trade for a long time) evoked. Such a tradition was prone to being identified with cheapness, and not with distinction. The Indian carpets, thus, acquired that end of the market which minded economy more than style. Recalling the early history of exports, the *Imperial Gazetteer* stated that, immediately after the Great Exhibition, 'patterns were . . . sent out, the quality prescribed, and the price fixed at an almost impossibly low figure. The result could hardly have been other than a steady deterioration in . . . artistic merit.'[17] In the 1890s, the southern carpets were adjusting to a demand that required the products to be cheap, above everything else.

The new custom also resulted in a clash of different aesthetic practices. This was a general problem: 'not want of weavers or diminution of talent for hard labor, but only indecision as to the character of art to create.'[18] In part, the carpet weavers had to learn to simplify. They had to alter designs meant to decorate rooms generally bare of furniture, or

[15] In Mirzapur at the turn of the century, 'the knowledge of how to dye fast appears to be rapidly decaying': A. W. Pim, *A Monograph on the Woollen Fabrics in the North-Western Provinces and Oudh* (Allahabad, 1898), 15.

[16] H. T. Harris, *A Monograph on the Carpet Weaving Industry of Southern India* (Madras, 1908); and H. J. R. Twigg, *A Monograph on the Art and Practice of Carpet-Making in the Bombay Presidency* (Bombay, 1907), 80–1. See Mumford, *Oriental Rugs*, 49, for the interesting text of the prohibitory order in Persia.

[17] *Imperial Gazetteer*, 214.

[18] Dilley, *Oriental Rugs*, 169; see also *ibid.*, 245, on tastes, with reference to Persian rugs.

to be hung upon the wall, to suit a sharing of floor with furniture. It meant a great reduction in average dimensions, a simpler plan, the cutting out of detail, an emphasis on the outline, and other innovations that were, at least in India, consistent with a certain de-skilling, the use of coarser material,[19] and even with the alteration of the basic knots, thereby weakening the foundation of the carpet.

Partly the problem was that the orientality of 'oriental carpets' began to be defined in London:

Every fresh trained textile designer, with the signature on his South Kensington or other diploma hardly dry, must try his hand at a new carpet design 'in my own combinations of form and colour' and this the trade often calls 'an Oriental Carpet'.[20]

The weaver was not a passive receptacle of these designs. The usual outcome was conflict and hybrid designs.[21] Worst off as a result of this process seem to have been those places of the south which had evolved a truly original style, but which were not large enough to resist shifting preferences. A segment of the southern industry was identifiable with geometrical designs using masses of deep-toned colours to suit the quality of local material, coarse tannery wool that took dye badly. The trade names 'Coconada' and 'Bangalore', the latter referring to carpets of Arcot and/or Tanjore due to an association with patronage from Tipu Sultan, belonged in this class. George Birdwood named them the 'Euphratean prototype', as opposed to the hybrid, the 'Italianesque-Persian'. In a very general sense, Caucasian carpets used more geometrical, and Persian more meandering, designs. The bold patterns on the Ayyampet carpets did not appeal to those who, 'in their painful anxiety to eschew anything vulgar or in bad taste, fall back on the . . . "aesthetic" muddiness of colour and monotony of pattern'.[22] In 1908, the 'Coconada' patterns were no more than modifications of cheap English carpet designs.[23] Previously, the dyeing practices ensured, in all of Asia in fact, the use of a lot of broken colours, that is, slightly varying shades

[19] Twigg, *Monograph on the Art and Practice*, 78.

[20] Harris, *A Monograph on the Carpet Industry*, 61.

[21] Percy Brown, Principal of the Mayo School of Art at Lahore, wrote that the artisan 'is only too willing to criticize the products of his workshop and laments deeply the use of these hybrid combinations': 'The Artistic Trades of Punjab and Their Development', in *Report of the Fourth Industrial Conference Held at Madras* (Madras, 1909), 175. It is probable that many of these designs were occidental records or interpretations of antique oriental designs, which did establish a very indirect connection between British powerlooms and the Indian hand-knotted, one that is occasionally visible in the reports (see note 19 above). But the influence of Gallic or Italianesque carpets on the oriental is virtually unknown.

[22] Edgar Thurston, *Monograph on the Woollen Fabric Industry of the Madras Presidency* (Madras, 1898), 3; the latter citation is from a report by Ernest Havell, in *ibid.*, 5.

[23] Harris, *Monograph on the Carpet Industry*, 6.

adjacently placed. This had evolved because, with vegetable dyes, it was always easier to obtain different shades of the same basic colour than different colours. 'The British carpet-dealers have changed this old Indian system, and introduced hard combinations' that not only departed from the smooth transitions between the border and the field that distinguished the Coconada, but probably hastened a change in dyeing material and techniques as well.[24] In a second burst of exports in the 1890s, when the American traders began to buy from northern India, the crisis apparently worsened.[25] When the pattern departed too much from received conventions, the work of the weaver, who was never quite adept at thinking in abstract terms, was 'a facsimile . . . but stiff'.[26]

One factor in the adoption of mineral dyes, despite the fact that quality mattered a great deal more in carpets than the small cost advantage the new dyes offered, was received patterns. Under the rule of the design book, colours were recommended at the same time as patterns. Britain's notion of carpet colours had far less relation with the Indian dyer's repertoire than it had with the German dye-maker's catalogue. The carpet samples involved a wide range and shades, and the weaver had no time for the costly experiments that would have been needed for the native knowledge to become competitive. He received a carpet sample in one hand, and, in the other, hundreds of new shades sent to him by the European dyers every month. There was 'no necessity for combining . . . colours, [but] . . . merely to take the colours and put them into a basin and use them'.[27]

In 1907 in Agra, 'designs are crude . . . no patterns or design-books are kept . . . the cheaper aniline dyes are used'.[28] Jhansi and Amroha had similar problems. In Mirzapur, Birdwood found deterioration in the 1870s.[29] There, in about 1900, the designs are either 'stiff and conventional', or 'of an occidental type which the weaver does not understand and consequently fails to render with skill'.[30] They were also 'identified with whatever is inferior in the name of dye or design'.[31] Kunwar Jagdish Prasad, in his 1907 monograph on the carpets of the United Provinces, devoted an entire chapter on 'Deterioration in Artistic

[24] *Ibid.*, 61.   [25] Twigg, *Monograph on the Art and Practice*, 80.

[26] George Birdwood, *The Industrial Arts of India* (London, 1887, reprinted Calcutta, 1992), 288.

[27] *Indian Industrial Commission*, vol. V, evidence of Shaikh Gulam Sadik, carpet manufacturer, 308.

[28] A. C. Chatterjee, *Notes on the Industries of the United Provinces* (Allahabad, 1908), 59.

[29] Birdwood, *The Arts of India*, 294–5.

[30] Pim, *Monograph on the Woollen Fabrics*, 10; and Chatterjee, *Notes on Industries*, 63.

[31] G. D. Ganguli, 'The Art Industries of the United Provinces', in *Report of the First Indian Industrial Conference (Benares, 1905)* (Allahabad, 1906), 351.

Quality'.[32] In 1898, in Eluru, 'the good work', defined as adherence to the older designs most characteristic of the place, 'is not at all easy to obtain'. Already, in 1880, the 'once glorious carpets of Masulipatnam have sunk to a mockery and travestie of their former selves'. Older designs were replaced by patterns and materials supplied by the British exporters, with the result that 'crude, inharmonious masses of un-meaning form now mark the spots where formerly varied, interesting and beautiful designs blossomed as delicately as the first flowers of spring'.[33] In 1900, Masulipatnam had been reduced to an imitation of Eluru carpets, but with 'indifferent workmanship'.[34] In 1908, the eastern coastal products no longer justified the words of praise that Birdwood and others had bestowed on them thirty years before. Dyeing deteriorated. Designs were lost. In a free departure from time-tested colour schemes, old designs were recoloured, 'often to the entire debasement of pattern'. Designs suited for narrow widths were applied to broader width carpets. Designs for wall hangings were applied on floor coverings resulting in 'ill-bred' variations.[35] Of the Kashmir industry in the 1880s, it was written: 'the modern craze for cheapness spoilt [the craft].' New designs were partly to blame, but 'the greatest evil' was wrought by the dyes.[36]

To these conditions was added competition from the jails. Roughly from the 1860s, carpet manufacture was introduced in various jails of the country to occupy the convicts. From a remark of Birdwood's, it appears that the rise of jail carpets followed the suppression of the Thuggees and the Pindaris in central India. Indeed, a rush of long-term inmates probably explains the massive scale of the craft: no other jail industry had the impact or the notoriety of carpets. And the long sentences might explain the choice of carpets, a craft needing time to learn. No direct proof seems to exist of the notion that the first-generation jail weavers were retired Thugs. But, in fact, the men who were put to this work were recruited from the 'lifers'.[37] Those among

---

[32] Kunwar Jagdish Prasad, *Monograph on Carpet Making in the United Provinces* (Allahabad, 1907), chapter III.

[33] Birdwood, *The Arts of India*, 295–6.

[34] Thurston, *Monograph on the Woollen Fabric*, 2, 5.

[35] Harris, *Monograph on the Carpet Industry*, 6, 61.

[36] A. Mitra, 'Notes on the Arts and Industries in Kashmir' in *Report of the Fifth Indian Industrial Conference Held at Lahore, 1909* (Amraoti, 1910), 366–7.

[37] A good description of the jail industry can be found in Edgar Thurston, *Monograph on Woollen Fabric*, 3–7. It has been suggested, in a recent study on the policy and practice of jail manufactures in south India, that carpets were probably an exception to the rule of allowing only such manufactures inside the jails as would cater mainly to government demand: Padmini Swaminathan, 'Prison as Factory: A Study of Jail Manufactures in the Madras Presidency', *Studies in History*, New Series, 11, 1 (1995).

them who came out of the prison included a few artisans trained almost as well as any professional. Around the turn of the century, their contribution in the revival of Amritsar and Eluru carpets was acknowledged.

The work appealed to the prisoners, though spinning, considered women's work, was hated.[38] As a business, it had several advantages. The jail premises were more spacious and well-lit than usual workshops.[39] The jail industry bore none of the transactions costs that arose in a market. Carrying of inventory was easy in the jails. And, finally, the token return on labour paid to the weavers bore no relation to the price. Major carpet towns usually had carpet weaving inside their jails. Many other towns had them as well. For example, Vellore was not a carpet town, but its jail employed 135 workers, taught by a convict from Eluru, working on thirty looms in 1898. There were worksheds of comparable size in Agra, Madras, Bangalore, and Rajahmundry.[40]

The intensity of jail competition was uneven. It was evidently more serious in the south than in the north or west. In Bombay, which had little of its carpet tradition left by the turn of the century, jail products were charitably received by the consumers.[41] The north had less to fear. In Agra, released convicts worked in the private industry. In Amritsar, jail products carried better quality, and even created the brand name which later helped the commercial side of the industry.[42] As long as both a jail and a private industry co-existed (in the late nineteenth century), the jail industry subdued the private industry. But, with the closure of carpets inside jails, the private industry flourished significantly, in which growth the reputation of jail goods and labour played a role.[43] In the south, where the industry outside the jails was smaller and weaker, opinions about the 'Thug carpets' were especially hostile.

The controversy about the jail carpets anticipates some typical debates about the public sector: problems of quality and of fairness. Jails had no indigenous patterns and inherited knowledge to defend, so freely borrowed designs, and, on the assumption that the most respected masters of the art were a rarity in the prisons, had access to the inferior ones. The costs of production being entirely notional, the final price

---

[38] Harris, *Monograph on the Carpet Industry*, 21.

[39] N. G. Mukherji, *A Monograph on Carpet-Weaving in Bengal* (Calcutta, 1907), 8–9 on the conditions in the jail factories.

[40] Thurston, *Monograph on the Woollen Fabric*, 4–5.

[41] Twigg, *A Monograph on the Art and Practice*, 28.

[42] C. Latimer, *Monograph on Carpet Making in the Punjab, 1905–06* (Lahore, 1907), 18, 20.

[43] Description of a carpet factory in Amritsar (Khan Bahadur Shaikh Gulam Hussun and Co.) in Somerset Playne, *The Bombay Presidency, United Provinces, Punjab, Kashmir, etc.* (London, 1917–20), 616.

could adjust easily to the adverse outcomes of such experiments. The results ranged from 'respectable level of mediocrity' to 'clumsy imitations . . . outrageous colouring and corrupt designs'.[44] The jails also suffered from the rarity of expert dyers in vegetable products, and contributed to the dyeing problem. The effect of selling a bad product cheaper was doubly deplorable. It created unfair competition, and corrupted work practices outside the jails.[45] Whether as a result of the adverse publicity it received from influential writers, or the reduced numbers of long-sentence convicts, or, in keeping with the growth of the bureaucracy, the conscription of more and more jail labour to the task of printing official forms, the issue of jail competition more or less died out by the First World War.[46]

The scale of the export trade in carpets and rugs after 1900 is shown in Table 7.1. For the first twenty years in this time series, figures for the quantity of export are not available. Nor do we have figures for carpet prices as such. A rough idea about changes in volume can be formed by comparing the values with the movement in general prices. Such a comparison suggests that, until the middle of the First World War, the trade was stagnant in volume, but, thereafter, the expansion in volume was dramatic. Between 1916–20 and 1935–8, the average annual volume of carpet exports, according to this calculation, might have increased four or five times. It will be seen below that this period, in particular, was associated with the most significant changes in the industry, in terms of scale of employment as well as in terms of industrial organization. The significance, especially, of the 1930s will be seen from time to time.

Production

What, therefore, happened in the late nineteenth century was a commercialization, but a stressful one. The stresses derived from commercialization itself. There occurred three sets of changes on the supply side, which can be inferentially attributed to the attempts by the trade to deal with these problems. These were (i) a shift from auctions to contracts at final sale; (ii) relocation; and (iii) the emergence of new production and exchange contracts on a foundation of older practices.

---

[44] Thurston, *Monograph on the Woollen Fabric*, 4–5.

[45] That designs outside were sensitive to what was turned out in the jails can be seen from a design developed in Eluru, called Rohde, possibly after an Inspector-General of jails: Harris, *Monograph on the Carpet Industry*, 13.

[46] The living testimony of carpet-weaving in the jails by then was a small cluster of weavers in Shahjahanpur whose leading figure was an ex-convict: *Indian Carpets* (Bombay, undated), 29.

Table 7.1 *Export of carpets and rugs by sea from India, 1901–1938*

	Quantity (million lbs)		Value (million Rs.)		
	Total	Annual average	Total	Annual average	Average annual change in prices (percentage)
1901–5	–	–	12.2	2.4	–
1906–10	–	–	12.4	2.5	8.9
1911–15	–	–	11.9	2.4	3.3
1916–20	–	–	21.7	4.3	10.8
1921–5	20.8	4.2	43.7	8.7	11.4
1926–30	23.0	4.6	41.0	8.2	–
1931–5	43.9	8.8	36.3	7.3	–
1935–8	29.9	10.0	27.0	9.0	–

Notes: The value figures for 1901–5 to 1921–5 include export of woollen manufactures. In the data after 1920, this item constituted about 5 per cent of combined carpet and wollen export. The prices are weighted agricultural prices.
Sources: India, *Annual Statement of the Sea-Borne Trade of British India with the British Empire and Foreign Countries*, vol. I, Director of Commercial Intelligence and Statistics (Calcutta, various years); India, *Statistical Abstract for British India* (Calcutta, various years); M. McAlpin, 'Price Movements and Fluctuations in Economic Activity (1860–1947)' in Dharma Kumar (ed.), *The Cambridge Economic History of India*, vol. II, *c. 1757–c. 1970* (Cambridge, 1983).

Decline of auction

All over Asia, long-distance trade in carpets was subject to a tension between two alternative systems of final sale: auction and contract. Under auction, popular in India until the end of the nineteenth century, carpets of all grades formed the 'consignments' sent to the Auction Sale Warehouse in London, where they were sold at prices which a fixed supply, variable grade, and somewhat unpredictable demand would fetch for them. The resultant prices were highly variable, as one would expect, and had enough of a cyclicality to attract speculators. Occasional offers of good prices created:

artificial demand, with the result that carpets – good, bad and indifferent, some inelegantly dyed and utilizing dead wool – were exported. Prices came down and large number of bales remained unsold in the godowns of Cutler's Street.[47]

Intermittent violent crashes drove many auctioneers and agents 'to the wall', but brought others into the trade who were willing to gamble for a

---

[47] United Provinces, *Industrial Survey of the United Provinces* (Allahabad, 1922–4), Mirzapur District, 22.

year or two, and/or collude to keep prices above what the qualities would justify.[48]

And yet, auctions can be seen as a rational adaptation to the initial conditions of the trade, that changed only slowly. First, the true offer price of carpets was largely unknown to the traders for a long time. As in any emerging market, the volumes traded were small in relation to the potential consumption, and new customers were entering the market every day. And yet, anyone with the slightest acquaintance with the trade knew that the cost price was so low that almost any likely sale price would justify the risk of auction.[49] The second factor behind auctions was the great difficulty foreigners in Asia faced in enforcing contracts that specified quantity, time, and quality. Bad communications, poor information, the task of monitoring dispersed producers, the latter's stubborn refusal to work to any kind of schedule, and the credibility of local intermediaries, all contributed to the repeated termination of attempts at contract. Under patronage in pure forms, the Indian artisan was a salaried member of a palace. The sedate pace of that life did not disappear even as the patrons did. Thus, the weaver asked for time, and was as a result shunned by the exporter because he had neither the authority nor the knowledge to ensure the fulfilment of contracts, by the British officer on furlough who found the wait too long and 'jail articles . . . good enough for their purpose for taking home',[50] and by members of the new elite who grew impatient of advancing money. The pace was faster in larger centres. The Nepal Durbar, thus, shifted orders from Patna to Mirzapur for this reason.

It appears from prewar records that, several episodes of speculative surge and crash later, the Indian trading firms who dominated the export trade at source until about 1900, and mainly worked on consignments, yielded to European and American firms who worked on order from London or New York trading firms. It is not quite clear whether this shift was wholly a reflection of the indifferent quality supplied by the Indian firms, or of trade practices on behalf of the foreigners. Possibly both factors were involved in the shift. The Indians still continued with consignments, but as minor actors. By 1908, the consignment system was unpopular, and was followed only when the Indian agents and suppliers certified the quality of the carpets. It was being replaced by

---

[48] A. Tellery, 'The United Provinces Carpet Industry', in *Report of the Fourth Industrial Conference of United Provinces Held at Benares* (Benares, 1910), 144. See on 'puffing', or the prearranged hike of bids in the London auctions, Dilley, *Oriental Rugs*, 278. Puffing, however, could make the subsequent crash, when inevitable, the more painful.

[49] Dilley, *Oriental Rugs*, mentions this gap between probable offer and costs, and explains the seemingly arbitrary quotations in an oriental bazaar in the same terms.

[50] Mukherji, *Monograph on Carpet-Weaving*, 3.

sale 'on order'.[51] Contractual sale, which implied price stability, worked better with identifiable brands, and these were supplied by trading-firms-turned-factories. The best known of them were European, later American. Several had multinational operations.

Relocation

Between 1880, when Birdwood published his treatise, and 1930, the industry became concentrated. The list of extinctions is long and curious, for it includes some almost mythical names. From the north, Jabbalpur carpets declined due to an unfortunate departure from the conventional knot, and Jhansi 'hardly deserve[s] mention' for similar reasons. In the interwar period, a few of the workers in the central Indian railway workshops traced their ancestry to Jhansi carpets.[52] Amroha and Jewar were mentioned for the last time by Ganguli.[53] A small tradition in Bahawalpur became extinct between the 1890s and 1916, when it was briefly mentioned in an article in the *Journal of Indian Art*. In western India, Bijapur and the enigmatic *zamorin* of Malabar were merely remembered, with no extant specimen, in 1900. Specimens did not exist for the 'Goa' either, mentioned briefly in Vincent Robinson's collection of plates.[54] A Cambay carpet, exported to Europe in the seventeenth century, was also legend.[55] The carpets of Gujarat, carried on in isolated factories at Ahmedabad, Surat, and Broach, declined as all available labour was absorbed by the cotton mills. Waves of famine over the Deccan plateau in the last quarter of the nineteenth century finished off the dispersed communities of carpet weavers in Bombay Presidency. In 1880, an industry in Ahmadnagar, 'on a very small scale . . . the Amritsar of [Bombay] Presidency', died out.[56] It seems that a considerable trade in carpets made in the Bellary area of the southern Andhra region disappeared in the latter half of the century. The ill-defined carpets of Warangal were 'past every efforts to revive them' in the face of competition from the jails.[57] Warangal did revive, but probably in cotton carpets. By 1900, Arcot and Masulipatnam were much reduced. In eastern India, small settlements in Patna and Calcutta

[51] Two sources on the change are Prasad, *Monograph on Carpet Making*, 30; and Harris, *Monograph on the Carpet Industry*, 15.

[52] United Provinces, *Industrial Survey*, Jhansi District, 1923, 34.

[53] Ganguli, 'The Art Industries', 351.

[54] Vincent Robinson, *Eastern Carpets* (London, 1893).

[55] Watt, *Dictionary*, 'Carpets and Rugs', 180–1. The Dutch naturalist and explorer, John Hayghen von Linschoten, is the source on the Cambay carpet.

[56] Twigg, *Monograph on the Art and Practice*, 6, 7.

[57] See Birdwood, *The Arts of India*, 294–5, on 'Jubbulpore', *zamorin* and Warangal, in particular.

were no more heard of in 1940, and the relatively well-known Obra-Daudnagar area was no longer prosperous. Most cases of decline are associated with the reason of 'the absence of continuous direction by any one who is in touch with the requirements of the largest consumers'.[58] When the dust settled, the significant concentrations left were Agra, Amritsar, and Srinagar in the north, a cluster of villages in the Mirzapur area in the eastern United Provinces, isolated towns in the south, and a few small satellites of each of these. These three broad clusters need to be described in more detail.

The Mirzapur area is significant in the history of carpet for two reasons. First, it is the only major example in this book of rural industrialization. Secondly, it is an example of a successful market adaptation in which a former luxury learnt, by skilfully degrading itself, to cater to middle-class consumers. Together, these conditions led to a very rapid expansion of weaving in the Mirzapur area in recent times. It seems that the area had about 3,500 workers in 1907, 9–10,000 about 1920, and the majority of the 20,000 workers in the entire province in the 1930s.[59] In 1953, the complex engaged 12,000 looms, or 50,000 workers. The 1961 census produced a lower figure.[60] But, in the middle of the 1970s, the count of Mirzapur workers had risen to 73,420,[61] and by best conjectures, in the middle of the 1990s to about 2–300,000.

The origin of the industry in Mirzapur is believed to be a sixteenth-century Persian craftsman who took refuge from bandits in one of these villages, and stayed on. The region had cotton, and a *durrie*-weaving tradition. The woollen carpet may have come later. Several weaving villages, notably Ghosia and Madho Singh, and Mirzapur town itself, were located on India's most frequented pilgrim track. Travellers halted here to buy mats and carpets. The district bordered on the Maharaja of Benares' domains. Local patronage might have been available.[62] In the nineteenth century, Mirzapur was a major trading town. It was the farthest port which heavy steamboats from Calcutta could reach by the Ganges. The east–west traffic between Bengal and Bombay–Deccan

[58] Watt, *Dictionary*, 'Carpets and Rugs', 180. Two contemporary attempts to patronize carpets were that of the Nizam in Warangal, and Scindia in Gwalior. But neither quite succeeded.

[59] Based on Chatterjee, *Notes on Industries*, 61; Tellery, 'The United Provinces Carpet Industry', 143; United Provinces, *Industrial Survey*, Mirzapur, 21; Prasad, *Monograph on Carpet Making*; Indian Tariff Board, *Written Evidence Recorded During Enquiry Regarding the Woollen Textile Industry* (Delhi, 1936), 309.

[60] Census of India, 1961, *Woollen Carpet*; India, *Indian Carpets in World Market*, All India Handicrafts Board (New Delhi, undated).

[61] India, *Report of Panel on Economic Conditions of Craftsmen in Carpets and Other Floor Coverings*, mimeo, All India Handicrafts Board (Delhi, 1976), 6.

[62] *Uttar Pradesh District Gazetteer*, Mirzapur District (Lucknow, 1988), 120.

followed the river and the Grand Trunk Road up to Mirzapur, and then branched southwards. Cotton was a major article in this trade. In Mirzapur many substantial cotton merchants and *arhatias* (stock-holders) lived and dealt with parties of Banjaras who carried these goods overland. In the 1860s, Mirzapur and Benares were linked with Calcutta by the railways. This ended its special importance as a trading town. But by then a woollen carpet industry and trade had developed in the area.[63] Since European investments in Indian carpets began roughly from this time, one can presume that carpet exports from this region flourished because of the railways and access to Calcutta's port.

Two nineteenth-century assessments suggest that Mirzapur carpets suffered a decline in quality and in scale thanks to hybrid designs and bad dyes.[64] And yet, there was expansion in the long run. This was made possible by clever adjustments in quality. In the interwar period, Mirzapur carpet was known to be a well-accomplished but medium-grade product, the range of threads rarely exceeding twenty per inch. 'Mirzapur' brand did not signal refinement. But it was an acceptable carpet sold for a very attractive price. Once this niche was defined, the capitalists paid closer attention to some of the standard problems that beset carpet production elsewhere. Designs, spinning, and dyeing all improved.[65] Much of this capability took shape in the premises owned by foreign merchants. In the interwar period, dyeing was the focus of technological initiatives, and the European factors led in this. In the long run, there was also a transition towards more evenly spun yarn prepared in the Kanpur mills, away from the country-spun ones. In the interwar period, a local dyeing school offered facilities and training. In fact, government action in the matter of quality control dated back to the turn of the century when the office of the Commercial Intelligence introduced a scheme for certification of dyeing in Mirzapur.[66] During another phase of expansion, in the 1940s, a quality marking scheme was introduced.[67]

[63] The origin of the woollen carpet industry is traced to the first quarter of the nineteenth century by William Crooke, 'A Note on the Art Industries of Mirzapur', *Journal of Indian Art (and Industry)*, 5 (1892–4), 56. Fanny Parks mentioned that this area was famous for carpets 'often sent to England': *Wanderings of a Pilgrim in Search of the Picturesque* (London, 1850, reprinted Karachi, 1975), 445–7.

[64] Crooke, 'Note on the Art Industries'; and Birdwood, *Arts of India*, 293–4.

[65] See on growth, Pim, *A Monograph on the Woollen Fabrics*, 10; United Provinces, *Industrial Survey*, Mirzapur, 21. The creation of a brand drove smaller towns to the service of the brand. An early example is Shahjahanpur: Census of India, 1961, *Woollen Carpet*, 27. More recently, not only most towns in Uttar Pradesh, but also one as distant and as historically unlike Mirzapur as Eluru, has been serving this brand.

[66] Chatterjee, *Notes on Industries*, 63.

[67] Census of India, 1961, *Woollen Carpet*, 7.

As the industry grew, the number of Indian traders increased rapidly and traders and trading firms multiplied. Many began as speculators, 'to buy at whatever cost . . . and through shipping agents at Calcutta . . . send them up to London',[68] which always left one segment of the market under the auctioneer. Those among them who acquired steady customers performed some crucial stages of manufacture, but did not usually start weaving.[69] In 1950, Indian and foreign firms with offices in Benares, Bhadohi, and Mirzapur towns contracted with *karkhanadars*. The former included carpet traders with varying interests in wool and yarn. The *karkhanadars* were a mix between middlemen and loom-owners. Invariably, they were people who had the ability to recruit, employ, train, and supervise weavers. The premises of the average large trader was mainly a storehouse, sometimes a factory, and frequently a shed with the facility to perform skilled tasks such as dyeing, designing and clipping, the three most highly paid jobs in the industry.

Increasingly, Mirzapur's expansion was met by farming families. It is almost certain that the industry began with the Julahas, remained in their hands until 1914,[70] and opened up to Hindu peasant castes in the interwar expansion. Growth, from then on, involved a greater number of households rather than an expansion in scale for a few of them.[71] Growth was not, however, entirely met by domestic labour. An average carpet loom required 4.1 workers (1.5 weavers, 1.6 part-time workers in wool sorting and picking, and about one full-time worker in the form of clippers, dyers, designers, and wool-carders), or more if spinning is done on the same premises. Clearly, even the smallest unit needed to hire-in workers or hire-out work.[72] Besides, the larger towns in that area, which functioned as points of trade, had also seen the start of several larger factories. Therefore, growth created a general shortage of skilled labour. To this condition, the factory side of the industry adapted by various means of informal labour-tying. The common instruments were consumption debts, apprenticeships, and kinship.[73] Apprenticeships and *ustads* in the northern sense were rare in this area. Some of the *ustad*'s functions were taken over by the multi-task 'middleman'.[74]

[68] Indian Tariff Board, *Written Evidence*, 259.
[69] On contractual relations and technical developments in the 1920s, see United Provinces, *Industrial Survey*, Mirzapur, 22, and Jaunpur, 29; on contracts in the 1950s, see Census of India, 1961, *Woollen Carpet*, 2.
[70] Tellery, the factor, wrote that Hindus had not taken much interest in carpets: 'The United Provinces Carpet Industry', 143.
[71] United Provinces, *Industrial Survey*, Mirzapur, 21.
[72] The average unit in Mirzapur town in 1947 had about three looms, but the rural units probably had less. See Ahmad Mukhtar, *Report on Labour Conditions in Carpet Weaving*, Labour Investigation Committee (Delhi, 1947), 7–10.
[73] *Ibid.*, 10.   [74] For example, India, *Report of Panel on Economic Conditions*, 7.

Eventually, a segmentation of factories and households developed. A score or so factories paid better wages, offered good working conditions, were located in the towns, and integrated processing shops that employed the best paid workers in the industry. Most satisfied the Factories Act and the Minimum Wages Act.[75] But, alongside, there arose a vast hinterland of rural workshops. They were under contract to town merchant firms, and produced simpler goods. The family and the village muted class formation, but not entirely. The rise in the cost of living during the Second World War put pressure on labour markets throughout the country. In many artisan towns, decisive changes in work practices can be traced to this period, and so can the incipient, almost invisible trade unions of the actual weavers or *qalinbafs*. In the factories at Mirzapur, the period saw the increasing employment of women in subsidiary processes. There was a shift from piece to time rates. There was also, reportedly, some discontent among the workers who felt that the piece-wages did not make sufficient allowance for the services that every man in the workshop performed as routine.[76]

By contrast with the semi-rural Mirzapur industry, Srinagar, Amritsar, and Agra were the home of the factory system in carpet. Carpet weaving in Kashmir began in the fifteenth century. In recent histories of the product there is little reference to antique Kashmir carpets or to the styles that distinguished them, but it seems that access to Central Asian wool, and seemingly a greater adherence to some Central Asian designs, were features that distinguished Kashmir from the plains. Organizationally, the industry in Srinagar was similar to that in Amritsar and Agra, and these towns can be discussed as one group. In 1931 in Srinagar, there were six firms with 715 looms in total, or about 3,000 workers. In 1947, five firms owned seven factories and employed 753 workers, the largest with 366.[77] The number of looms must have been 150–200. Thus, active looms after 1947 were fewer than in the 1930s.[78] Loomage later increased, but no reliable count seems to be available.

It is known that migrant Kashmiri artisans started carpet weaving in Amritsar.[79] At first they made shawls for export to Europe, but shifted to carpet when the shawl market crashed, apparently due to a problem

---

[75] See, on these, India, *Report of Panel on Economic Conditions*, pp. 7–8; and Uttar Pradesh, *Linkages Between Formal and Informal Sectors. A Study of Handloom and Carpet Industrial Units of Varanasi Division*, Perspective Planning Division, State Planning Institute (Lucknow, 1983).

[76] Mukhtar, *Report on Labour Conditions*, 11.

[77] A. F. Barker, *The Cottage Textile Industries of Kashmir* (Leeds, 1933); and Mukhtar, *Report of Labour Conditions*, 19–25.

[78] M. Ganju, *Textile Industries in Kashmir* (Delhi, 1945).

[79] Shaikh Gulam Hussun, cited in Playne, *Bombay Presidency*, 616.

Figure 7.1 Loom operated by young apprentices, Shaikh Gulam Hussun's factory, Amritsar, *c*.1915. The owner's great-grandfather was a Kashmiri migrant shawl weaver. The switch from shawl to carpet occurred about 1880.

of quality. The switch was encouraged by the fact that Amritsar was then known for its jail carpets. In the 1880s, the shift seems to have been complete, for shawls were then unknown in the town, but several large carpet factories were at work. The largest had fifty looms and employed 300, 'the greater part of these are boys, apprentices or *shágirds*, who are learning the trade'.[80] At the turn of the century, the city engaged 5,000 persons, mostly in factories of eight to ten looms each. European merchants engaged 'wealthy Hindus' who owned many of the larger factories, and who in turn engaged 'Muhammadan weavers all working on the contract system and entertaining their own staff of workers'.[81] In 1916, foreigners owned some of the most important factories of Amritsar.[82] There is no estimate of scale for the interwar period, but, by 1947, the industry had dramatically shrunk. One immediate sign of

---

[80] *Gazetteer*, cited in George Watt, *Dictionary*, 'Sheep and Goats', vol. VII, 618.
[81] George Watt and Percy Brown, *Indian Arts and Crafts*, Official Catalogue of the Indian Art Exhibition (Delhi, 1904), 430.
[82] Shaikh Gulam Sadik, who appeared before the *Indian Industrial Commission*, vol. V.

decline was the relative rarity of young apprentices.[83] In the middle of the 1970s, the Indian Punjab had an estimated 100 handlooms left in carpets, and only one factory still in operation at Amritsar.[84]

In Agra, the recent history of carpet weaving begins with the establishment of factories owned by European merchants, the most important being the Otto Weylandt. Many of the workers were former convicts. Persistent labour shortages before the war led to the employment of women, but the experiment failed because of resistance from the men. The system that did seem to stabilize eventually was the time-tested apprenticeship. Young boys were recruited by labour contractors, called *mistries* as well as *ustads*. These contractors came from both weaver and non-weaver backgrounds. How closely such systems resembled the customary apprenticeship is unknown. The older custom itself is better observed in the smaller centres such as Jhansi or Amroha, where the markets remained local, where masters were not yet full-fledged labour contractors, and where not only did they recruit workers, but they retained a great deal of authority on entry and graduation of workers.[85]

The southern industry was different from the northern in several ways. It was always a smaller and more dispersed industry than the northern. The southern industry used mainly local wool, which was rougher than average and a poor dye-taker. The quality of the fabric, and its decorative component, had to adjust to this factor. Most southern carpet designs were therefore simpler, and in their use of plain geometric motifs, quite distant from the Persian influence that pervaded the north. At the same time, the south's legendary facility with vegetable dyes helped carpets. The northern and the southern industries might have served somewhat different markets. The north had a mainly local clientele until the 1850s. But the south, especially the coastal products, always had an export trade. By the middle of the nineteenth century, the south served the export firms under the brand names 'Coconada' and 'Madras rugs'. But the axis of maritime trade in Indian carpets had by then shifted from Masulipatnam to Calcutta. Not surprisingly, the coastal carpets became marginal and less visible as exportables.

The main centres in the south were Eluru and Masulipatnam on the eastern coast, Walajahpet in North Arcot about fifty miles west of Madras, Ayyampet about ten miles north of Tanjore town, and a relatively recent industry at Bangalore. Of these, Ayyampet was mainly a

[83] Mukhtar, *Report on Labour Conditions*, 39.
[84] Punjab, *Punjab District Gazetteers*, Amritsar District (Chandigarh, 1976), 199.
[85] Prasad, *Monograph on Carpet Making*, 38. On *ustad–shágird* contract, see Shaikh Gulam Sadik's evidence, *Indian Industrial Commission*, vol. V, 308–9; and Mukhtar, *Report of Labour Conditions*, 43.

silk carpet centre. The main advantage of Masulipatnam was its foreign trade, and the eastern coast's proficiency with colours, which found spectacular uses in cloth printing and painting. The chief product may have been meant for specific uses. One of the most famous Masulipatnam manufactures in cotton was the 'Asia' or *'telia rumal'*, popular with *haj* pilgrims in the nineteenth and twentieth centuries. Not surprisingly, a tradition in prayer rugs developed here.[86] In 1679, Streynsham Master, the chief agent of the East India Company in Coromandel, travelled via Eluru. He found a carpet industry, worked by 'a race of Persians' said to have come there 'over above 100 years ago'.[87] His description suggests that there were then factories in Eluru that followed practices similar to those in Kashmir.[88] In 1900, Eluru carpets were of two styles: copies of Persian; and a unique but rather coarse floral design known as 'Ram Chandra'. A tour in 1903 unearthed a very old rug, 'which I regard as the original style of Rajahmundry and Ellore'. Remarkably, it was modelled after an indigenous grass mat.[89] In the same decade, Alfred Chatterton found 100 *karkhanas*, possibly 400 looms, and 3,000 workers engaged in Eluru. In large workshops, production conditions resembled those in north India, except that domestic workers were more common in the south.[90] In 1935, there were 600 looms.[91] But no further details were available until much later.[92]

The Walajahpet industry was established by a group of Muslim silk weavers in 1799, who fled Mysore after the city fell, and whom Hyder Ali had originally brought from Tanjore in 1761 and converted. In the nineteenth century, the carpets were known as 'Bangalore' carpets, and possibly consumed locally. In the early 1900s, the industry had shrunk, but as export demand revived between the wars, two European firms, Arbuthnot (who also dealt in Eluru–Masulipatnam products) and

---

[86] The connection between prayer rugs and carpets appears in most towns of northern India, but became obscure as the export trade in carpets grew. On northern India, see Prasad, *Monograph on Carpet Making*, 8.

[87] John Irwin and P. R. Schwartz, *Studies in Indo-European Textile History* (Ahmedabad, 1966), 40–1.

[88] Harris, *Monograph on the Carpet Industry*, 4.

[89] Watt and Brown, *Indian Arts and Crafts*, 440.

[90] A. C. Chatterton, 'Carpet Weaving at Ellore', in Harris, *Monograph on the Carpet Industry*, 14, 52; see also Thurston, *Monograph on the Woollen Fabric*, 4.

[91] Indian Tariff Board, *Written Evidence*, 304.

[92] During the late-1980s export boom, Eluru was the largest centre of southern India. In 1990, there were about 2,000 workers, a quarter in workshops, but the majority engaged in small and probably family-run units. The extent of subcontract under the Benares merchants was notable. And the use of north Indian wool had spread in a region that earlier relied on southern wool. Dastkar, 'Eluru Field Notes' (unpublished, 1989–90).

Leighton, began to buy from here. The tanneries at Arcot became a major local wool supplier. Under these conditions, the industry revived. The production of carpets received new capital, most notably that of a Sourashtra factor who invested in mechanized processing.[93] But the forty-nine looms at work in the middle of the 1930s probably represent the peak the Arcot industry ever reached.

New firms and new contracts

In the northern towns, and elsewhere in a subdued form, conditions of both trade and production changed dramatically. The period was the interwar years, when trade expanded greatly in scale. Where earlier, the old master-weaver interacted directly with palace representatives, now at least four tiers intervened between the weaver and the consumer. These were: the local trading firm; the shipping agent at Calcutta, Bombay, or Karachi; the London trading firm; and the retailer. Indian firms could not hope to penetrate the London trade. But the local arena was contested between foreigners and Indians. Here, survival was a matter of who could take the risks of trade better.[94] On the side of production, the relationship between the masters and the ordinary workers was earlier more or less strictly governed by implicit contracts which now partially loosened or readapted.

The early history of the foreign firms is obscure. In Mirzapur area, some former indigo planters seemed to have taken up the trade after 1860.[95] But, in general, many of the first factories were German, which indicates an entry of carpet traders into ownership of the factory. Otto Weylandt, who owned a sixty-loom factory in Agra, was one of them, with operations in both Turkey and India. In the craft monographs produced between 1890 and 1910, these factories were mentioned favourably, as the result of an attempt by the industry to expand scale, centralize control, establish a reputation in the use of raw material and dyes, and, with all that, establish a brand name.[96] The First World War destroyed many factories in Persia and Turkey, which were owned by some of the India-based firms. In the interwar period, therefore, Indian-owned enterprise became more visible. Otto Weylandt had been bought

---

[93] Census of India, 1961, *Druggets and Carpets of Walajahpet*, vol. IX, Part VII-A, No. vii (Delhi, 1965), 3–4.

[94] See, on increased intermediation, and increased fluctuations in place of 'the small, steady, and persistent demand which characterized the old forms of industry', in Mirzapur, Prasad, *Monograph on Carpet Making*, 14.

[95] *Indian Carpets*, 27.

[96] For example, Latimer, *Monograph on Carpet*, 21, on Amritsar, and Prasad, *Monograph on Carpet Making*, 31, on Agra.

over by East Indian Carpets, the largest in the business, with four units in Amritsar, and factories or trading posts in West Asia.[97] C. M. Hadow, which started in 1888, dominated Srinagar. Tellery, an export firm based in Bombay, had contracts with the sole surviving carpet factory in Ahmedabad, and themselves owned a factory at Mirzapur.[98] Apart from that, a Hindu firm of Amritsar, Devi Sahai Chamba Mull, later renamed, owned a large factory. Why did factories arise in this industry?

Partly, the idea of a central workshop was related to investment in quality control, especially in dyeing. Otto Weylandt employed an expert dyer, enforced control on the dyes, and compiled a large collection of old designs.[99] Tellery of Mirzapur invited expert dyers from Punjab to ensure fast dyeing.[100] The Kashmir trade was largely in the hands of C. M. Hadow and Devergne, with whose attempts to revive designs came 'a fresh impetus'.[101] Other traders, the Eluru agent of the English exporter Arbuthnot and Co. for example, were also known to take part in design and dye initiatives.[102] The premium on reliable dyeing was reflected in the high wages of dyers in the cities, which encouraged many master weavers to appropriate the operation. It thus happened that certain matters of basic quality were probably better taken care of in India than in Persia. All Indian carpets were copies of Persian, but increasingly they were authentic copies, such that Amritsar became indistinguishable from Kermanshah or Sultanabad.[103] In general, the extent of the division of labour in processing probably increased. The workshop form allowed carding, spinning, and dyeing to develop as separate industries, and accounts for a quicker transition to machinery in wool spinning in India, while resistance to machinery in spinning continued elsewhere.[104]

[97] *Royal Commission on Labour in India*, vol. II (Part 2) (London, 1931), 89–90.

[98] B. A. Brendon, *A Monograph on the Woollen Fabrics of the Bombay Presidency* (Bombay, 1899), 10, on the Ahmedabad factory.

[99] Chatterjee, *Notes on Industries*, 59.

[100] Pim, *Monograph on the Woollen Fabrics*, 15.

[101] Mitra, 'Notes on the Arts and Industries in Kashmir', 366–7.

[102] Thurston, *Monograph on the Woollen Fabric*, 5.

[103] Hawley, *Oriental Rugs*, 254–8.

[104] On resistance, see Mumford, *Oriental Rugs*, 37–8. In India, 'traders began to reorganize the cottage industry of carpet-making . . . and some mills were set up . . . whose chief function was to spin the carpet yarn': Indian Tariff Board, *Report of the Indian Tariff Board on the Woollen Textile Industry in India* (Delhi, 1935), 8; India, *Indian Carpets in World Market*. The evidence recorded during the Tariff Board enquiry reported initiatives by the largest Amritsar factory, East Indian Carpets, to diversify into the spinning and weaving of wool in the early 1920s. The weaving shop typically had both powerlooms and handlooms. Shaikh Gulam Sadik, a leading north Indian manufacturer of carpets, interviewed by the Indian Industrial Commission in 1916, and by the Tariff Board exactly twenty years later, reported a similar move. This decade witnessed great strides in the woollen yarn industry, the import of worsted

But these investments do not really explain the factory. It can be argued that they were, in turn, enabled by factory organization. One explanation for the factory is economies of scale in the use of space, especially where large dimensions were produced. Thus, Agra and Amritsar carpets were much larger than those made in the Mirzapur area. Correspondingly, the average size of a workshop in the former was larger than in the latter. A second explanation is 'agency costs', the fact that 'the weavers [are] not sufficiently reliable to be trusted to weave in their own houses'.[105] This, in fact, is a frequently cited reason for the rise of the factory in crafts that used expensive inputs, such as silks. Thirdly, whether due to their greater capital or due to higher productivity, the factories usually paid better wages. Where the factory and putting-out co-existed, the better weavers sometimes preferred the factory because 'the European firms can pay better wages, and give greater continuity of work'.[106] A yet fourth factor could be, the factories efficiently utilized the relics of an old industrial organization familiar to artisans in north Indian towns.

Old roots of new organizations

It is quite clear that the factories, even those owned by foreigners, had old roots. The factory (or *karkhana*) as such was not new. Nor was one part of the work contract it used, the apprenticeship system, a new feature. The new elements were merchants as owners, the identity of the merchants, and the relationship between the merchants and the intermediaries. To differentiate these elements, it is necessary to look closely at the shop floor.

The employment contract in the factory was not a wage contract at all. It involved three or four parties and not two: the owner, a master, and workers. Typically, the owner contracted on piece-rate with the intermediary, also called the *ustad* or *karigar*. The latter created his team. The team consisted of both trained men, and young apprentices called *shágirds* or disciples. The former sometimes appear as partners of the *ustad*, sometimes as his employees. The latter were almost always engaged on time rates, for the tasks they did were wide-ranging and ill-defined. In the large factory, the *ustad* was an intermediary. In smaller factories, the *ustad* and the owner (called *karkhanadar*) often became

yarns, and the rise of woollen hosiery and garments in Punjab. The broad-based tendency seems to have coincided with a move by carpet firms to diversify.
[105] *Royal Commission on Labour*, 89.
[106] Prasad, *Monograph on Carpet Making*, 31.

indistinct. The *karkhanadar* was technically one who owned the factory, but, in practice, he was an owner with an artisanal background. The large factory was not a factory in the modern sense: it was the shed where a putting-out contract was implemented. The employer received the benefit of terminable, putting-out contracts as a strategy towards risk. The employer avoided one disadvantage of a factory, having to communicate with and monitor the direct producer. The shed ensured that the work progressed under their eyes. All these features suited the European factor very well.

The weaver-intermediary symbolized two elements, of which one was old and one new. The old element was his function as a repository of skills, one of the main senses of the term *ustad*. In this sense, the work contract explicitly accommodated learning. Workers were supervised by a super-worker who had their trust and respect. When the master moved from one factory to another, he took a whole team with him. This complex of features, jointly implied by *ustad*, was a relic of the past when carpets were woven in royal *karkhanas*. It is significant that the factory prevailed in towns where urban artisans were used to such patronage. On the other hand, the *ustad* was a contractor under the merchant or *karkhanadar*. When he worked under a European factor, the *ustad* was a result of foreign trade. Once again, the remnants of ustadhood suited the European factors, who would be looking for contractors who could guarantee quality.

The form of this contract varied in minor ways in carpets. In Punjab and Kashmir, the *ustad* worked inside a factory owned by the merchant. The latter remained distant from production, and the master remained a contractor. This division of labour persisted even when the owner was an Indian. Towards plainer and simpler types of work, the *ustad* became a more diluted category, and was replaced by ordinary *karkhanadars* without the special aura of proficiency. The system dissolved completely in Mirzapur, where much of the actual production took place in closely situated villages and in family firms. The employer was the head of the household, and most workers were members of it. Unlike in western United Provinces, in Mirzapur, the old patronage was never a dominant historical experience.

Three types of customary relationship, cooperation, credit, and apprenticeship, gave security to north Indian *karkhanadari*. The first occurred among *ustads* or among *karkhanadars*. The second occurred between the *ustad* and his merchant employer, or between the skilled workmen and their *ustad* or *karkhanadar*. The third bound unskilled workers and new entrants to the *ustads*. These relationships enabled the securance of trust, the supply of labour, and the formation and retention of skills and helped producers respond to expanded markets with relative ease.

Cooperation, or what Jagdish Prasad called 'guilds', is a state where masters of apprentices combined to regulate wages, quality, 'limit[ed] supply to demand', and 'settle[d] trade disputes'. In the prewar decade, such controls could still be seen in places where the industry was in decline.[107] But, in towns that were growing very rapidly, there is very little trace of informal guilds of this kind, not to mention formal ones. In the long run, such customary forms of cooperation came under pressure from sustained new entry into carpets, the ownership of factories by merchants, the decline of the old type of apprenticeship system (see below), and the entry of rural families in carpet production, as in the Mirzapur area. By and large, even within the period of this book, cooperation seems to have given way to market-mediated coordination systems in which the European firms played a major role.

'Indebtedness' evokes powerful negative images of the crafts in present-day India. Post-independence official statements about small-scale industry unfailingly equate debts with exploitation of the generic artisan in the hands of the generic capitalist. The existence of debts tends to be seen as a sufficient ground to replace private trade networks by government-aided cooperatives. In colonial India, debts were endemic in the urban crafts. But they appeared in a manner that cannot be boiled down to the term 'exploitation'. Usually, debts represented an exchange of privileges. It offered the employers an instrument to secure steady labour supplies, but that instrument came at a cost. Its effectiveness depended on the condition of the industry and the worker in question.

The trader who wanted a stable contract had to offer a banking service to his *ustads*. In Amritsar, the former could be compelled to take over the weaver's debts to the moneylender. For, otherwise, a hard-up weaver often went into hiding, looked for alternative jobs, and became irregular at the factory.[108] Indebtedness, in this case, reflected competition for the master-worker's services, and could rise so high in good times as to put the employer at risk in bad ones.[109]

The smaller factory owner or *karkhanadar*, similarly, never actually paid out a sum to his employees-cum-partners or employees-cum-apprentices at the end of a task. Regularity in payments was a feature of the trader–*karkhanadar* contract, but almost never of the employer–

---

[107] Prasad, *Monograph on Carpet Making*, 6. Jhansi is an example.

[108] *Royal Commission on Labour*, 90.

[109] For a speculatory episode in the 1890s in Amritsar, see Latimer, *Monograph on Carpet*, 16–17.

worker contract. The worker withdrew money as he needed. The employer wrote his dues as the tasks were completed. The employer kept an account that was, all descriptions concur, transparent to both parties. Disputes, and the charge of breach, were unheard of. The financial status of a *karkhanadar*, and of the best workers he employed, were similar enough to ensure roughly equal bargaining power. The account was checked about four times a year, on four festive days, and finally settled on one of these. They were interest-free. The Muslim artisan had an aversion to interest. But nor did the Hindus, forced by competition or by custom, indulge in usury.

The *baqi*, as such loans were called, thus, performed an essential banking service to the workers. It smoothed transactions, and enabled them to provide security to their savings. And this service was freely available. In carpets, the system existed in Amritsar and Agra, and probably also in Mirzapur. It was rarely seen in small places. The urban worker, unlike the peasant, did not possess collateral, and thus needed a banker willing to lend without tangible security. The only pledge he could offer was a commitment to work, and the only person who could cash that pledge was, not a moneylender, but the *karkhanadar*. The cities that looked for a stable labour force invariably offered this arrangement.

The skilled artisan, however, was always a valuable asset in industries like carpet. Thus, *baqi* was also the means to control labour. The supply of loans was a means to enforce quality, where, for example, deductions were made for bad work. It was a means to retain the best workers.[110] The towns displayed not only a reputation for honesty in accounts, but respect for the rule that no employer would engage a worker who was indebted to another *karkhanadar*, except by repaying that loan himself. In practice, the average worker was perpetually indebted, but the best ones were clearly so out of choice. For it was never a problem for a good worker to clear off debts from current incomes.

This ambiguity was an essential feature of the system. Employers could be obliging, or use debts to bargain wages. The combination of loan account and piece-rate payments was potentially a complication the workers might fail to understand. It could also lead to a condition where the workers remained tied even when there was neither work nor wages. Whether the system favoured the workers or was used against their interest depended on the demand for labour. In a rising industry, employers needed to secure the labour supply, but debts as an instrument for labour-tying became loosely enforceable. A good worker

---

[110] Mukhtar, *Report on Labour Conditions*, 16.

invariably had employers competing for him. For the interwar period in general, *baqi* in the United Provinces towns appears to have been driven by a persistent shortage of skilled labour. But, during periods of decline, workers might not be able either to leave or to earn. And, as the decline itself might make credit supply more monopolistic, they faced harder bargaining on wages and interest rates. Echoes of these adversities came from small towns in decline.[111]

The other inseparable institution, and equally ambiguous, was apprenticeship. This involved the *ustad* and young boys under training. The apprentice was a *shágird*, a student, and never 'the household drudge of the master'.[112] The training aspect was reflected in the generally accepted durations specified for an apprentice to be recognized as an *ustad* in the making. Significantly, the time was the shortest in weaving itself, on average three to six months in Mirzapur, though it could extend, in towns such as Amritsar or Srinagar reputed for more complex work, to two to four years. But the time was on average longer in designing (four to ten years), dye preparation (two to ten), and dyeing (one to five years).[113] A credit account was started as soon as an apprentice was taken. It began with an exchange. Gifts to the *ustad* were returned in the form of a loan to the worker.[114] In most cases, the talented worker could repay the loan. But, more often, he persuaded the next employer to take it over. Training fees in the case of the young student evolved into *baqi* as the student grew up.

Frequently the apprentice was a young boy. In fact, in no other craft were children more extensively employed outside the family. Whether inside the family firm or in *karkhanadari*, the ordinary carpet weaver in India was a boy. The possibility of employing children derived partly from the work itself, and partly from tradition. There are three levels in a decorative craft: the conception of the design; the execution or the pure physical labour; and the coordination of the two. In most complex crafts, the first level is separable from the others, whereas the latter two are variously tied in the labours of the main artisan, the handloom weaver for instance. In carpets, *all* three levels were in principle separable. The task of knotting piles was simple and not too exhausting. And, by a few ingenious devices, it did not need the reference of the whole carpet. One such device was the presence of the *ustad*. Another, more important, was *talim*, a system that came from Kashmir, but had distant

---

[111] For one among several descriptive accounts on these nuances, see Prasad, *Monograph on Carpet Making*, 12–14.
[112] Census of India, 1961, *Woollen Carpets*, reference to Shahjahanpur, 19.
[113] Mukhtar, *Report on Labour Conditions*, 8–9, on apprenticeship.
[114] *Ibid.*, 16.

relations in Central Asia. Repeatable sections of a design were transferred onto graph paper (called 'cartoons' in West Asia), which worked
as a reference for the weaver, where he or she is an adult. Where he was
too young, the matrix was written out, in a coded script to avoid piracy.
With the help of this graph, each knot could be coordinated by oral
instruction.[115] These tasks needed separate and literate groups of
workers. Once these tasks separated from weaving, the weaving itself
could be done by persons skilled only in tying knots. These were boys
between nine and fourteen. They followed a 'reader' behind them, who
dictated the oral instructions in a rhythmic chant.

Usually, a normal-sized loom in an Amritsar factory involved four
persons, two of them were boys under twelve years, the third a boy in
late teenage, or a senior apprentice, and the fourth the master
himself.[116] Apprentices were divided and hierarchized according to
whether they were domestic, hired, or quasi-domestic, and according to
the age of entry and the duration of stay. It is possible that some of these
differences derived from the condition of the industry: good times
induced quicker entry. The usual age of entry into apprenticeship was
nine, though six year olds were not unknown. In most other factories,
work practices broadly resembled Amritsar. The boys earned an income
about half that of an adult weaver. On becoming an expert weaver, a
distinction attained in late teens, they earned a wage somewhat above
the average in textile crafts. As they reached this stage, the chances
increased of their leaving for a new job, 'just as they are beginning to be
really useful'. There were abuses, too. In Amritsar, for example, the
wages of the boys remained rigid as they rapidly improved as workers.[117]
This, however, was not the general case: there are examples of produc-
tivity-adjusted apprentice earnings.

The Amritsar data shed some light on the process of recruiting a child
into a carpet factory. It involved an intriguing contract, in which
apprenticeship, tied labour, and debts are so closely intermeshed that it
is impossible to say which was the dominant compulsion. Typically, a
man, not infrequently a weaver himself, brought his son or grandson to
the master, and took a loan from him, to be repaid from the wages of the
boy. The boy worked as an apprentice for a few years and, if a good
worker, was considered an adult entrant into the labour force like any

---

[115] For a sample text, see *Indian Carpets*, section titled 'Kashmir'.

[116] *Report of the Royal Commission on Labour in India* (London, 1931), 97.

[117] *Ibid.*, evidence of masters Muhammad Ramzan and Rajbai, 104–5. Some aspects of
the arrangement will be dealt with below, and are also described in a recent book on
Pakistan, where the typical interwar Indian contracts seem to have remained more
unaltered than in India itself. See the excellent report, Shah, *Hand-Knotted Carpet*,
8–40.

other. Merely the existence of an advance does not signify the motive for the contract: *all* apprenticeships start with a ritual gift exchange. In less commercial and more tradition-bound crafts (such as music), the apprentice had to make substantial gifts. In a commercial craft like carpets, the *ustad* seemingly paid a higher amount. In either case, there was no trace of usury in these transactions.

With children, however, the contract expressed entirely the wish of the elders. A sample from Amritsar showed that the son of a guard of the town pledged two of his own sons to a carpet weaver, against an advance from the weaver, and monthly wages. The amount of the debt was small, about four months' wages, which suggests that the attraction of a steady income was a stronger motive than distress borrowing. Rs. 16 (the monthly wage of the boys), indeed, would count as a good income in 1930 by any standard. The contract makes no mention of the term, or repayment of the debt, possibly because the weaver was sure of recovering it in unpaid labour. If these inferences are correct, we are justified in seeing in the boys a valuable asset, further implying the not-so-trivial option for the elders of grooming a carpet weaver in a city like Amritsar.[118]

But, like *baqi*, apprenticeship was a double-edged weapon. In the normal course, it was above all a learning process, and, as such, the *ustad*'s economic power remained relatively intact. Being a child worker at ten meant being an entrepreneur at twenty or thirty, even *ustad* status for the talented ones. In fact, when markets were rising, the *ustad*'s economic power could be undermined by young apprentices beginning to contract and compete. Good times induced the quicker graduation of apprentices into independent contractors, if not into ustadhood.[119] On the other hand, in bad times, or in a state of decline of custom, apprenticeship could degenerate into exploitation of new entrants and weak workers, without necessarily the promise of a better future. The

[118] The contract read as follows:

> I, booter son of Chakli, Chowkidar of Amritsar, owe Rs 57 off, of which half is Rs 28–8–0, which I have borrowed from Booty, weaver, in advance. I agree that my grandsons N and F, should be handed over for the purposes of carpet weaving. N is to get Rs 9 per month and F is to get Rs 7 per month. I will take the wages monthly. I will not break this agreement. If I break this agreement I will return all the money I have borrowed to the man who has lent it to me.

Royal Commission on Labour, 92. If the contract were broken, say if the boy ran away with or without parental consent, the chit could be presented to the court. Such cases were rare, but, if they did arise, the chit was considered a proof of the debt, but not the commitment on work.

[119] For example, Prasad writes of the prewar decades in northern India: 'the great demand for labour makes the instruction less thorough and, very often, raw workmen are turned out', who obviously competed with their masters: *Monograph on Carpet Making*, 9.

first serious alarm developed about 1930, when the market was depressed, and labour legislation became a credible threat. Who would bear the cost of the substitution of children by adults, if labour laws came to that? The managers of East Indian Carpets, when probed by the Royal Commission on Labour, tried first to shrug the whole thing off, then pointed at the *ustad*, who was solely responsible for employment contracts.[120] That solution was consistent from the merchant's point of view, but inconsistent from the *ustad*'s point of view. For the child apprentice was the counterpart of the *ustad*: one could not be sacrificed without the other.

The problem did not need immediate action in the 1930s, especially since the market for Indian carpets abroad revived greatly. But, after 1947, two circumstances affected these customary transactions vitally. First, numerous artisans, especially the *ustads*, emigrated from India to Lahore, Multan, and Lyallpur. The effect in Amritsar in particular was devastating. And, secondly, the formal sanction on child labour now became too strong to ignore. From the 1950s, the north Indian factories began to decline. The *karkhanas* and *karkhanadari* contract became obscure, and with it went many of the *ustads* and aspiring *ustads*. And yet, interestingly enough, child labour did not disappear. It merely reincarnated inside the family firms.

Since 1950, and especially after the Iranian revolution, carpets greatly prospered in South Asia. Pakistan expanded in West and Central Asian styles, and India, as before, proceeded in an eclectic direction. In India, all older locations have seen growth, such as Agra, Amritsar, Warangal, and Eluru. Jaipur has developed a relatively new industry. As conditions stabilized, labour laws made the survival of children in the factories unsustainable, though it was tolerated in practice when not too visible. The result was a retreat of carpets into households or small workshops, a proliferation of intermediaries, and the advent of putting-out in place of the *karkhanadari*. At this point, the Indian and Pakistani carpets probably diverged somewhat. Pakistan seemed to receive, along with Muslim migrant weavers, vestiges of the institutions that formerly governed urban weaving in northern India, but the major concentration in India came to be the relatively rural complex of Mirzapur–Bhadohi, with mainly Hindu artisans from cultivating castes, and quite different work practices. [121]

---

[120] *Report of the Royal Commission*, 97–8; and *Royal Commission on Labour*, 90.

[121] See on Pakistan, Shah, *Hand-Knotted Carpets*, 33–4, 41. In the rare instances in southern India where children were formerly employed, and which could not adapt, the industry declined. At Walajahpet in Arcot, carpet factories were apparently run under family cooperatives, and children employed as domestic workers. The Factories Act ended the employment of children and, by breaking up the family work unit,

In a classic example of 'proto-industrialization', nearly 90 per cent of Indian carpet exports in recent times originates from the rural production and urban market system of the Mirzapur area.[122] The de-urbanization in India led to the meteoric rise of this cluster, and a new class of workshops which had evolved out of peasant weaver families, and employed surplus labour from one of the most densely populated, high-illiteracy, and impoverished agrarian zones, north Bihar. These workshops continued to employ children, since that was technically possible. But they were no longer employed as part of a more or less formal master–apprenticeship system; rather, they were employed as the hired component in the family firm. The mobility from employee to contractor was as a rule truncated. Their young age reflected not studentship, but the extreme vulnerability of the eastern Indian labour in general.

Interestingly enough, the historical association between carpets and child labour does provide an ideological continuity. When today's employers are pressed into explaining why they employ young boys, their answer echoes what the 1930s *ustad* told the Royal Commission, that young persons have 'nimble fingers' ideally suited for carpets. This is evidently a lie, for the association between young worker and carpet weaving is not a feature of the industry as such, but of the South Asia region. Child labour is the preferred institution in this area. In this area, furthermore, the institutional context of child labour in carpets has vitally changed in the last fifty years.

Conclusion

Carpets carry three lessons for the general themes of this book. First, carpet is an example of a rise of export trade. In this respect, it resembles leather. But, carpet was a skilled craft, and not a semi-processed input like tanned hides. The second feature follows. One outcome of trade was changes in craftsmanship and related strains. Thirdly, there were adaptations in trading and production systems. Thus, carpet illustrates how apprenticeship systems evolved, and how the *ustads*, once quasi-teachers, assumed a variety of capitalistic roles. In the interwar period, this transformation took place in the premises of the European factories and Indian *karkhanas*, probably the most visible

'played an important role in hastening the decline of the industry'. It needs to be noted that the children moved into more unskilled occupations, and did not necessarily leave the labour market to get educated, as a result. *Census, 1961, Madras, Druggets and Carpets of Walajahpet*, 20.

[122] India, *Indian Carpets in World Market*.

example of 'manufacture' in India. In short, the dynamism of crafts-manship and the karkhana in its clearest form made carpets a useful example in the study of sources and forms of organizational change. Having finished with the examples, it is to these general attributes of the transition that we return.

8   Conclusion

The examples studied in chapters 3 to 7 suggest three general points. At a purely empirical level, they suggest that major types of traditional industry in colonial India experienced 'commercialization' and, as a result, experienced changes in their organization, which on the whole improved their capability. The examples also bear on two analytical problems: the historical roots of underdevelopment, and the distinction between 'modern' and 'traditional' elements in Indian industrialization. In relation to the first, the book disputes an influential belief that exposure to free trade destroyed or devitalized the Indian artisan, and, in this way, was regressive in its impact on the economy of colonial India. The transition outlined here is not qualitatively very different from the experience of traditional industry during the early stages of industrialization in Western Europe or Japan. It follows that the roots of underdevelopment in South Asia cannot be found in some special distress that trade or markets caused only in South Asia. Rather, the roots should be sought in those specific South Asian conditions that prevented industrialization from securing rapid growth in average incomes. These conditions might be rapid population growth or social backwardness.

In relation to the second problem, the belief that colonialism devitalized traditional industry implies that 'modern' and 'traditional' industries are essentially different, unrelated, and incompatible species. This, in effect, is the view of the Marxists, as well as that of many of their critics. This view can be challenged based on the evidence gathered in this book. It can be argued instead that 'traditional' industry represents one root of 'modern' industry in India. This hypothesis is hinted in current employment statistics. It finds support in recent urban experiences. Many of the dynamic industrializing towns in present-day India rely on old 'artisanal' activities such as textiles and leather. The examples in this book lend further support to the hypothesis by showing how capital accumulation in artisanal activities 'began' so to speak.

Having said that, a qualification is necessary. The term 'modern' is used above in a chronological sense. In a technological or organizational sense, the modernity of these industries in post-colonial India is open to interpretation. While traditional industry has evolved, it has rarely become a high-wage or mechanized industry. And yet, small-scale industry of artisanal origin has moved a long distance from its origins. In what way, then, is post-colonial India different from the colonial? There is far too little research available on industrial organization in small-scale industry after 1947 to generalize on these evolutions with any certainty. Still, some broad drifts can be captured, based on the recent experience of the industries that figure in this book.[1]

The growth and agglomeration of these industries in terms of employment are more visible now than 100 years ago. In some cases, the growth of the craft towns that figured prominently in the foregoing narrative has been truly enormous in the last fifty years. Surat at the turn of the century probably employed about 5–6,000 weavers in silk and lace. Today, the direct descendant of weaving, the powerloom, provides employment to about half a million. Moradabad brass engaged 7–8,000 full-time workers in 1924. In the 1990s, an estimate places the town's metal workers at 150,000. Not more than a few thousands were found in the carpets in the Mirzapur–Bhadohi area in the interwar period. 300,000 is the approximate figure in the 1990s. By the most recent report (a television documentary of 1997) Firozabad glass employs 400,000, many times the number it did sixty years ago. These cases, it has been suggested earlier, capture a steadily increasing share of the informal sector in industrial wage labour.

Along with staggering orders of employment growth, there has been modernization in infrastructure – marketing, credit, and input supplies. There has also been some modernization in capability. The main work of Moradabad is now generalized brass-casting; the main work of pottery centres is industrial ceramics; that of glassware centres is bottles rather than bangles; and that of textile centres is rayon *saris*, polyester shirting, and cotton cloth for exportable casual wear, rather than old-style bordered cotton *saris*.

Trading networks began to change soon after independence. In

---

[1] The overview that follows is mainly based on post-1947 published reports on specific industries. Most of these have been cited in previous chapters. The impression drawn from them has been supplemented with occasional descriptions in the mass media, and a few scholarly works. The information content of state-sponsored craft surveys tends to be poorer in the post-1947 era, even as their number and frequency have increased. For their aim is rarely to create a knowledge base, as it was with such pre-1947 classics as the *Fact-Finding Committee* on textiles, or the craft monographs prepared at the turn of the century. The aim is now either to evaluate specific policies like cooperation, or analyse specific features of industrialization like the employment of children. While the surveys have narrowed in focus, the industries have grown in scale and complexity.

carpets, and partly in hides, the original export firms were of foreign origin, with privileged access to information on demand. Their operation in India was dependent on Indian agents, partners, *karkhanadars* and *ustads*, who knew the workers and suppliers. The Second World War, and finally political change, weakened the old-style export firm, and strengthened the Indian side of the business, while global communications reduced barriers to access of the final markets. This has seen, in a number of crafts studied here, a substantial increase in the mobility of trade and traders. They spread out from industrial towns to greater distances. In *jari*, the migration and settlement of Surati merchants in south Indian textile towns is one example of this drift. Another effect of 1947 was a shift, in north India especially, from Muslim towards Hindu enterprise, somewhat slowly in management and labour, but at a faster pace in capital.

Recent descriptions of the worksite lead one to speculate the following changes. On the one hand, tiny factories, typically with an employment of eight to ten workers, seem to be the dominant organization in most of these industries, whereas the family firm has steadily receded. In this respect, wage labour has become more extensive than in the colonial period. Only in handloom weaving does the artisan family still have a considerable presence. But this is, at least partly, one of several anomalies created by the protection the industry has received from the government. Elsewhere, as in carpets, factories sometimes involve family labour, but are rarely pure family-labour units. Wage labour expanded in post-1947 India. This is the lesson of employment statistics, and the experience of major sectors. In this extension of wage labour, there is continuity between the colonial and post-colonial periods, and similarity between agriculture and industry in post-colonial India.

But in respect of the size of unit, there is apparently a break. In the 1940s, it was usual for a craft observer to talk about the steady growth of the factory. But the large craft factory, officially recognized as a factory, is today rather rare. There has been an expansion of small backyard workshops, rather than 'factories' registered as such. Why did the trend stop or slow down? Why is wage labour being employed increasingly in tiny workshops? The answer should consider both the structural and the regulatory forces acting on organization. But we know rather little about the former. At least one reason why the larger factories disappeared from view is political. There is systematic underreporting of factories in post-1947 India. Fear of the regulatory regime, which can be both tough and arbitrary on the weaker capitalist, is pervasive in small-scale industry.

Coming now to the shopfloor, there has been a proliferation of new tasks where training is not a critical resource. Old-style apprenticeship, and, in turn, the sway of ustadhood have clearly decayed. The intermediary in employment is typically a 'labour contractor', and not a master in the old sense of the term. The term *ustad* is remarkably rooted. But it does not necessarily carry the 1920s meanings. One likely reason why it does not is the further division of labour that reduced the importance of the skilled supervisor. Another possible reason is de-skilling and casualization across the new tasks. A third factor, and related to the other trends, has been the great increase in employment of vulnerable labour like children.[2] Finally, labour is far more mobile now than before. There has been a very large increase in the migration of labourers from the poorest, agrarian, and overpopulated states in India.[3] Before 1947, artisan migration involved mainly the artisan castes and communities. Thus, the Padmasalis of southern India and the Momins of the north came to populate and activate textile towns in western India. But the typical migrant labourer in northern India today is likely to be of agrarian origin, a labourer working for a subsistence wage, a migrant from Bihar, and possibly a teenager. All this is a world away from the *ustads* and *shágirds* of the interwar period. In western India, the picture would differ only in minor detail. In south India, such vast pools of surplus labour are scarcer, but limited and short-distance migrations, between semi-arid countryside and industrial towns, have been a typical channel of labour supply. Whereas, in many instances, the artisan migrant in the interwar period ended up as an entrepreneur or a factor, the average migrant today is likely to end his career as a casual labourer.

This brief sketch of the situation after 1947 suggests several changes, and a basic continuity, in the character of the industrialization depicted in this book. What has been happening after 1947 is surely an

---

[2] Studies on child labour in these clusters suggest some patterns of change in the labour market. The child worker in northern India today is usually employed in household workshops and not factories; for example, in carpets they are employed in rural households to perform agricultural and industrial labour; he or she does not originate in the city but is an immigrant from distant and impoverished villages; is nowhere mentioned as a 'trainee', 'student', or 'apprentice', but universally as cheap labour. See, for example, B. N. Juyal, *Child Labour and Exploitation in the Carpet Industry: A Mirzapur–Bhadohi case study* (New Delhi, 1987). In a survey of Khurja pottery, Burra was told that the child-turned-adult earns less than an adult entrant into labour, Neera Burra, *Born to Work* (Delhi, 1995), 131. If generalizable, this is the opposite of what any apprenticeship employment of children must imply, and shows that the motive for employing children is the vulnerability of the segment they are from, rather than potential incomes from training.

[3] For an insightful and detailed descriptive survey of supply of labour and conditions of work in some major artisan clusters in north India, see Burra, *Born to Work*. On the labour market and employment practices in the informal industry of Surat town, see Jan Breman, *Footloose Labour* (Cambridge, 1996).

industrialization on a large scale, building upon a foundation of traditional industry. But it is industrialization in a limited sense, that of expansion in employment without a significant rise in income or productivity. Despite the manifest dynamism, this industrialization continues to be nourished by primitive resources like informal training, informal credit, and simple excess supply of unskilled labour. Long-distance trade created it. But it has been maintained by, on the one hand, crushing rates of population growth, and, on the other, by deficient investment in human beings.

References

Abe, Takeshi, 'The Japanese Cotton Industry: A Study of the Cotton Spinning Enterprise During the Interwar Period', in conference on Cotton as Prime Mover in Global Industrialization, 1600–1990, Manchester, 1997

Allāmī, Abù'l-Fazl, *The Aín-i Akbarí*, vol. I (trans. H. Blochmann), third edition. New Delhi, 1977

Amsden, Alice, *Asia's Next Giant*. New York and Oxford, 1989

Anand, R. L. and Ram Lal, *Tanning Industry in the Punjab*, Board of Economic Inquiry Publication No. 61. Lahore, 1931

Andrews, F. H., 'One Hundred Carpet Designs', *Journal of Indian Art (and Industry)*, 9, 89–94 (1906)

Anonymous, 'Defects in Indian Art Ware', *Journal of Indian Art (and Industry)*, 15–16 (1912–14)

Anonymous, 'Researches in Tanning and the Calcutta Research Tannery', *Journal of Indian Industries and Labour*, 1, 1(1921)

Ansari, G., *Muslim Caste in Uttar Pradesh*. Lucknow, 1960

Baden-Powell, B. H., *Handbook of the Economic Products of the Punjab*, 2 vols. Lahore, 1872

Badenoch, A. C., *Punjab Industries, 1911–12*. Lahore, 1917

Bagchi, Amiya Kumar, *Private Investment in India*. Cambridge, 1972
'Deindustrialization in India in the Nineteenth Century: Some Theoretical Implications', *Journal of Development Studies*, 12, 2 (1976)
The Political Economy of Underdevelopment. Cambridge, 1982

Bairoch, P., 'International Industrialization Levels from 1750 to 1980', *European Journal of Economic History*, 11, 2 (1982)

Baker, Christopher, *An Indian Rural Economy: The Tamilnad Countryside*. Delhi, 1984

Balakrishna, R., *Survey of Handloom Industry in Madras State, 1955–6*. Bombay, 1959

Baran, Paul, *The Political Economy of Growth*. Harmondsworth, 1978

Barker, A. F., *The Cottage Textile Industries of Kashmir*. Leeds, 1933

Barratt-Brown, Michael, *The Economics of Imperialism*. Harmondsworth, 1974

Bayly, C. A., *Rulers, Townsmen and Bazaars: North Indian Society in the Age of British Expansion, 1770–1870*. Cambridge, 1983
'The Origin of Swadeshi (Home Industry): Cloth and Indian Society, 1700–1930', in A. Appadurai (ed.), *The Social Life of Things: Commodities in Cultural Perspectives*. Cambridge, 1986

Bengal, *Report on the Survey of Cottage Industries in Bengal.* Calcutta, 1924
   Report on the Survey of Cottage Industries in Bengal, second edition. Calcutta, 1929
   The Report on the Survey of Handloom Weaving Industry in Bengal. Calcutta, 1937
   Handloom Cotton Weaving Industry in Bengal. Calcutta, 1941
Berg, Maxine, *The Age of Manufactures, 1700–1820. Industry, Innovation and Work in Britain,* second edition. London and New York, 1994
Bernier, François, *Travels in the Mogul Empire.* London, 1914
Bhattacharya, Ardhendu, 'Extracts from a Survey of the Small Urban Industries of Lucknow', in United Provinces, *The United Provinces Provincial Banking Enquiry Committee,* Evidence, vol. II. Lucknow, 1930
Bhattacharya, Jogendranath, *Hindu Castes and Sects.* Calcutta, 1896 (reprinted 1968)
Birdwood, G. C., *The Industrial Arts of India,* Part II. London, 1887
Black, David and Clive Loveless (eds.), *The Unappreciated Dhurrie.* London, 1982
Blunt, E. A. H., *The Caste System of Northern India.* Lucknow, 1931
Bombay, *Report of the Bombay Economic and Industrial Survey Committee, 1938–1940.* Bombay, 1940
   Report of the Bombay Leather Survey. Bombay, 1960
Bose, Sugata (ed.), *Credit, Markets and the Agrarian Economy of Colonial India.* New Delhi, 1994
Breman, Jan, *Footloose Labour.* Cambridge, 1996
Brendon, B. A., *A Monograph on the Woollen Fabrics of the Bombay Presidency.* Bombay, 1899
Briggs, G. W., *The Chamars.* Calcutta, 1920
Brown, Percy, 'The Artistic Trades of Punjab and Their Development', in *Report of the Fourth Industrial Conference Held at Madras.* Madras, 1909
Buchanan, Francis, *An Account of the Districts of Bihar and Patna in 1811–1812.* Patna, 1934 (reprinted Delhi, 1986)
Burden, E., *Monograph on the Wire and Tinsel Industry in the Punjab.* Lahore, 1909
Burra, Neera, *Born to Work.* Delhi, 1995
Census of India, 1901, *Bombay,* vol. IX, Part I (Report). Bombay, 1902
Census of India, 1901, *Madras,* vol. XV, Part I (Report). Madras, 1902
Census of India, 1911, *India,* vol. I, Part II (Tables). Delhi, 1912
Census of India, 1931, *India,* vol. I, Part I (Report). Delhi, 1933
Census of India, 1931, *India,* vol. I, Part II (Tables). Delhi, 1933
Census of India, 1931, *United Provinces of Agra and Oudh,* vol. XVIII, Part I (Report). Allahabad, 1931
Census of India, 1961, *Art Metal Wares of Tanjavur,* vol. IX, Part VII-A, No. iii. Delhi, 1964
Census of India, 1961, *Brass and Copperware Industry in Uttar Pradesh,* vol. XV, Part VII-A, No. 4. Delhi, 1964
Census of India, 1961, *Druggets and Carpets of Walajapet,* vol. IX, Part VII-A, No. vii. Delhi, 1965
Census of India, 1961, *Woollen Carpet and Blanket Industry in Uttar Pradesh,* vol. XV, Part VII-A, No. 1. Delhi, 1964

Central Leather Research Institute, *Symposium on Tanning as a Small Scale and Cottage Industry.* Madras, 1959

Central Provinces and Berar, *Report of the Industrial Survey of Central Provinces and Berar.* Nagpur, 1908–9

Report of the Industrial Survey Committee. Nagpur, 1939

Chandavarkar, Raj, 'Industrialization in India before 1947: Conventional Approaches and Alternative Perspectives', *Modern Asian Studies,* 19, 3 (1985)

The Origins of Industrial Capitalism in India: Business Strategies and the Working Class in Bombay, 1900–1940. Cambridge, 1994

Chandra, Bipan, *The Rise and Growth of Economic Nationalism in India.* New Delhi, 1966

Chandra, Rowland N. L., *Tanning and Working in Leather in the Province of Bengal.* Calcutta, 1903

Chapman, S. D., *The Early Factory Masters: The Transition to the Factory System in the Midlands Textile Industry.* Newton Abbot, 1967

Chatterjee, A. C., *Notes on the Industries of the United Provinces.* Allahabad, 1908

Chatterjee, Ruma, 'Cotton Handloom Manufactures of Bengal, 1870–1921', *Economic and Political Weekly,* 22, 25 (1987)

Chatterton, A. C., *A Monograph on Tanning and Working on Leather in the Madras Presidency.* Madras, 1904

'Carpet Weaving at Ellore', in H. T. Harris, *A Monograph on the Carpet Weaving Industry of Southern India.* Madras, 1908

Chaturvedi, V. P., *Moradabad mein Pital ke Bartanon ka Gharelu Udyog wa Vyavasaya* [The Cottage Industry and Trade in Moradabad Brassware]. Allahabad, 1950

Chaudhuri, K. N., 'Foreign Trade and Balance of Payments', in Dharma Kumar (ed.), *The Cambridge Economic History of India,* vol. II, *c.1757–c.1970.* Cambridge, 1983

'Markets and Traders in India During the Seventeenth and Eighteenth Centuries', in Sanjay Subrahmanyam (ed.), *Money and the Market in India 1100–1700.* Delhi, 1994

Chitra, V. R. and V. Tekumalla (eds.), *Cottage Industries of India (Guidebook and Symposium).* Madras, 1948

Choksey, R. D., *Economic Life in the Bombay–Deccan (1918–1939).* Bombay, 1955

Clark, Colin, *Conditions of Economic Progress.* London, 1951

Cohn, B., 'Cloth, Clothes and Colonialism: India in the Nineteenth Century', in A. Weiner and J. Schneider (eds.), *Cloth and the Human Experience.* Washington and London, 1989

Colebrooke, H. T., *Remarks on the Husbandry and Internal Commerce of Bengal.* Calcutta, 1804

Corbett, Jim, 'Chamari', in *My India.* Delhi, 1991

Crooke, William, 'A Note on the Art Industries of Mirzapur', *Journal of Indian Art (and Industry),* 5 (1892–4)

The Tribes and Castes of the North-Western Provinces, 2 vols. Calcutta, 1896

Races of North India. London, 1907

The Natives of Northern India. London, 1907

Crouzet, François, *The First Industrialists. The Problem of Origins.* Cambridge, 1985

'France', in M. Teich and R. Porter (eds.), *The Industrial Revolution in National Context. Europe and the USA.* Cambridge, 1996

Cumming, J. G., *Review of the Industrial Position and Prospects in Bengal in 1908* (Part II of Special Report). Calcutta, 1908

Dampier, G. R., *A Monograph on the Brass and Copper Wares of the North-Western Provinces and Oudh.* Allahabad, 1894

Darling, M. L., *Wisdom and Waste in the Punjab Village.* Bombay, 1934

'Prosperity and Debt', in Sugata Bose (ed.), *Credit, Markets and the Agrarian Economy.* Delhi, 1994

Das, B. M., 'Researches in Tanning and the Calcutta Research Tannery', *Journal of Indian Industries and Labour*, 1, 1 (1921)

Das Gupta, Ranajit, 'Factory Labour in Eastern India: Sources of Supply, 1855–1946. Some Preliminary Findings', *Indian Economic and Social History Review*, 13, 3 (1976)

Dastkar, 'Eluru Field Notes', unpublished, 1989–90

Datta, V. N., *Amritsar: Past and Present.* Amritsar, 1967

Davies, R. H., *Report on the Trade and Resources of the Countries on the North-Western Boundary of British India.* Lahore, 1862

The Trade of Central Asia. London, 1864

Deane, Phyllis, 'The British Industrial Revolution', in M. Teich and R. Porter (eds.), *Industrial Revolution in National Context.* Cambridge, 1996

Digby, William, *The Famine Campaign in Southern India*, 2 vols. London, 1878

Dilley, A. U., *Oriental Carpets and Rugs.* New York and London, 1931

Dobb, Maurice, *Studies in the Development of Capitalism.* London, 1946

Duplessis, Robert S., *Transitions to Capitalism in Early Modern Europe.* Cambridge, 1997

Dutt, R. C., *The Economic History of India*, vol. I, *Under Early British Rule, 1757–1837.* London, 1901

The Economic History of India in the Victorian Age. London, 1906

Dutt, R. P., *India To-day.* Bombay, 1947

Edwardes, S. M., *A Monograph upon the Silk Fabrics of the Bombay Presidency.* Bombay, 1900

Edwards, M. V., R. L. Badhwar, and A. C. Dey, *The Vegetable Tanning Materials of India and Burma*, Indian Forest Records (New Series), Chemistry and Minor Forest Products, vol. I, No. 2. Delhi, 1952

Ellis, T. P., *Monograph on Ivory Carving Industry in the Punjab.* Lahore, 1900

Epstein, S. A., *Wage Labor and Guilds in Medieval Europe.* Chapel Hill, NC and London, 1991

Frank, André Gunder, *On Capitalist Underdevelopment.* Bombay, 1975

Frankau, G. N., 'The Gilt Wire and Tinsel Industry at Burhanpur, Central Provinces', *Journal of Indian Industries and Labour*, 1, 1 (1921)

Fraymouth, W. A., 'Note on the Progress of Researches to Apply the Natural Tanstuffs of Northern India to the Production of War Leathers', in Indian Munitions Board, *Industrial Handbook.* Calcutta, 1919

Gadgil, D. R., *Sholapur City: Socio-economic Studies.* Bombay, 1965

Industrial Evolution in India in the Recent Times. Delhi, 1971

Gadgil, D. R. and R. K. Patil, *Gold and Silver Thread Industry in Surat*. Surat, 1953

Gaitonde, Y. R., *Report on the Village Tanning Industry in the Bombay Presidency*. Bombay, 1930

Ganguli, G. D., 'The Art Industries of the United Provinces', in *Report of the First Indian Industrial Conference (Benares, 1905)*. Allahabad, 1906

Ganju, M., *Textile Industries in Kashmir*. Delhi, 1945

Gazetteer, Bombay District, Ahmadnagar District. Bombay, 1884

Gazetteer, Bombay District, Nasik District. Bombay, 1884

Gazetteer, Bombay District, Thane District. Bombay, 1884

Gazetteer of the Bombay State, Poona District. Bombay, 1954

Gazetteer, Haryana District, Ambala District. Chandigarh, 1984

Gazetteer of India, The Imperial, The Indian Empire, vol. III (Economic). Oxford, 1907

Gazetteers, Maharashtra State, Nasik District. Bombay, 1975

Gazetteers of India, Uttar Pradesh, Varanasi District. Allahabad, 1965

Gazetteer, Uttar Pradesh District, Mirzapur District. Lucknow, 1988

Gerschenkron, A., *Economic Backwardness in Historical Perspective*. Cambridge, 1962

Ghate, B. G., *Changes in the Occupational Distribution of the Population*. Office of the Economic Adviser, Government of India. Delhi, 1940

Goldsmith, Raymond W., *The Financial Development of India, 1860–1977*. New Haven and London, 1983

Goody, Jack, 'Comparing Family Systems in Europe and Asia: Are There Different Sets of Rules?', *Population and Development Review*, 22, 1 (1996)
The East in the West. Cambridge, 1996

Grant, A. J., *Monograph on the Leather Industry of the Punjab, 1891–92*. Lahore, 1893

Griggs, William, *Relics of the Honourable East India Company*. London, 1909

Grove, Linda, 'Rural Manufacture in China's Cotton Industry, 1890–1990', in conference on Cotton as Prime Mover in Global Industrialization, 1600–1990, Manchester, 1997

Grover, B. R., 'An Integrated Pattern of Commercial Life in the Rural Society of North India During the Seventeenth and Eighteenth Centuries', in Sanjay Subrahmanyam (ed.), *Money and the Market in India 1100–1700*. Delhi, 1994

Guha, Sumit, 'The Handloom Industry of Central India: 1825–1950', *Indian Economic and Social History Review*, 26, 3 (1989)

Guthrie, A., *Report on Leather Industries of the Bombay Presidency*. Bombay, 1910

Gwynne, C. W., *Monograph on the Manufacture of Wire and Tinsel in the United Provinces*. Allahabad, 1910

Habib, Irfan, 'Potentials for Capitalistic Development in the Economy of Mughal India', *Journal of Economic History*, 29, 1 (1969)

Hadaway, W. S., *Monograph on Tinsel and Wire in the Madras Presidency*. Madras, 1909

Hajnal, J., 'Two Kinds of Preindustrial Household Formation System', *Population and Development Review*, 8, 4 (1982)

Hamilton, Alexander, *A New Account of the East Indies*. London, 1739

Harnetty, Peter, 'Deindustrialisation Revisited: The Handloom Weavers of the Central Provinces of India, c.1800–1947', *Modern Asian Studies*, 25, 3 (1991)

Harris, H. T., *A Monograph on the Carpet Weaving Industry of Southern India.* Madras, 1908

Hawley, W. A., *Oriental Rugs.* London, 1913

Haynes, Douglas, 'The Dynamics of Continuity in Indian Domestic Industry: *Jari* Manufacture in Surat, 1900–47', *Indian Economic and Social History Review*, 23, 2 (1986)

'The Logic of the Artisan Firm in a Capitalist Economy: Handloom Weavers and Technological Change in Western India, 1880–1947', in Burton Stein and Sanjay Subrahmanyam (eds.), *Institutions and Economic Change in South Asia.* Delhi, 1996

'Urban Weavers and Rural Famines in Western India, 1870–1900', mimeo, 1996

'Weavers' Capital and the Origins of the Powerlooms: Technological Transformation and Structural Change Among Handloom Producers in Western India, 1920–1950' (annual meeting of the Association of Asian Studies, Washington DC, 1996)

Haynes, Douglas and Tirthankar Roy, 'Conceiving Mobility: Weavers' Migrations in Precolonial and Colonial India', *Indian Economic and Social History Review*, 36, 1 (1999)

Hicks, John, *A Theory of Economic History.* Oxford, 1969

Hobson, E. A., *Cotton in Berar.* Nagpur, 1887

Hoey, William, *A Monograph on Trade and Manufactures in Northern India.* Lucknow, 1880

Holder, Edwin, 'Brass and Copper Ware of the Madras Presidency', *Journal of Indian Art (and Industry)*, 6, 46–53 (1896)

Hudson, Pat, *The Genesis of Industrial Capital. A Study of the West Riding Wool Textile Industry, c.1750–1850.* Cambridge, 1986

Ibbetson, Denzil, *Panjab Castes.* Lahore, 1916

Imperial Institute Committee for India, *Reports on Hides and Skins.* London, 1920

India, *Annual Statement of the Sea-Borne Trade of British India with the British Empire and Foreign Countries*, vol. I, Director of Commercial Intelligence and Statistics. Calcutta, various years

Statistical Abstract for British India (Calcutta, various years)

Statistical Abstracts for India, Central Statistical Organisation. Delhi, various years

Report of the Indian Famine Commission. Simla, 1898

Report of the Indian Famine Commission. Calcutta, 1901

Minutes of Evidence Recorded by the Indian Fiscal Commission. Calcutta, 1923

The Hides Cess Enquiry Committee, vol. I (Report) and vol. II (Evidence). Delhi, 1929

Report of the Fact-Finding Committee (Handloom and Mills), Commerce Department. Calcutta, 1942

Report of the Indian Tariff Board on the Continuance of Protection to the Silver Thread and Wire Industry, Ministry of Commerce. Bombay, 1948

Report on the Marketing of Hides in India, Ministry of Food and Agriculture. Delhi, 1952

Report on the Survey of the Brocade Industry at Varanasi, All India Handicrafts Board. Delhi, 1960

Report on the Jari Industry at Important Centres, All India Handicrafts Board. Delhi, 1961

Report of the Powerloom Enquiry Commission, Ministry of Industry. New Delhi, 1964

Report on Cast Metal Industry in Dariapur, All India Handicrafts Board. New Delhi, 1964

Report on the Survey of the Brassware Industry at Moradabad, All India Handicrafts Board. New Delhi, 1964

Report of Panel on Economic Conditions of Craftsmen in Carpets and Other Floor Coverings. All India Handicrafts Board. Delhi, 1976

Report on the Working Conditions of Workers in the Jari Industry at Surat (Gujarat), Labour Bureau. Chandigarh, 1978

Report on the Working and Living Conditions of Workers in the Metalware Industry at Moradabad, Ministry of Labour and Rehabilitation. New Delhi, 1982

Annual Report, 1994–5, Ministry of Labour. Delhi, 1996

Indian Carpets in World Market, All India Handicrafts Board. New Delhi, undated

Indian Carpets. Bombay, undated

Indian Industrial Commission, Minutes of Evidence, 5 vols. Calcutta, 1916–18

Indian Leather Trades and Industries Year-book. Madras, 1967

Indian Munitions Board, *Industrial Handbook.* Calcutta, 1919

Indian Tariff Board, *Cotton Textile Industry Enquiry*, vol. I (Report), vols. II–IV (Evidence). Calcutta, 1927

Evidence Recorded During Enquiry Regarding Gold Thread Industry. Calcutta, 1931

Report of the Indian Tariff Board Regarding the Grant of Protection to the Cotton Textile Industry. Calcutta, 1934

Report of the Indian Tariff Board Regarding the Grant of Protection to the Sericultural Industry. Delhi, 1934

Oral Evidence Recorded During Enquiry on the Grant of Protection to the Sericultural Industry. Delhi, 1935

Report of the Indian Tariff Board on the Woollen Textile Industry in India. Delhi, 1935

Written Evidence Recorded During Enquiry on the Grant of Protection to the Sericultural Industry. Delhi, 1935

Written Evidence Recorded During Enquiry Regarding the Woollen Textile Industry. Delhi, 1936

Oral Evidence Recorded During Enquiry on the Grant of Protection to the Sericultural Industry. Delhi, 1939

Written Evidence Recorded During Enquiry on the Grant of Protection to the Sericultural Industry. Delhi, 1939

Irwin, John, *Shawls.* London, 1954

Irwin, John, and P. R. Schwartz, *Studies in Indo-European Textile History.* Ahmedabad, 1966

Johnstone, D. C., *Monograph on Brass and Copper Ware in the Punjab, 1886–87.* Lahore, 1888

Joshi, N. M., *Urban Handicrafts of Bombay Deccan.* Poona, 1936

Juyal, B. N., *Child Labour and Exploitation in the Carpet Industry: A Mirzapur–Bhadohi Case Study.* New Delhi, 1987

Kaiwar, V., 'Property Structures, Demography and the Crisis of the Agrarian Economy of Colonial Bombay Presidency', in David Ludden (ed.), *Agricultural Production and Indian History.* Delhi, 1994

Kakade, R. G., *A Socio-economic Survey of the Weaving Communities in Sholapur.* Poona, 1947

Katiyar, T. S., *Social Life in Rajasthan.* Allahabad, 1964

Kellenbenz, H., 'The Organization of Industrial Production', in J. Habakkuk and M. Postan (eds.), *Cambridge Economic History of Europe,* vol. V. Cambridge, 1977

Kendrick, A. F. and C. E. C. Tattersoll, *Hand-Woven Carpets: Oriental and European.* London, 1922

Kessinger, Tom, *Vilayatpur, 1848–1968: Social and Economic Change in a North Indian Village.* Berkeley, 1974

Kipling, J. L., 'Brass and Copper Ware of the Punjab and Kashmir', *Journal of Indian Art (and Industry),* 1, 1–16 (1886)
    'The Industries of the Punjab', *Journal of Indian Art (and Industry),* 2 (1887–8)

Kriedte P., H. Medick, and J. Schlumbohm, *Industrialization before Industrialization. Rural Industry in the Genesis of Capitalism* (trans. Beate Schempp). Cambridge, 1981

Krishnamurty, J., 'Changing Concepts of Work in the Indian Censuses: 1901–61', *Indian Economic and Social History Review,* 14, 3 (1977)
    'Occupational Structure', in Dharma Kumar (ed.), *The Cambridge Economic History of India,* vol. II, *c.1757–c.1970.* Cambridge, 1983
    'Deindustrialization in Gangetic Bihar: Another Look at the Evidence', *Indian Economic and Social History Review,* 22, 4 (1985)

Kumar, Dharma (ed.), *The Cambridge Economic History of India,* vol. II, *c.1757–c.1970.* Cambridge, 1983
    'The Forgotten Sector: Services in Madras Presidency in the First Half of the Nineteenth Century', *Indian Economic and Social History Review,* 24, 4 (1987)

Kumar, Dharma and J. Krishnamurty, 'The Evolution of Labour Markets in India, 1857–1947', mimeo, Employment and Rural Development Division, World Bank, Washington DC, 1981

Lal, Deepak, *The Hindu Equilibrium,* vol. I, *Cultural Stability and Economic Stagnation: India 1500BC–1980.* Oxford, 1988
    The Hindu Equilibrium, vol. II, *Aspects of Indian Labour.* Oxford, 1989

Latimer, C., *Monograph on Carpet Making in the Punjab, 1905–06.* Lahore, 1907

Ledgard, H., 'The Hide, Skin and Leather Trades and Boot and Shoe Manufacturing in India', *Journal of Indian Industries and Labour,* 1, 2 (1922)

Lockwood, W., *The Economic Development of Japan.* Princeton, 1954

Ludden, David (ed.), *Agricultural Production and Indian History.* New Delhi, 1994

Maconochie, E., *A Monograph on the Pottery and Glass Industries of the Bombay Presidency*. Bombay, 1900?

Madras, *Report of the Madras Famine Code Revision Committee, 1938*, vol. I, *Report* and vol. II, *Appendices*. Madras, 1940

Majumdar Choudhury, S. N., 'Extracts from a Survey of the Small Urban Industries of Benares', *United Provinces Provincial Banking Enquiry Committee*, Evidence vol. II. Allahabad, 1930

Mansuri, I. M., 'Picker Industry in India', in Central Leather Research Institute, *Symposium on Tanning as a Small-Scale and Cottage Industry*. Madras, 1959

Mantoux, Paul, *The Industrial Revolution in the Eighteenth Century*. London, 1928

Martin, J. R., *Monograph on Tanning and Working in Leather in the Bombay Presidency*. Bombay, 1903

Marx, Karl, 'The British Rule in India', *New York Daily Tribune*, 25 June 1853, reprinted in Marx and Engels, *Collected Works*, vol. XII. Moscow, 1979

Mathias, Peter, *The First Industrial Nation: An Economic History of Britain, 1700–1914*. London, 1969

Mathias, Peter and John A. Davis (eds.), *Agriculture and Industrialization*. Oxford and Cambridge, MA, 1996

Maxwell-Lefroy, H. and E. C. Ansorge, *Report on an Inquiry into the Silk Industry in India*, 3 vols. Calcutta, 1917

McAlpin, M., 'Price Movements and Fluctuations in Economic Activity (1860–1947)', in Dharma Kumar (ed.), *The Cambridge Economic History of India*, vol. II, *c.1757–c.1970*. Cambridge, 1983

Medick, Hans, 'The Proto-industrial Family Economy: The Structural Function of Household and Family During the Transition from Peasant Society to Industrial Capitalism', *Social History*, 1 (1976)

Mehd, P. V., 'Tanning Industry, its Development in India', in *Proceedings of the Ninth Indian Industrial Conference at Karachi, 1913*. Amraoti, 1914

Mehta, V. N., *Gilt Wire and Tinsel Industry*, Bulletin of Indian Industries and Labour No. 25. Bombay, March 1922

Mensinkai, S. S., *A Survey of Handicrafts in Eight Districts of the Mysore State*. Dharwar, 1961

Mines, Mattison, *The Warrior Merchants: Textiles, Trade and Territory in South India*. Cambridge, 1984

Mir Hassan Ali, Mrs, *Observations on the Mussulmans of India* (ed. W. Crooke). London, 1917

Mitchell, B. R., *International Historical Statistics. Europe 1750–1988*. New York, 1992

Mitra, A., 'Notes on the Arts and Industries in Kashmir', in *Report of the Fifth Indian Industrial Conference Held at Lahore, 1909*. Amraoti, 1910

Morris, Morris D., *The Emergence of an Industrial Labor Force in India: A Study of the Bombay Cotton Mills, 1854–1947*. Berkeley and Los Angeles, 1965

    'Values as an Obstacle to Economic Growth in South Asia: An Historical Survey', *Journal of Economic History*, 27, 4 (1967)

    'Towards a Reinterpretation of Nineteenth Century Indian Economic History', *Indian Economic and Social History Review*, 5, 1 (1968)

    'The Growth of Large-Scale Industry', in Dharma Kumar (ed.), *The Cambridge Economic History of India*, vol. II, *c.1757–c.1970*. Cambridge, 1983

Mukharji, T. N., *Art-Manufactures of India*. Calcutta, 1888

A Monograph on the Brass, Bronze and Copper Manufactures of Bengal. Calcutta, 1903

Mukherjee, Meera, *Metalcraftsmen in India.* Calcutta, 1978

Mukherji, N. G., *A Monograph on the Silk Fabrics of Bengal.* Calcutta, 1903

A Monograph on Carpet-Weaving in Bengal. Calcutta, 1907

Mukhtar, Ahmad, *Report on Labour Conditions in Carpet Weaving*, Labour Investigation Committee. Delhi, 1947

Mumford, J. K., *Oriental Rugs.* New York, 1900

Nakamura, Takafusa, *Economic Growth in Prewar Japan* (trans. R. A. Feldman). New Haven, 1983

Nanjundayya, H. V. and L. K. Ananthakrishna Aiyar, *The Mysore Tribes and Castes.* Mysore, 1931

Naqvi, H. K., 'Industrial Towns of Hindustan in the Eighteenth Century', in M. K. Chaudhuri (ed.), *Trends in Socio-Economic Change in India, 1871–1961.* Simla, 1969

Nissim, J., *A Monograph on Wire and Tinsel in Bombay Presidency.* Bombay, 1910

Ogilvie, S. C. and M. Cerman (eds.), *European Proto-industrialization.* Cambridge, 1996

Ohkawa, Kazushi and Mutsuo Tajima, 'Small–Medium Scale Manufacturing Industry: A Comparative Study of Japan and Developing Nations', International Development Center of Japan. Tokyo, 1976

Otsuka H., *The Spirit of Capitalism, the Max Weber Thesis in an Economic Historical Perspective.* Tokyo, 1982

Pandey, Gyanendra, 'The Bigoted Julaha', in *The Construction of Communalism in Colonial North India.* Delhi, 1991

Pandit, Y. S., *Economic Conditions in Maharashtra and Karnatak.* Poona, 1936

Parks, Fanny, *Wanderings of a Pilgrim in Search of the Picturesque*, London, 1850 (reprinted Karachi, 1975)

Patel, Raoji B., 'Handloom Weaving in India', in *Proceedings of the Industrial Conference at Baroda.* Madras, 1906

Perot, Michelle (ed.), *A History of Private Life.* Cambridge, MA, 1990

Pilgrim, J. A., 'The Future of Tannin Extract in India', in Indian Munitions Board, *Industrial Handbook.* Calcutta, 1919

Pim, A. W., *A Monograph on the Woollen Fabrics in the North-Western Provinces and Oudh.* Allahabad, 1898

Piore, Michael, 'Technological Trajectories and the Classical Revival in Economics', in Michael Storper and Allen J. Scott (eds.), *Pathways to Industrialization and Regional Development.* London and New York, 1992

Pitke, H. R., 'Hides and Skins Industry in Berar', in *Proceedings of the Ninth Indian Industrial Conference at Karachi, 1913*, Amraoti, 1914

Playne, Somerset, *The Bombay Presidency, the United Provinces, Punjab, etc.: Their History, People, Commerce and Natural Resources.* London, 1917–20

Southern India: Its History, People, Commerce, and Industrial Resources. London, 1914–15

Bengal and Assam Behar and Orissa: Their History, People, Commerce, and Industrial Resources. London, 1917

Prasad, Kunwar Jagdish, *Monograph on Carpet Making in the United Provinces.* Allahabad, 1907

Punjab, *Report of the Punjab Provincial Banking Enquiry Committee, 1929–30.* Lahore, 1930

Report on Industrial Survey of Punjab. Chandigarh, 1960

Quddus Pal, K., 'The Punjab Tanning Industry', unpublished report prepared for the Punjab Government. Lahore, 1940

Raffé, W. G., 'Industrial Art Education', *Journal of Indian Industries and Labour,* 3, 1 (1923)

Raj, K. N., N. Bhattacharya, S. Guha, and S. Padhi (eds.), *Essays on the Commercialization of Indian Agriculture.* Bombay, 1985

Ranga, N. G., *The Economics of Handlooms.* Bombay, 1930

Rao, D. Narayana, *Report of the Survey of Cottage Industries in the Madras Presidency.* Madras, 1925

Rao, G. N., 'Changing Conditions and Growth of Agricultural Economy in the Kistna and Godavari Districts 1840–90', PhD dissertation, Andhra University, Waltair, 1975

Rau, B. R., *The Economics of the Leather Industry.* Calcutta, 1925

Ray, B. M., *A Monograph on Wire and Tinsel Industry in Bengal,* Calcutta, 1900?

Report of the Royal Commission on Labour in India . London, 1931

Risley, H., *The People of India.* Calcutta, 1908

Rivett-Carnac, J. H., 'Specimens of Indian Metal-Work', *Journal of Indian Art (and Industry),* 9, 70–80 (1902)

Robinson, Vincent, *Eastern Carpets.* London, 1882 (First Series) and 1893 (Second Series)

Rosovsky, H. and Kazushi Ohkawa, 'The Indigenous Components in the Modern Japanese Economy', University of California, Institute of International Studies. Berkeley, 1961

Roy, Tirthankar, 'Acceptance of Innovations in Early Twentieth Century Indian Weaving', in conference on Cloth, the Artisans and the World Economy, Dartmouth College, New Hampshire (1993)

Artisans and Industrialization. Indian Weaving in the Twentieth Century. Delhi, 1993

'The Pattern of Industrial Growth in Interwar India, *Journal of Indian School of Political Economy,* 6, 3 (1994)

'Capitalism and Community: A Study of the Madurai Sourashtras', *Indian Economic and Social History Review,* 34, 4 (1997)

'Development or Distortion? Powerlooms in India, 1950–97', *Economic and Political Weekly,* 33, 16 (1998)

(ed.), *Cloth and Commerce: Textiles in Colonial India.* New Delhi, 1996

Royal Commission on Labour in India, Evidence, vol. II (Part 2). London, 1931

Russell, R. V. and Hira Lal, *The Tribes and Castes of the Central Provinces and Berar.* Nagpur, 1916

Rutten, Mario, *Farms and Factories.* Delhi, 1995

Sabel, Charles and Jonathan Zeitlin, 'Historical Alternatives to Mass Production: Politics, Markets and Technology in Nineteenth-Century Industrialisation', *Past and Present,* 58, August (1985)

(eds.), *World of Possibilities.* Cambridge, 1997

Sahai, Raghbir, *Report on the Survey of the Handloom Weaving and Dyeing Industries in HEH Nizam's Dominion.* Hyderabad, 1933

Sastry, K. R. R., *South Indian Gilds*. Madras, 1925
The Madura Saurashtra Community. Bangalore, 1927
Satyanarayana, A., 'Expansion of Commodity Production and Agrarian Markets', in David Ludden (ed.), *Agricultural Production and Indian History*. Delhi, 1994
Schlumbohm, J., 'Proto-industrialization as a Research Strategy and a Historical Period – A Balance Sheet', in S. C. Ogilvie and M. Cerman (eds.), *European Proto-industrialization*, Cambridge, 1996
Schmitz, H., 'On the Clustering of Small Firms', *IDS Bulletin*, 23, 3 (1992)
Shah, P. G., 'The Copper and Brass Industries in India', in *Report of the Eighth Indian Industrial Conference, Bankipore, 1912*. Amraoti, 1913
Shah, S. M., *Hand-Knotted Carpet Industry of Pakistan*. Peshawar, 1980
Sharma, Harish C., *Artisans of the Punjab*. Delhi, 1996
Sheridan, Jr., George J., *The Social and Economic Foundations of Association Among the Silk Weavers of Lyons, 1852–1870*. New York, 1981
Sherring, M. A., *Hindu Tribes and Castes*. Calcutta, 1879
Shukla, Shanti Prasad, 'A Survey of Small Urban Industries of Allahabad City', in United Provinces, *United Provinces Provincial Banking Enquiry Committee*, Evidence vol. II. Allahabad, 1930
Simmons, C. P., 'Recruiting and Organizing an Industrial Labour Force in Colonial India: The Case of the Coal Mining Industry, c.1880–1939', *Indian Economic and Social History Review*, 13, 4 (1976)
Singh, Baljit, *The Economics of Small-Scale Industries. A Case Study of Small-Scale Industrial Establishments of Moradabad*. Bombay, 1961
Singh, Chowdhry Mukhtar, *Cottage and Small-Scale Industries*. Allahabad, 1947
Sivasubramonian, S., 'Income from the Secondary Sector in India 1900–47', *Indian Economic and Social History Review*, 14, 4 (1997)
'Revised Estimates of the National Income of India, 1900–1901 to 1946–47', *Indian Economic and Social History Review*, 34, 2 (1997)
Sovani, N. V., *Social Survey of Kolhapur City*, 2 vols. Poona, 1951
Specker, Konrad, 'Madras Handlooms in the Nineteenth Century', *Indian Economic and Social History Review*, 26, 2 (1989)
Stevenson, M., *Without the Pale, the Life Story of an Outcaste*. Calcutta, 1930
Stokes, Eric, 'Dynamics and Enervation in North Indian Agriculture: The Historical Dimension', in David Ludden (ed.), *Agricultural Production and Indian History*. Delhi, 1994
Strachey, John, *The End of Empire*. London, 1959
Sugihara, Kaoru, 'Agriculture and Industrialization: The Japanese Experience', in Peter Mathias and John A. Davis (eds.), *Agriculture and Industrialization*. Oxford and Cambridge, MA, 1996
Swaminathan, Padmini, 'State Intervention in Industrialisation: A Case Study of the Madras Presidency', *Indian Economic and Social History Review*, 29, 4 (1992)
'Prison as Factory: A Study of Jail Manufactures in the Madras Presidency', *Studies in History*, New Series, 11, 1 (1995)
Sweezy, Paul, *et al.*, *The Transition from Feudalism to Capitalism*. London and New York, 1992

Teich, M. and R. Porter (eds.), *The Industrial Revolution in National Context. Europe and the USA*. Cambridge, 1996

Telang, S. V., *Report on Handloom Weaving Industry in the Bombay Presidency*, Bombay, 1932

Tellery, A., 'Embroidery, Braiding, Lace, etc.', in *Report of the Fourth Industrial Conference of the United Provinces Held at Benares*. Benares, 1910

'The United Provinces Carpet Industry', in *Report of the Fourth Industrial Conference of United Provinces Held at Benares*. Benares, 1910

Tennant, William, *Indian Recreations; Consisting Chiefly of Strictures on the Domestic and Rural Economy of the Mahommedans and Hindoos*. Edinburgh, 1803

Thankappan Nair, P., 'Civic and Public Services in Old Calcutta', in S. Chaudhuri (ed.), *Calcutta. The Living City*, vol. I. Calcutta, 1990

Thorner, Daniel and Alice Thorner, '"De-industrialization" in India, 1881–1931', in *Land and Labour in India*. Bombay, 1962

Thrupp, Sylvia, 'The Gilds', in J. Habakkuk and M. Postan (eds.), *Cambridge Economic History of Europe*, vol. III. Cambridge, 1977

Thurston, Edgar, *Monograph on the Woollen Fabric Industry of the Madras Presidency*. Madras, 1898

Monograph on the Silk Fabric Industry of the Madras Presidency. Madras, 1899

Tribes and Castes of Southern India. Madras, 1909

Tiwari, R. D., 'Leather Industry: Its Transport Problem', *Journal of the University of Bombay*, 6, 4 (1938)

Tripathi, Dwijendra, 'Indian Entrepreneurship in Historical Perspective: A Reinterpretation', *Economic and Political Weekly*, 7 (1971)

Trivedi, A. B., *Post-War Gujarat*. Bombay, 1949

Twigg, H. J. R., *A Monograph on the Art and Practice of Carpet-Making in the Bombay Presidency*. Bombay, 1907

Twomey, M. J., 'Employment in Nineteenth Century Indian Textiles', *Explorations in Economic History*, 20, 3 (1983)

United Provinces, *Industrial Survey of the United Provinces*. Allahabad, 1922–4

Report of the Director of Industries. Allahabad, 1922–3

Report of the United Provinces Provincial Banking Enquiry Committee. Allahabad, 1930

Report of the Industries Reorganisation Committee. Allahabad, 1934

Uttar Pradesh, *Linkages Between Formal and Informal Sectors. A Study of Handloom and Carpet Industrial Units of Varanasi Division*, Perspective Planning Division, State Planning Institute. Lucknow, 1983

van Zanden, J. L., 'Industrialization in the Netherlands', in M. Teich and R. Porter (eds.), *Industrial Revolution in National Context*. Cambridge, 1996

Venkatraman, K. S., 'The Handloom Industry in South India', supplements to *Journal of the University of Bombay*, 7, 1 (1935) and 8, 1 (1936)

'The Economic Condition of Handloom Weavers', *Journal of the University of Bombay*, 11, 1 (1942)

Verma, Tripta, *Karkhanas under the Mughals*. Delhi, 1994

Vicziany, Marika, 'The Deindustrialization of India in the Nineteenth Century: A Methodological Critique of Amiya Kumar Bagchi', *Indian Economic and Social History Review*, 16, 2 (1979)

Visaria, Leela and Pravin Visaria, 'Population (1757–1947)', in Dharma Kumar (ed.), *The Cambridge Economic History of India*, vol. II, *c.1757–c.1970*. Cambridge, 1983

von Tunzelmann, G. N., *Technology and Industrial Progress*. Aldershot and Brookfield, 1995

Wales, J. A. G., *A Monograph on Wood Carving in the Bombay Presidency*. Bombay, 1902

Wallerstein, Immanuel, *The Capitalist World-Economy*. Cambridge, 1979

Walton, H. G., *A Monograph on Tanning and Working in Leather in the United Provinces of Agra and Oudh*. Allahabad, 1903

Washbrook, David, 'Agriculture and Industrialization in Colonial India', in Peter Mathias and John A. Davis (eds.), *Agriculture and Industrialization*. Oxford and Cambridge, MA, 1996

Watson, John Forbes, *The Textile Manufactures and the Costumes of the People of India*. London, 1866

Watt, George, *A Dictionary of the Economic Products of India* vols. I and II. London and Calcutta, 1889 and 1890

Watt, George and Percy Brown, *Indian Arts and Crafts* (Official Catalogue of the Indian Art Exhibition). Delhi, 1904

Weber, Max, *General Economic History* (trans. F. H. Knight). New York, 1961

Williamson, O. E. 'The Organization of Work: A Comparative Institutional Assessment', *Journal of Economic Behaviour and Organization*, 1 (1980)

Williamson, O. E. and S. G. Winter (eds.), *The Nature of the Firm. Origins, Evolution, and Development*. New York and Oxford, 1991

Yanagisawa, Haruka, 'The Handloom Industry and its Market Structure: The Case of the Madras Presidency in the First Half of the Twentieth Century', *Indian Economic and Social History Review*, 30, 1 (1993)

Yusuf Ali, Abdullah Ibn, *A Monograph on Silk Fabrics Produced in the North-Western Provinces and Oudh*. Allahabad, 1900

Zelliot, Eleanor, 'Mahars and the Non-Brahmin Movement in Maharashtra', *Indian Economic and Social History Review*, 7, 3 (1970)

Index